THE CENTURY OF DECEPTION

ALSO BY IAN KEABLE

The Usborne Complete Book of Magic

Usborne Book of Magic Tricks

The Big Book of Magic Fun

Stand-Up:
A Professional Guide to Comedy Magic

Magic Shows:
30 Years of Programmes from Daniels to Derren

Charles Dickens Magician:
Conjuring in Life, Letters & Literature

THE CENTURY OF
DECEPTION

*The Birth of the Hoax
in Eighteenth-Century England*

Ian Keable

The Westbourne Press

THE WESTBOURNE PRESS
An Imprint of Saqi Books
26 Westbourne Grove, London W2 5RH
www.westbournepress.co.uk
www.saqibooks.com

First published 2021 by The Westbourne Press

A full CIP record for this book is available from the British Library.

ISBN 978 1 908906 44 1
eISBN 978 1 908906 45 8

Printed and bound by CPI Mackays, Chatham, ME5 8TD.

Dedicated to Dr Tony Keable-Elliott (1924–2020),
who I like to think would have been pleasantly surprised and proud.

CONTENTS

* * *

PROLOGUE

I

A professional magician is always looking for the perfect publicity stunt. In 2017 I needed one badly. After successfully performing my one-man comedy magic show at art centres and small theatres, I had ambitiously booked an evening of entertainment at the Theatre Royal Haymarket in London. Featuring a solo appearance at a West End venue on my website would impress future clients. It was going to be a tough sell, given that the theatre's capacity was 893, over ten times the size of my usual audience. But if I got in touch with all my existing contacts, including friends who had previously used my services, I thought I could make up the numbers. It turned out I had miscalculated.

One person after another gave an excuse as to why they were unable to buy a ticket. The potential downside of the venture was eye-watering. Initially I hoped the theatre would agree a box-office split, with proceeds divided between venue and performer. The management pointed out they would only consider such a deal with a show guaranteed to be a success – and mine did not remotely fall into that category. My only option was a buy-out for the evening. This meant that, although I kept all of the ticket sales, I had to pay £25,000 upfront. I decided to risk it. If I sold all the seats at £30 a head and made some additional money on selling programmes and other merchandise, I could come away with a small profit. But with the prospect of no audience I was facing a huge loss.

In turning this around, I had to overcome a seemingly

insurmountable problem: no one had heard of me. If I were well
known, like the mind-reader Derren Brown, I could have obtained
publicity with a slot on a television programme such as *The One Show*
or *Good Morning Britain*. I did try telephoning several production
companies but got no further than the receptionist. Emails and text
messages were ignored. I sent out a press release to all the major
newspapers, both national and local. The *Islington Tribune* was the
only one that published it, accompanied with a sarcastic comment
about the hubris of one of its borough residents.

With one month to go I had sold ten tickets. In desperation I
contacted a few close friends to brainstorm my options. We met at
the headquarters of The Magic Circle, which is located just behind
Euston Station. Many drinks went down, and I am uncertain who
it was that first came up with the ingenious solution. I like to think
it was me, but I am probably flattering myself. Neal Austin later
said it was him, so it's only fair I give him a name check. Of course,
many of you reading this will already know what I'm about to tell
you. Because for a brief period in January 2017 I, or at least my
pseudonym, was seriously trending.

It all started with an advertisement that appeared on Facebook.
The demographic spread of those who received it was potential
London theatre-goers in the higher-income bracket, aged between
twenty-five and forty. The notice stated that, on Monday 16 January
2017, an unknown performer was going to climb inside a bottle of
Prosecco on the stage of the Theatre Royal Haymarket. It stressed
it was an ordinary-sized bottle and, in case anyone suspected any
subterfuge, it could be examined in advance. Once the entertainer
was inside the bottle, he would sing a medley of songs. Furthermore,
the bottle could be passed around the audience to check all was fair.

Readers were also informed that this same person would borrow
a walking stick and play a tune on it as if it was a musical instrument,
and he would reveal the names of audience members, even if they
were masked. It was pointed out that he had performed in Europe,
Asia and Africa at exclusive private functions. The implication was

that this would be the last occasion on which he would make a public appearance. To reassure everybody they would get their money's worth it was noted the show would last at least two-and-a-half hours. The cost of the tickets, which could only be bought on the night, was at the top end of West End prices, the same as you would pay to see *The Lion King* or *The Book of Mormon*. My thinking was that all this gave the show an air of exclusivity and the semblance of respectability. What's more, it was happening at one of London's most prestigious theatres. Surely such a venerable institution would not be party to some sort of deliberate fraud?

The advertisement appeared only five days before the actual performance. Delaying any publicity until the last moment was a deliberate ploy on my part. It created enough time to provoke interest and intrigue, in particular fuelling curiosity as to the performer's possible identity – but insufficient for anybody to address rationally the absurdity of what the person was claiming he could do. In any event, I surmised, was climbing inside a wine bottle any more impossible than walking on the Thames, living in a Perspex box for forty-four days without food, or making the Statute of Liberty disappear? These had all been done respectively by the magicians Dynamo, David Blaine and David Copperfield.

I knew I was on to something when an anonymous genius came up with the hashtag 'Bottle Conjurer'. It was posted on my Twitter feed, linked to the advertisement. As a result, whether it was on this social network or others, everybody seemed to be talking about the magician entering the bottle. His other proposed feats were ignored. I was a little concerned when somebody wrote a spoof notice stating that a man jumping down his own throat would be on the same bill. But it just got the Bottle Conjurer talked about even more. Given the success of the advertisement I decided to leave it unaltered, thus not publicly acknowledging the buzz surrounding it. My only amendment came, on 13 January; I added a note that there would be security present at the theatre. This hinted that there might be problems on the night, given the demand for tickets. When

I discovered the cost of hiring bouncers, I abandoned the idea. But I disingenuously retained the wording, because the feedback I was seeing online suggested it was giving extra confidence to those contemplating attending.

It was all coming together better than I could have expected. But on 16 January it began to unravel. So caught up was I with the publicity and the promotion that I hadn't got around to thinking how I could even begin to meet the audience's expectations. I did speak with my friend Paul Kieve, who has devised many brilliant theatrical illusions for shows such as *Ghost the Musical*, *Matilda* and *The Invisible Man*. He couldn't think of any magic principle that would genuinely convince spectators that a fully-grown man was inside a litre bottle.

My intended solution was that I would go on stage and treat it as a joke. The Bottle Conjurer hadn't made it as he had been persuaded earlier in the evening to give a private performance. Someone had corked him inside a bottle, and he couldn't escape. After the laughter had subsided, I would then do my normal show. But I could tell, when eavesdropping on the queuing audience, that this was not going to work. I heard one couple agreeing with another that all they wanted to see was a person entering a bottle. A man was proclaiming that, while he knew it was not physically possible, he was expecting to see a credible representation of the stunt: he had seen similar on YouTube, so why not in real life? I confess I lost my nerve. Props in hand, I slipped out of the stage door. I left the theatre staff to deal with the consequences.

The unfortunate circumstances of that night were widely reported in the media. I really hadn't anticipated such anger from those attending. My faint hope was they would still accept the non-appearance of the Bottle Conjurer as an amusing jest. The rioting was set off by a heckle. When a nervous member of staff told the audience that they would get their money back if the show didn't go ahead, someone yelled out, 'For double the price he'll climb inside a medicine bottle!' Scuffles immediately broke out in the theatre and continued outside as the disgruntled ticket holders exited onto the street. The fracas was not helped by a mocking crowd who were waiting there to hear how the performance had gone.

All the newspapers had a field day, with headlines such as the 'Bubble Bursts leaving the Audience Flat' and 'The Miracle of the Invisible Performer'. Even I had to smile at a cartoon in the *Daily Mail* with the caption 'Ye're all Bottled'. There were rumours Prince Harry had attended the show. Although his name was never specifically mentioned in the press, there were vague references to a 'distinguished member of the royal family' being present. Fearful of getting sued by aggrieved attendees, and the Theatre Royal's claim for damages caused by the brawls, I lay low and kept quiet. I had had the foresight to secure the booking of the theatre through an overseas associate (it was a tax dodge). The Facebook advertisement was posted from an untraceable email account. It meant there was no paper trail back to me. There was speculation that either the theatre's management, or the producer of Shakespeare's *Much Ado About Nothing*, which was showing there for the rest of the week, had dreamt up the Bottle Conjurer as a promotional gimmick. Both issued press statements denying culpability.

This is the first time I have confessed my role in the affair. I refute the allegation made by some that I have chosen this moment to go public in order to promote *The Century of Deception*.

II

As befits a book about hoaxes, what you have read so far is fiction. But only to the extent that I have updated events of 1749 to the present day. You will discover in a later chapter that in all the essential elements, including the attempt by one enterprising author to pretend to be the Bottle Conjurer, the above scenario is identical to what happened over 270 years ago. However one aspect of my imaginary stunt is true: I am a professional magician who specialises in comedy magic. And part of my fascination with hoaxes is that the best of them comprise both aspects of my chosen form of entertainment: they are fooling and amusing.

A hoax is a different animal from a con or a financial swindle, of which there were plenty in the eighteenth century. The most common was obtaining goods or monies under false pretences, either by claiming to represent another party — the so-called 'false servant' — or by passing yourself off as someone to whom credit could be extended. An example, unique to this period, was obtaining naval prize money. This was due to those who had participated in the seizure of a ship. Sailors were allowed part of the proceeds of selling off its cargo and the vessel itself, together with any ransom money received for returning enemy captors to their homeland. The fraud was achieved by pretending to be an entitled crew member or related to a deceased mariner.

Another potential means of illicitly obtaining money was through the lottery. State lotteries had been introduced by a Parliament Act in 1694 and continued through to 1826. The money raised was used to reduce the capital and interest on national debt, as well as pay for specific projects. One deception was the presentation of a forged lottery ticket. A more ambitious scheme was launched in 1722 when the directors of the Harburg Company attempted to sell off lottery tickets to the value of £1,500,000, with the aim of distributing prize money of one million pounds and keeping the remainder. The House of Commons called it 'an infamous and fraudulent undertaking' and Lord Barrington, a member who had been instrumental in promoting the project, was expelled. As so often happens, perpetrators of massive fraud fare rather better than those stealing relatively small amounts. William Dodd, an Anglican clergyman, was arrested in 1777 for discounting a bill of exchange allegedly drawn by the Earl of Chesterfield. Despite Samuel Johnson, among many others, interceding on his behalf, he was hanged.

Instigating a hoax in order to financially benefit is rare. In only one of the cases that I consider was money the main incentive for the deception. Even then it is hard to know how it could have succeeded. A couple of the others did generate income for the perpetrator but that was through chance rather than any foresight. That is not to say that the remaining hoaxes were benign; far from it. Possibly three were done in order to get the upper hand over, or exact revenge on, someone else (as we will discover, the exact motive behind a hoax is often hard to unravel). Another three were carried out for personal ambition. Two had loftier aims to expose wrongs in society. Only one hoax therefore fits tidily into my definition, akin to a good illusion, of amicably spoofing people for the sheer joy of it.

You would have thought that one difference between a magic trick and a hoax is that with the latter it is obvious how it is done. However, many of the best hoaxes are far more intricate and sophisticated than they first appear. This is reflected in that some continue to be believed even after they have been exposed. With others there are details, which contributed to the schemes' success, that require almost a forensic investigation to properly understand them. Confessions, whether through admittance, interrogation, court trial or writing books, therefore play a large part in getting to the bottom of many of the hoaxes. In one instance the alleged culprit went to her grave denying any involvement, which means there are still many unanswered questions relating to it – even to the extent of being unclear whether it was a hoax at all.

In that one, as indeed in all the hoaxes I look at, you cannot blame a lack of available evidence for any failure to comprehend the entirety of the story. The sheer volume of contemporary data can seem, at times, almost overwhelming. Before 1700 this was not the case, with facts about supposed hoaxes being sparse and often questionable. For instance, it is still not known whether the Cerne Abbas Giant – a chalk figure of an enormous naked man with an erect phallus carved into the side of a hill in Dorset – was drawn in the seventeenth century or earlier. Similarly, it is uncertain whether the seer responsible for *The Prophesie of Mother Shipton* published in 1641, eighty years after she was said to have died, even existed.

One of the most authenticated, pre-eighteenth-century hoaxes was conducted by William Perry. Otherwise known as the Boy of Bilson, he claimed in 1620 that he was bewitched, as a result of which he began to vomit 'rags, thred, straw, crooked pinnes'. Jone Cocke was accused of casting a spell on him and was sentenced to death. But a Bishop intervened and persuaded the thirteen-year-old to admit he had faked his symptoms. All of our knowledge relating to the case is limited to, and wholly dependent on, two pamphlets: there are no newspapers, trial transcripts, theatrical reconstructions or satirical cartoons to provide any supporting testimony.

Another 100 years after Perry's bizarre behaviour, there is an abundant paper trail available on all major hoaxes. From 1678, trials at the Old Bailey were regularly published. The first daily newspaper, *The Daily Courant*, appeared in 1702. An exponential growth in other papers, and then journals, followed thereafter. These brought about in their turn, through advertising, an escalation in the production of pamphlets. Drama, too, was more easily promoted. From 1714 onwards there were at least two London theatres competing during the winter months. The evening's entertainment was extended, so that there was both a full-length play and an afterpiece. These short farces or pantomimes incorporated contemporary news items, including hoaxes. Satirical prints, the equivalent of today's topical cartoons, came into their own from 1720, the year William Hogarth's career began. Only a couple of the hoaxes that I feature failed to be depicted in an engraving, with both Hogarth and his great successor, James Gillray, each illustrating three of them.

Alongside the increase in reliable information about hoaxes came an equivalent preoccupation in the subject matter generally. As each new hoax unfolded, it seemed to many to further prove the inherent gullibility of the populace – they were 'perpetual testimonies of English credulity'. The phrase 'English credulity' originated in 1749 and was constantly reprised through to the end of the century. When a number of gentlemen were duped into parting with money for an alchemist-type scheme to make gold, it was labelled as a 'modern instance of English Credulity'. Readers were informed that a man had taken 'Advantage of English Credulity' by pretending he had slept for four months without food or water. A surgeon announced a successful operation enabling a cripple to walk, raising the question of whether this had been dreamt up in order to ridicule 'English Credulity'. A 'pretty strong instance of English credulity' was demonstrated when a crowd had gone to see 'a wonderful creature' found in a sewer, which turned out to be a hedgehog.

Overseas visitors were said to be taking advantage of this perceived ailment. A German who was tried for fraud had 'for some time past lived upon English Credulity'. French adventurers with fake 'titles of Marquis, Comte, Vicomte and Chevalier' entered this country 'to prey on English credulity'. The Dutch, Italians, Swedes and Hungarians were encouraged to come over with their 'whims' as the English were 'one great pack of fools'. 'Foreigners have repeatedly laughed at the English for their credulity,' reported one paper. Occasionally certain sectors of the populace were highlighted as being especially susceptible. 'The lower class of people' were more ready to 'believe the grossest absurdities'. 'Particularly the Londoners' possessed 'a much greater share of gross credulity'. But usually it was generalised. 'Credulity is a part of the English character,' claimed an author. A correspondent thought that 'no people are more credulous than the English in swallowing [hoaxes]'. In summary, there was a 'hold which credulity retained on the national character'.

Given this self-flagellation, tinged with more than a hint of xenophobia, intellectuals and thinkers were keen to develop the tools to convincingly expose a hoax. It was important that any related incident was 'authentic', which came increasingly to be a buzzword of the eighteenth century. Relying on 'taste' – in other words an instinctive reaction as to whether a story was true or not – was insufficient. English law, in order to convict someone of a crime, no longer insisted on there being an actual eyewitness. Circumstantial evidence was now accepted, which changed the system of proof from 'demonstration' to 'beyond reasonable doubt'. Evidence had to be collected and weighed up. Once in play it then had to be scrutinised to check it was consistent both with itself and with external facts and observations.

One area of significance was the reliability of witnesses. Did they have a reason to lie? For instance, so as not to implicate themselves, or because they were bribed? Did they have an accurate recall of what happened? The concept of false memories, or the dangers of forgetting due to lapse of time, was known about. Were they giving sufficient detail in relating their side of events? The lack of it could be an indication of falsehood. Nevertheless, in spite of the increasing knowledge in such matters – and in figuring out one or two of the hoaxes there was an element of applying these 'modern' principles – the majority were only really solved to everybody's satisfaction through a confession from the perpetrator.

First-time reliable reporting, contemporary fascination with the subject matter, and the development of methods to expose them might all seem reasons to support the thesis that the birth of hoaxes happened in the eighteenth century. But I would not have wanted to write this book unless I considered the hoaxes themselves to be intriguing in their own right. And in this respect the era does not let me down. In 1899 a query was raised as to whether there were any hoaxes that had occurred in the past 100 years that bore comparison with those of the previous century. A correspondent came back with four suggestions: John Payne Collier, Sir William Courtenay, the *Bathybius haeckelii* and Sir Roger Tichborne. The first was a Shakespearian forger, a mere amateur in contrast to his counterpart discussed in the final chapter. Sir William Courtenay maintained that smugglers accused of stealing the contraband from one of Her Majesty's ships were innocent. Not so much a hoax as a direct lie. He was imprisoned for perjury. *Bathybius haeckelii* was a substance discovered by the British biologist Thomas Huxley that he genuinely thought was the source of all organic life. So, an error of judgement with no intention of deliberate deceit. The Tichborne affair, concerning a man called Arthur Orton who claimed he was the missing heir to the Tichborne baronetcy, captivated Victorian society for nearly a decade. But, basically, it was an attempt at impersonation in order to obtain money and a title.

So, stand by not just to be educated but, more importantly, to be entertained by far more enterprisingly duplicitous stunts than these. In the process you will learn plenty about the society of the 1700s; the involvement of historical names such as Jonathan Swift, Henry Fielding, the Duke of Cumberland, Benjamin Franklin and Samuel Johnson; how hoaxes impacted on the religion, politics, wars and monarchy of the times; the myriad ways and reasons why some people were credulous and others were sceptical; and the sheer inventiveness of our predecessors to come up with imaginatively deceptive schemes. Welcome to a rollicking ride, accompanied by gasps and laughs, through eighteenth-century hoaxes.

ONE

'LATELY ARRIVED
FROM FORMOSA'

* * *

I

Hoaxes tend to be short-lived, overturned by an inevitable revelation, newly acquired information or a forced confession. It takes a special person to sustain a singular pretence over a lifetime, even though most people have forgotten about it and the potential for exploiting any gain is long gone. In this respect George Psalmanazar stands out as exceptional, surely one of the greatest liars of the eighteenth, or indeed any other century – a man who was able to convince London society that, despite an appearance that contradicted his assertion and without any evidence to support his claims, he came from a far eastern island that upheld barbaric religious customs. And yet he was also somebody seemingly without malice or a desire to cause harm to others. Praise does not come much higher or from a more respected source than Samuel Johnson. Psalmanazar was 'the *best* man he had ever known' and the one person he would seek out to 'sit with him at an alehouse'.

George Psalmanazar [Fig. 1] (as he called himself – his real name has never been discovered) was born in 1679 and brought up in Southern France as a Catholic. His father deserted the household before his son had reached the age of five, moving more than

Fig. 1: Portrait of George Psalmanazar, taken from his
posthumously published *Memoirs*.

500 miles away. A combination of an excellent education and an
'uncommon genius for languages' resulted in fluency in Latin and
Greek. He left school at the age of sixteen, seeking employment in
Avignon as a tutor, his early choice of career. This did not work out
well, with a relative of one of his pupils making sexual overtures to
him. He was eventually dismissed and found himself desolate, unable
to obtain another position. He had no alternative but to return to his
mother. However, he was faced with the problem of how to pay for
his food and lodgings on the journey back.

In his *Memoirs*, published posthumously, Psalmanazar says that
from an early age he learnt to gain sympathy by pretending that he
had too great an attachment to the Church, blaming his absent father

for this. He was convincing, with friars in particular showing him 'pity and admiration'. He decided for his homebound trip to exploit this acquired skill of exaggerating his religious devotion. He took on the character of a Roman Catholic on a pilgrimage from Ireland to Rome. A forged certificate, showing he was a student of theology, established his credentials. He also carried a stolen cloak and staff, and spoke in Latin. In this guise he requested alms from clergymen and other sympathisers. He led such a good life on his travels that he seriously thought about continuing to the Vatican. Psalmanazar's life of reinventing himself had begun.

Arriving back home, he did not remain there long. His mother persuaded him to go and visit his father. He suspected it was a plan to get him out of the way while she was wooed by his cousin. She reassured him that she only wanted to find out if her husband was all right and that he was 'by no means to stay longer than a year from her', he writes, 'unless I could convince her that it was very much to my advantage'. Once again masquerading as an Irish pilgrim, Psalmanazar made his way to Germany and was reunited with his father. However, this parent, too, didn't seem keen on his son staying with him for any length of time. Psalmanazar acquiesced, knowing that his ignorance of German and his foreign pronunciation of Latin and Greek did not augur well for obtaining any work as a tutor. He was encouraged to go to the Low Countries, where he would have a better chance of getting a job. Never again would Psalmanazar see his family.

Psalmanazar's intended destination was Cologne. But he was wary about continuing to play the part of an Irishman. He was concerned he might meet another person from that country who would expose him as a fraud. He opted instead to be a native from the Far East. This time there was no obvious financial incentive in his choice of role, and Psalmanazar fails to address why he adopted it. The most likely assumption is that he genuinely got a kick out of recreating himself, realising that people were more liable to take notice of him if he was someone other than an unremarkable Frenchman with no money and little prospect of bettering himself.

Claiming he came from a part of the world of which few Europeans knew anything gave him a blank canvas for his 'fertile fancy to work upon'. And he made the most of it. He came up with his own alphabet, language and religion consistent with passing himself off as someone from Japan. To authenticate his new nationality, he altered his Irish certificate while retaining the same seal. His cover story was that he had been converted to Christianity by the Jesuits. They had sent him to Avignon to further his education and to avoid the dreadful punishment meted out to converts in his land of birth.

Passing cities on either side of the Rhine, he arrived at Cologne. He was recruited into the Dutch army by an officer he met at the garrisoned gate. By now he was calling himself Salmanazar after the King of Assyria referred to in the Second Book of Kings. He fully embraced his supposed Japanese roots, deliberating winding up his fellow Lutherans and Calvinist soldiers by praying to the sun, writing gibberish prose and muttering heathen incantations. He retrospectively excused this behaviour by saying he had been only eighteen and 'desirous of being admired and taken notice of'.

Travelling with the army he ended up in Sluis in Holland. Working alongside the Dutch was a Scottish regiment. Their chaplain was the Reverend Alexander Innes, whom he met at a dinner arranged by the colonel of the regiment. Innes was impressed by Psalmanazar's debating abilities and began to befriend him. From the outset the chaplain saw a means of boosting his career by claiming he had converted Psalmanazar from a pagan religion to the Anglican Church. The teenager was prepared to go along with the deception, having become tired of the soldier's life with its hard work for little pay. It was, though, Innes who masterminded what was to follow; and it was the clergyman who would reap most of the rewards both financially and in enhancing his prospects. 'What a consummate wretch must this Innes have been! Psalmanazar himself was an honest man in comparison,' wrote *The Monthly Review* after the hoaxer's death.

Changes, presumably initiated by Innes, were that he should call himself Psalmanazar and that he was born on the island of Formosa, later to be called Taiwan. It was even more obscure than Japan. As today, in the eighteenth century Formosa belonged to the Chinese, but Psalmanazar always insisted that it was part of Japan. He began to work on a Formosan language, which he adapted from his original attempts to create Japanese. He had already constructed an alphabet and had practised writing out sentences from right to left. It took him some time to be fluent. Innes caught him out by getting him to translate a passage from Cicero into his pretended language. He was asked to repeat the exercise. Comparing the two passages showed considerable discrepancies. Psalmanazar took the lesson on board and made sure that in future he could transcribe into 'Formosan' with assiduity.

Innes tested his protégé's plausibility as to his pretended change in religion by submitting him to examinations from 'learned gentlemen' and 'ministers'. Convinced he was able to withstand scrutiny, Innes wrote a letter to the Bishop of London telling him all about the miraculous conversion. While anxiously awaiting a reply, Psalmanazar was baptised by the clergyman. This was a traumatic event for the young man as he had already participated in the ceremony as a child. He described it as 'an abominable piece of irreligion' and it is an indication of Innes's selfish indifference to Psalmanazar's emotional well-being.

After several weeks the response from the Bishop of London arrived. It could not have been more positive. He was full of praise for Innes for his evangelical zeal and invited him and Psalmanazar to come to England. The Bishop was particularly enthusiastic as it was his intention to send Psalmanazar 'to Oxford, to teach the Formosan language to a set of gentlemen'. Afterwards, the missionaries would travel with their tutor to the island to convert the natives to Christianity. Psalmanazar's fear at this happening was trumped by the welcoming prospect of leaving the army. He hoped he would find other ways of making himself useful to the Bishop. This proved to be the case, because there is no more mention of this conscripted tutelage.

With the governor's permission Psalmanazar was formally discharged from the army. He set out with Innes to Rotterdam in preparation for sailing to England. Innes made sure that Psalmanazar was thoroughly tested, encouraging probing questions from some English ministers of the Church. A few were unimpressed by the account he gave of himself and his pretended country. His solution was extreme. He started eating raw flesh, roots and herbs. Blessed with a good constitution, he survived on this strange diet – the addition of peppers and other spices also helped – without prejudicing his health. It had the desired effect of stopping the sceptical interrogations. Psalmanazar faced another obstacle while crossing the Channel, when they encountered a fearsome storm. Innes was happy to abandon him, stepping into a lifeboat while leaving Psalmanazar on board with the prospect of sinking with the ship. Psalmanazar didn't seem to bear him any grudge, claiming that at the time he was far more concerned about the 'dreadful shipwreck' of his 'soul' resulting from the duplicitous course he was about to embark upon. Fortunately the weather calmed, and they safely landed at Harwich.

Once they had made their way to London, Psalmanazar was introduced to Henry Compton, the Bishop of London. If Innes was the instigator of the scheme to persuade English society that Psalmanazar was from Formosa, the Bishop was the catalyst in ensuring it succeeded. He was seventy-one when he met the twenty-four-year-old convert in the summer of 1703. A committed Protestant and strongly opposed to the Roman Catholics, he also had a profound dislike of the Jesuits. In 1669 he translated *The Jesuits' Intrigues* from the French. He received Psalmanazar 'with great humanity' and totally believed his story. As one commentator noted, he could not have possibly have supported Psalmanazar 'if there was the least Suspicion of his being a Cheat'. His endorsement convinced others and enabled the Formosan to establish friendships with both the clergy and the laity.

Innes was determined to take maximum advantage of the Bishop's goodwill. He ordered a reluctant Psalmanazar to translate the Church

Catechism into Formosan and give it to the Bishop. Although Compton received the gift 'with his usual candour and generosity', Psalmanazar disarmingly admitted that it 'deserved to have been condemned to the flames'. Innes then persuaded Psalmanazar to write a book about Formosa, which would be dedicated to the Bishop. It was to be financed by several of the clergyman's acquaintances. Innes knew that speed was of the essence as 'the town was hot in expectation'. Psalmanazar was given two months to write it. With remarkable understatement Psalmanazar notes, 'one might have imagined, that a task so arduous and dangerous would have startled such a raw young fellow as I was'. However, he took to it with relish, unencumbered by having to do much research. He resolved that his account of Formosa 'should be wholly new and surprising' and 'should in most particulars clash with all the accounts other writers had given of it'.

An Historical and Geographical Description of Formosa 'by George Psalmanaazaar, a Native of the said Island, now in *London*' appeared in early 1704. The book is in three sections. The first is titled 'An Account of the Travels of *Mr.* George Psalmanaazaar' and relates how he left Formosa. The principal villain in this scenario is a Japanese-speaking Jesuit called Father de Rode from Avignon who came to Formosa to tutor Psalmanazar. He tricks his impressionable student into leaving the island in order to explore the world. But his real aim is to convert the Formosan to Catholicism. This back-story enables Psalmanazar to show his fortitude in evading the physical restraints of those determined to make him pursue their own particular religions. He can also show off his intellectual ability by explaining why their faiths are flawed. He takes great delight in telling the doubtless already convinced reader why the Roman Catholic belief in transubstantiation is erroneous. It is only when he meets a 'Judicious and Honest Guide' – the unnamed Reverend Innes – that he discovers 'the Church of *England*'. This brings about his deliverance from 'the Errors and Superstitions of my *Pagan* Religion'.

The next section is titled 'The Grounds of the Author's Conversion' and is a lengthy diatribe showing how the Anglican religion is the only true one. He is directly appealing to his intended readership. The final part, 'A Description of the Island Formosa', is by far the most entertaining. It begins with its history, relating how the island became a dominion of Japan thanks to the nefarious deeds of the entirely fictitious Emperor Meryaandanoo. The Emperor installed his own new laws but also enforced the old, barbaric ones. Psalmanazar then details the activities of the island and its inhabitants. He lets his imagination rip with descriptions of their cities, houses, palaces and castles; their clothes, weapons, musical instruments, liberal and mechanical arts, money, food; animals on the island; diseases, weights and measures and manner of eating and drinking, smoking and sleeping. He even provides illustrations of some of the prominent buildings and how the people dress, from the King and Queen through to a 'Country Bumpkin'. There is a chapter on the language, which is similar to Japanese except inhabitants of Japan don't pronounce 'some Letters gutturally as the *Formosans* do'. Helpfully he gives his own translations of the Lord's Prayer and the Ten Commandments.

Psalmanazar is determined to make his homeland as heathen as possible, so as to render his conversion even more impressive. Christians aren't allowed to live on the island. Any who are found that don't renounce their faith are burnt alive. Murderers, thieves and robbers are whipped, hanged or crucified. On their first offence, adulterers are fined or beaten; caught a second time and they are beheaded. Striking someone superior to you results in having your limbs cut off; hit a priest and you are buried alive; lay hands on the King and you will be hanged by your feet, while having four dogs fastened to your body, tearing it to pieces. The result of all this was, apparently, 'a profound Peace'.

But Psalmanazar is only just warming up. In his religion they acknowledge one God, but he is so sublime that they dare not worship him directly, substituting the sun instead. On New Year's Day 18,000 young boys are sacrificed. This is done by cutting their throats and plucking out their hearts. In order to keep a constant supply of infants going, the men are allowed more than one wife; some of them have over six. The average age of a bride is between ten and fifteen, rendering them more compliant to their husbands. The promiscuous man must be careful though, for if he can't look after them properly, then he is executed. Psalmanazar wrote the book in Latin and, in his *Memoirs*, he pays tribute to his translator who he says, with no hint of irony, corrected many of his 'improbabilities'.

Psalmanazar was paid ten guineas for the book. It quickly sold out. He was asked to write a second edition [Fig. 2], in order to appease the 'avarice of the proprietor'. This was published in the summer of 1705 and he was paid twelve guineas. Doubtless the bookseller and Innes would have made considerably more. In the amended version, Psalmanazar was urged to make 'such alterations and vindications' that 'promote the sale, and satisfy at once the curiosity of the public'. He duly ratcheted up the paganism. He writes that he had forgotten to mention that the husband has the power of life and death over his wife. It is legal to kill her for crimes that include obstinate disobedience and cursing her spouse. She is either beheaded or stabbed through the chest with a dagger. Sometimes, as part of the ritual, he will take her heart out and eat it in front of her relatives. Another addition is that the Formosans apparently eat human flesh, although thankfully this is restricted to those enemies slain in battle or legally executed criminals.

A new chapter contends that the Formosans worship devils. They do this to abate seismic and extreme events like earthquakes or storms, as they are not permitted to appeal to the sun for deliverance from such natural ocurrences. Sacrifices are made at the feet of terrifying statues which are distributed all over the island. Some of them are so horrific that pregnant women aren't allowed near them in case they miscarry at their sight. An engraving is inserted so the reader has an idea of what one of the monstrosities looks like.

Apart from these augmentations, there were relatively few other changes to the first edition. However the layout was altered so that

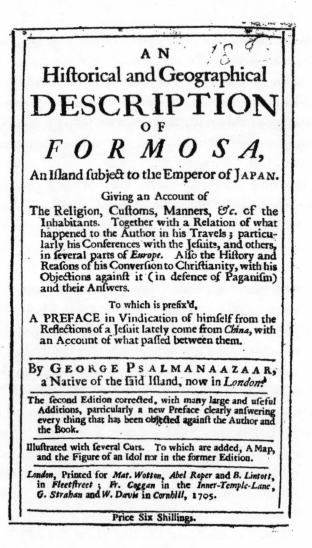

AN
Hiſtorical and Geographical
DESCRIPTION
OF
FORMOSA,
An Iſland ſubjeſt to the Emperor of JAPAN.

Giving an Account of

The Religion, Cuſtoms, Manners, *&c.* of the Inhabitants. Together with a Relation of what happened to the Author in his Travels ; particularly his Conferences with the Jeſuits, and others, in ſeveral parts of *Europe.* Alſo the Hiſtory and Reaſons of his Converſion to Chriſtianity, with his Objections againſt it (in defence of Paganiſm) and their Anſwers.

To which is prefix'd,

A PREFACE in Vindication of himſelf from the Reflections of a Jeſuit lately come from *China,* with an Account of what paſſed between them.

By GEORGE PSALMANAAZAAR, a Native of the ſaid Iſland, now in *London.*

The ſecond Edition correſted, with many large and uſeful Additions, particularly a new Preface clearly anſwering every thing that has been objected againſt the Author and the Book.

Illuſtrated with ſeveral Cuts. To which are added, A Map, and the Figure of an Idol not in the former Edition.

London, Printed for *Mat. Wotton, Abel Roper* and *B. Lintott,* in *Fleetſtreet* ; *Fr. Coggan* in the *Inner-Temple-Lane, G. Strahan* and *W. Davis* in *Cornhill,* 1705.

Price Six Shillings.

Fig 2: Title page of the second edition of *An Historical and Geographical Description of Formosa.*

the juicy section, the 'Description of Formosa', came first. This was followed by the 'Account of the Author's Travels'. The preachy 'Author's Conversion' was tagged on at the end. There was also a second preface where Psalmanazar set out and responded to twenty-five objections which 'unmerciful Criticks have rais'd against me and the Book'. Most of them were relatively nit-picking, but he did tackle the question of whether the island's population would be swiftly depleted given the annual sacrifice of 18,000 boys. His answer was that, although the law might demand it, in practice the number often fell far short of that target. Sometimes the yearly total might be as low as 1,000. Nobody dared question the priests' arithmetic as the punishment was to be burnt alive. Reassuringly the executioners were open to bribery if a family wanted to save their son. Finally, realising that there might not be enough boys around to satisfy the yearly sacrifice, he added that the priests could substitute young girls instead. This involved a complicated ritual of passing them twelve times through the four elements before taking them into the temple for their unspecified demise.

Psalmanazar made his amendments to the first edition while at Oxford University, where the Bishop of London enrolled him with all the privileges of a student. He said he did not take advantage of what was on offer, applying himself solely to church music. Fearing his tutors might think he was indolent, he kept his candle lit in his study window, and slept in a chair instead of his bed, to give the impression he was up all night working. He pretended he had gout caused by his lack of sleep. His limping gave him a 'kind of gravity, which I was not willing to part with'. According to Psalmanazar, gout was one of the most common diseases found in Formosa.

II

How did Psalmanazar evade exposure? One fundamental reason has already been mentioned: the belief by the influential Bishop of London, a figure of authority and impeccable credentials, that the Formosan was authentic. Many, in particular clergymen, took their lead from him. Psalmanazar's success in convincing the Bishop came down to his personality. He was likeable, mixed well in society and had a 'good-natured and charitable disposition'. By his own admittance he had no particular vices. He was not 'inclined to drinking nor gaming'. He was unostentatious in the way that he dressed and in his dietary requirements. He seemed indifferent to a wealthy lifestyle, satisfied with board and lodgings and a small amount of spending money. He did not canvas preferment in any way. When it came to women, he treated them with respect and avoided those who came on to him. He delighted in talking about, as well as practising, the restrictions of his new-found religion. Who could possibly think, he rhetorically asked, that 'a youth of so much sense and learning for his years, so seemingly free from ambition and other vices, could be abandoned enough to be guilty of such abominable an imposture and impiety'? In short, he was an exemplar of a converted Christian.

Psalmanazar needed to be a consummate liar. In this respect he possessed the major advantage of having a 'ready and retentive memory'. He knew that, if you lie, then it is vital to remember what you have said, so you don't give yourself away by saying something different at a later date. He applied this maxim consistently both in talking and in his writings about Formosa. Whatever he had previously related about the island, he made sure he would never contradict it in his book. A specific example of this was his claim, made 'inadvertently in conversation', that the yearly number of sacrificed infants was 18,000. Despite his awareness that this would result in a rapid depopulation of the island, together with the necessity for the existence of priests of breathtaking inhumanity, he 'could never be persuaded to lessen it'. As we have seen above, he did set out circumstances in which the total could be amended but, in doing so, he never corrected or withdrew his initial figure.

Alongside a phenomenal memory was an ability to argue well and think on his feet. Even when he was in the wrong, for instance claiming that Formosa was part of Japan rather than China, Psalmanazar managed to win the argument. 'I seldom found myself at a loss for a quick answer' he wrote. The most striking flaw in Psalmanazar's claim to be a Formosan was that he had a 'very fair' complexion. According to one source he 'looked like a young Dutchman'. So how could he possibly come from the Far East? His answer was that, as he came from a privileged family, he rarely ventured out of doors, thereby preventing him getting any darker. This fitted in with the racial stereotype of the time that the amount of exposure to the sun determined the colour of your skin. This myth was sustained because very few people from the Far East had made it as far as England to repudiate the theory.

It was pointed out that he had nothing to prove that he came from Formosa. His reply was that he had left in too much of a hurry to bring any documentation with him. And in any event, he retorted, if an Englishman ended up in Formosa without papers, how would he show where he came from? He was assisted in this respect by his accent. His 'idiom and pronunciation were so mixed and blended', whether he was speaking Latin, French, Italian or English, that it was impossible to place his country of birth. The physician Richard Mead postulated that he was of German or Dutch extraction. Psalmanazar crowed that he couldn't have chosen anywhere more unlikely.

One of his intellectual tussles was with Edmond Halley, later to be Astronomer Royal. When Psalmanazar met him in a tavern along with some other gentlemen, he had recently been appointed the Savilian Professor of Geometry at the University of Oxford. Halley decided to use his scientific knowledge to get the better of Psalmanazar. He innocently asked him if the sun shone down the chimneys in Formosa. No, was the reply. That's interesting, was the response, given that the island was directly under the line of the Tropic of Cancer. The reason, Psalmanazar explained, was because chimneys were built crooked in Formosa. Halley tried anew by asking how long Psalmanazar's shadow was when he stood in the hottest weather. 'Very short,' was the succinct reply. Halley finally gave up when, after asking his opponent how much twilight they had, Psalmanazar said they didn't use the term where he came from. 'I never heard of a distinguish'd time from Day and Night' before coming to England, he explained.

Making outrageous statements in debate is different from setting them permanently on record in a book. But Psalmanazar had a number of factors in his favour. Principal among them was a general ignorance about Formosa, enhanced by the knowledge that some of the other reports written previously to Psalmanazar's were equally absurd. An influential source was George Candidius, a Dutch reformed missionary. He lived on Formosa for ten years during the seventeenth century and wrote about his experiences. His most notorious claim was that women weren't allowed to have children until they were at least thirty-seven years old. If they became pregnant before that age, a priestess would induce a miscarriage. Psalmanazar enjoyed repeating this in his own book, concluding that it was 'a more barbarous Custom than what I affirm of the humane Sacrifices'.

Other contemporary accounts about Formosa lacked detail and therefore didn't directly contradict most of what Psalmanazar had imagined. His supporters pointed out that the island was inhabited by a number of different tribes, all with their own societal structures. Just because other Formosans led their lives in a certain way, it didn't nullify the behaviour of Psalmanazar's community. Dr James Pound, a clergyman who had served in the East India Company, raised the objection that, of the many Formosans he had spoken to, none of them backed up any of Psalmanazar's contentions. In so doing, he also stated that two thirds of the island were uncharted. So perhaps Psalmanazar came from one of those unexplored areas, was the response. Pound replied by saying the areas were full of naked savages. In which case they were not unknown, came the counter-argument. Caught out by his own logic, Dr Pound had to concede.

Another convincer was Psalmanazar's Formosan language. Its relative ease of understanding, combined with how different it was from the more complex and less approachable Chinese language, gave the impression of authenticity. When Psalmanazar translated the Church Catechism for the Bishop of London it was inspected by 'many persons of ingenuity and learning'. They found it to be regular and grammatical in relation to the words and the idiom, concluding 'it must be a real language, and no counterfeit, much less invented by such as stripling as *Psalmanazar*'. As late as 1748 his Formosan version of the Lord's Prayer appeared in a major collection, among 200 other languages and dialects. Horace Walpole wrote that Psalmanazar created a fake language 'that all the learned of Europe, though they suspected, could not detect'.

The trump card for Psalmanazar, though, was that he was perceived as a 'good Christian', appealing to the majority with his pro-Anglican faith and stressing his contempt for Catholics and Jesuits. He is deliberately coy about the sexual proclivities of his race. If he had expanded on this there might have been alarm that he would indulge in such activities in England. By his omissions he is indirectly proving he is moral, trustworthy and the epitome of a noble savage. The likes of Edmond Halley, Richard Mead and the naturalist John Woodward failed in their endeavours to expose him because they were perceived as 'free-thinkers' with an anti-religious agenda. Indeed, their eagerness to attack Psalmanazar only served to make others 'think the better of' him. Their opposition, it was felt, had nothing to do with labelling him a fantasist and all to do with 'their supposed disregard for Christianity'.

There were other detractors, untainted with agnosticism, but they were not especially vociferous in their scepticism. 'Various have been the Opinions of Men about this Gentleman, some looking upon him as an impostor,' begins a review of his *Historical and Geographical Description of Formosa*; but the writer refrains from making his own judgement on Psalmanazar's honesty. One diarist notes on the publication of the second edition that Psalmanazar was 'still taken to be a Cheat in London'. Letters to the philosopher John Locke as early as February 1704 show amusement at Psalmanazar's claims. Referring to 'one who says he comes from Formosa', writes the physician and collector of antiquities Sir Hans Sloane, 'I could make you very merry with what I have heard'. Another correspondent calls him a 'Rogue'. The minutes of the Royal Society reported at one of their meetings that some letters had been read from a Mr Griffith, who had stayed a long time in Formosa. In these he contradicted the 'account lately given of it by Mr George Psalmaanasaar'. But this, like the other writings, were kept private. For whatever reason, nobody took it upon themself to systematically and publicly expose Psalmanazar's narrative as a fraud.

III

On his return to London from Oxford, Psalmanazar found out that his co-conspirator, Reverend Innes, had been promoted by the Bishop of London to become chaplain-general to the English forces in Portugal. This was a reward for his successful conversion of the supposed Formosan. Innes doubtless thought that he had extracted all the money he could from the deception. Better to be out of the country when it all blew up. Psalmanazar claimed he was glad to see the back of him as Innes 'had an almost insurmountable propensity to wine and women'. Nevertheless, he must have felt very isolated now that the person who had conceived the deception, and had come up with creative ideas to further exploit the story, had deserted him.

Following the publication of the second edition of his *Historical and Geographical Account*, scepticism about Psalmanazar started to rise. In the absence of Innes, a group of his supporters attempted to defend his reputation. In April 1706 an advertisement appeared requesting that anybody who had 'any real scruple at, or fair Objection against' Psalmanazar or his book were to submit it to the publisher Bernard Lintott before 1 August. Readers were informed that another pamphlet was in preparation which would prove that all 'divers Reports spread abroad to his prejudice' against Psalmanazar were 'false and slanderous'. A similar advertisement appeared a month later, stating the booklet would also answer points raised against him by Monsieur d'Amalvy's recently produced tract. As this had been published only in French and, by Psalmanazar's own admission, had been seen by 'so few here in *England*', any response to it seemed pointless.

The resulting booklet, *An Enquiry into the Objections against George*

Psalmanaazaar of Formosa, came out on 18 July 1707. Before that, in February of the same year, another pamphlet emerged, written by Psalmanazar. This was called *A Dialogue between a Japonese and a Formosan, About some Points of The Religion of the Time.* Neither of them had anything significantly more controversial to add about Formosa. Psalmanazar later accepted that the publications made little difference to what people thought. 'I had the mortification to find,' he wrote, 'that my fabulous account was as much discredited by the greatest part of the world as ever.'

For the next few years Psalmanazar described his life as being 'mis-spent in a course of the most shameful idleness, vanity and extravagance', resulting in him continually falling into debt. He did embark on one scheme to try to extricate himself from his financial difficulties. Along with an entrepreneur called Edward Pattanden he attempted to sell enamelling for wainscots, tops of staircases and cabinets. Called 'White Formosan Work', it was constructed by a secret process, 'according to the right Japan way', only known to Psalmanazar. He said he agreed to be involved as much to convince his detractors of his origins as to make any money. The business collapsed owing to his partner charging too high a price for a shoddy product.

Following this failed venture, Psalmanazar's ability to profit from his supposed origins had all but dried up. His lack of perceived credibility was highlighted when *The Spectator* sent him up in a spoof advertisement, for a supposed opera called *The Cruelty of Atreus,* as an April fool joke. The '*Scene wherein* Thyestes *eats his own Children, is to be performed by the famous Mr* Psalmanazar, *lately arrived from* Formosa'. He tried a myriad of different occupations to earn a living. These included teaching modern languages, tutoring, being a clerk to a regiment, painting fans, translating books, learning Hebrew, all the time augmenting his income by accepting charitable payments from the dwindling few who still believed that he was a Formosan. It was only in the 1730s, by which time he claimed that he had truly found religion, that he found his vocation as an author, albeit anonymously. He ghost-wrote a book for the printer Samuel Palmer on the history of printing, published in 1732. He then contributed to the monumental *An Universal History, from the Earliest Account of Time*, which began appearing in 1747 and was produced in forty-four volumes through to 1766.

In spite of settling into his new life of hard work, frugal living and religious devotion, Psalmanazar could never bring himself to make a public confession of his wrongdoing. The closest he got to it was in *A Complete System of Geography*, where he wrote the sections on the Far East, including Formosa. In his *Memoirs* he claimed he had publicly acknowledged in this book 'the falsehood and imposture of my former account of that island'. However this is not backed up by a reading of the appropriate section, where he writes of himself in the third person. Psalmanazar 'now gives us Leave to assure the World, that the greatest Part of that Account was fabulous', he informs the reader, implying that maybe some of it might be true. And as for an authentic description of the island, he admits that most of the information comes from Candidius, even though 'upon serious Examination, this will be found to deserve as little Credit, as that of our pretended *Formosan*'.

Doubtless it was with relish that he reiterated Candidius's preposterous contention that women weren't allowed to have children until they were thirty-seven years old. To bring about any required miscarriages the Priestesses jumped and stamped on the bellies of the pregnant women. In his opinion such violence would permanently prevent the mother from having children in the future, especially in such a hot country where natural births didn't occur after the age of thirty. You can imagine many readers thinking that Psalmanazar's original text sounded more reliable. It is almost as if he is keeping alive the possibility of a retrospective re-evaluation of his account of Formosa which will once again thrust him back into the limelight.

It is probably around this time that Psalmanazar wrote his *Memoirs*. He makes reference to it in *A Complete System of Geography*, together with his intention of a posthumous publication. And the autobiography has very little information about his life beyond this period, even though he was to live for another sixteen years. The most notable part of his later years was his friendship with Samuel Johnson. Johnson especially admired his work ethic as a hack writer and his piety in leading what the lexicographer described as a 'regular' life. One subject they did not discuss was Psalmanazar's past life. When Johnson was asked if he ever brought up the subject of Formosa with his companion, he said 'he was afraid to mention even China'.

Psalmanazar died on 3 May 1763 aged eighty-four. There were no obituaries as such, but one correspondent recalled him in a letter several months later as 'a beastly Fellow' who 'lived on raw Meat, just as it came from the Butcher's' and 'took a monstrous deal of Snuff'. In his will, which had been written eleven years before, Psalmanazar left his possessions to his friend Sarah Rewalling. He asked that his *Memoirs* should be sold to the highest bidder in order to pay for any arrears on his lodgings and to defray his funeral expenses. The *Memoirs* were first available for sale in January 1765. A second edition swiftly followed and continued to be advertised through to April 1766.

Much of the narrative in this chapter has been based on Psalmanazar's *Memoirs*. This raises the question that, given he had previously written a tissue of lies about his life in his *Historical and Geographical Description of Formosa*, can we accept the truth of his final work? Psalmanazar wrote in his will that the reason for forbidding publication until after his death was that 'the author would be far out of the influence of any sinister motives that might induce him to deviate from the truth'. Conveniently, though, it also meant that he didn't have to answer any awkward questions, the most obvious being, what was your real name, who were your parents and where were you born? As one contemporary reviewer wrote, it is perhaps understandable why he might not want to give any information about his family, in order to protect future generations from embarrassment.

But to use that same excuse to redact the country where he was brought up was 'carrying his delicacy very far indeed!'

Nevertheless Psalmanazar deserves the benefit of the doubt as to whether he intended to genuinely undo all the mischief he had done, and produce 'a faithful account of every thing I could recollect'. His religious fervency suggests he was fearful of meeting his maker without a confession. How complete that confession is must be left for the reader to judge. My own conclusion is that the basic facts are probably correct but that he deliberately downplays the pleasure and excitement he must have obtained from deceiving so many. He could not possibly have sustained the deception over such a prolonged period unless he had enjoyed the process. Combined with that was the realisation that, once he was given an opportunity to better himself through playing the role of a converted Formosan, there was never really any reason or advantage in retracting the deception.

In demonstrating such remarkable perseverance, he deserves to be better remembered than his citation in another hoaxer's most controversial work. Psalmanazar was said to have inspired the scheme set out in Jonathan Swift's pamphlet *A Modest Proposal* of replenishing the lack of venison with the meat of children. But there again, to see your own deliberately nonsensical story being used to augment an equally absurd proposition by his adopted country's leading satirist must have given Psalmanazar some satisfaction, particularly given his humble beginnings. The two men might not have been equal as writers but, when it came to hoaxing, Psalmanazar was arguably in the same league as Swift. Whether or not he was greater, you can judge for yourself in the next chapter.

TWO

'BUT A TRIFLE'

* * *

I

How do you hoax a hoaxer? It's a question that Jonathan Swift must have asked himself in early 1708 when he contemplated duping a best-selling author of the day. The man he had in his sights was called John Partridge, and he was an astrologer.

Astrology was born out of common sense and verifiable data. Two-thousand years before Christ it was clear there was a link between the sun and the seasons of the year. It was not much of an imaginative leap, therefore, to conclude that other planets, together with meteors, comets and eclipses, might have an effect on events on earth – particularly as the thinking was that our world was at the centre of the universe. It was modern in its approach, as it rejected the idea that capricious gods were imposing their will on our actions. Rather it was the calculation of the constantly changing relationship of the stars to one another that could predict the consequences for man and nature.

Astrology made an impact on English society in the second half of the sixteenth century. Following the Reformation, clergymen were no longer thought to possess supernatural powers. For people looking for some sort of guidance, astrology therefore filled a gap that the parson had relinquished. Knowing the inter-planetary alignment at the time of your birth, your 'nativity', enabled the skilled practitioner to both work out your personality and determine your destiny. When it came to answering personal problems, such 'horary' questions were adjudicated on the basis of the position of the stars at the time of asking. 'Elections' comprised choosing the exact moment when the influence of the planets was most favourable for a decision, whether it was harvesting a crop or weaning an infant. In many respects, therefore, astrology was a relatively benign belief. One-to-one consultations, although they did not do much good, didn't do much harm either. The problem was that astrologers found a means of influencing not just an individual, through a personal reading, but potentially great masses of the populace. They did this through the Christian's equivalent of the Bible, the astrologer's almanac.

The first almanac to be published in England was probably the work of William Parron, at the end of the fifteenth century. It took another fifty years before they proliferated and also became gradually standardised. They tended to be around forty-eight pages in length, containing a calendar and details of the movements of planets; an image of man divided into twelve areas corresponding to the signs of the zodiac; lists of fairs, festive occasions and saint's days; prognostications on the weather, farming and medical matters; and short pieces of prose and verse. The opportunity to include propaganda in the forecasts came about with the Civil War of 1642. Previously, if you failed to back the monarchy, you were labelled a traitor. There was now scope for partisanship. Embracing political predictions proved to be a winning formula for astrologers. The most successful exponent was William Lilly. As he was a Parliamentarian, his anti-Royalist prognostications were in line with public opinion. By the time of the execution of Charles I in 1649, he was selling 30,000 copies of his yearly almanacs.

Lilly died in 1681. His successor as the favourite almanac writer of his generation was John Partridge [Fig. 3]. Partridge was born in East Sheen in Surrey in 1644 and began life as a shoemaker, a profession that Swift would later enjoy teasing him about. He had an inquiring mind and taught himself Latin, and some Greek, and then began to

Fig. 3. Portrait of John Partridge with his astrological birth chart.

study astrology and medicine. He turned both of these to his financial advantage in 1677 when he moved to London, making a living selling quack remedies and publishing almanacs. The latter quickly became popular as he revealed his pro-Parliament and anti-Catholic astrological prognostications, almost to the point of republicanism. After James II came to the throne in 1685, he was forced to flee abroad and live in Holland for three years. He continued to produce his almanacs from the safety of the Continent. In one of them he made his most notorious forecast anticipating the death of a king in 1688. As Partridge had been confidently predicting the end of Louis XIV for some years, this could be seen as foreseeing the demise of the King of France, rather than of England. But Partridge was quick to take credit when William of Orange deposed James II in December of that year. He got around the problem that James II was still alive by stating his exile was a 'Civil Death', an event 'worse than Death'.

Following the Glorious Revolution, Partridge's time had come, and he became the foremost astrologer of the 1690s. He regularly published his *Merlinus Liberatus,* continuing his anti-papal reformist agenda. He earned a substantial income from these almanacs, with annual sales averaging 25,000, along with the lucrative off-shoot from his sales of medicine – which were naturally advertised within its pages.

Sceptics, having tried over many years, knew that astrology was a slippery beast to try to pin down and somehow discredit. Seemingly the most obvious way was to compare the prognostication with the actuality and draw attention to its non-fulfilment. But astrologers had learnt numerous strategies with which to respond to this critique. Most often used was invoking God's goodwill. If a forecast disaster did not arise, then God, in his infinite kindness, had decided to give us a reprieve. If an unanticipated catastrophe occurred, then it was God punishing us for our sins. When William Lilly failed to predict the Restoration of Charles II, he passed it off by writing that 'God is just and we must acknowledge so much.' In addition there was always the fallback, as espoused by Lilly, that 'the stars incline, but do not compel'.

Many of the predictions were deliberately cryptic or ambiguous, sufficiently malleable for the astrologer to be 'correct' irrespective of what took place. 'News from *France*; good enough if it prove true, though perhaps all may not be of my opinion.' Making a statement in the form of a query – 'Why not an ecclesiastical person, or lawyer, promoted to great honour?' – meant you were right whatever the outcome. Repeating the same forecast year in, year out, ensured that eventually you would be spot-on in your assertion. And when you were, attention was focused on the accurate prediction, with the multiple failures quietly forgotten. Astrologers were adept at explaining away blatant errors. John Gadbury, a rival to Partridge, said that in the years of the Great Plague and the Fire of London, he had anticipated only small discontents because he 'wished them so'. Lilly simply blamed the 'wicked people' of the Scottish nation who had 'deluded me' in his failure to predict the Scottish invasion of 1648. When his almanacs were redacted he turned that to his advantage. In 1655 he wrote that he would love to tell more but 'loves not a prison'. In 1673 he told his readers that many of his previous years' predictions had been right, despite his inability to write them down in advance because of the censor.

Nevertheless attempts were made to ridicule Partridge's forecasts. George Parker, a long-time opponent of Partridge, in his *Parker's Ephemeris for the Year of our Lord 1708*, went through each month of Partridge's 1707 predictions to show how inaccurate they were. For instance, his forecast that the kings of Poland and Sweden would be at war, even though in reality they had enacted a peace treaty. Or that the predictions were merely stating the obvious: anticipating the destruction of shipping in October, when it was well known to be the season of storms and tempests. Or that Partridge was playing the odds: forecasting the death of a prince who was 'the Troubler of *Europe*'.

Another attempt to mock Partridge was through a satirical parody of his almanac. This was tried by Thomas Brown in 1700 in *A Comical View of the Transactions That will happen in the Cities of*

London & Westminster. They were published weekly from October to December under the supposed authorship of Silvester Partridge, so incorporating ridicule of another astrologer called John Silvester. Two of his predictions were that, if it is raining, few prostitutes will be seen in Cheapside, and from eight to nine there will be bell ringing all over the City. Brown enjoyed explaining why some of his prognostications the previous week hadn't come true or why he had got the timing slightly wrong. And he also had fun inserting phony advertisements from Silvester Partridge for personal readings, elixirs, medical pills and restorative charms, including '*a Ring to prevent Cuckoldom, very useful for all married Persons*'. It was all very amusing but hardly likely to trouble Partridge to any great degree.

Jonathan Swift [Fig. 4] therefore faced a formidable task if he was going to land a blow on Partridge, necessitating a new approach that no one had previously thought of. Before looking at his inspired solution, and to fully appreciate its subtleties, it is necessary to understand why Swift wanted to confront the astrologer. The predominant reason was that Partridge had a religious outlook that was directly contrary to Swift's core beliefs. Swift was ordained in the Anglican Church in 1694 at the age of twenty-six. His first position was as a prebendary in Kilroot in the county of Antrim in Northern Ireland. Later, in 1700, he was appointed a vicar at Laracor in Southern Ireland. Both of these jobs showed him how hard it was for lowly clergymen to make a living. The core parishioners were in decline owing to the influx of Presbyterians and dissenters, who were hostile to Swift's own tenets of the Church of England liturgy and the rule by the bishops. This gave an excuse for many landlords to fail to pay the tithes due to the curates and vicars.

Swift mistrusted the Presbyterians because of their involvement in the rebellion against the Church and State during the years of the Civil War and afterwards, including the beheading of the King. Dissenters, those who opposed state interference in religious matters, were associated with 'enthusiasm', the claim by individuals to be inspired by the voice of the Holy Ghost. They were rebelling against

Fig. 4. Portrait of Jonathan Swift, an engraving by George Vertue, from a painting by Charles Jervas, around 1709–10.

the episcopal authority of a legally established church of which Swift was a representative. This came to a head in 1707 when Swift was sent over to London by the Irish bishops to lobby for the remission of two taxes which were burdensome to the poorer clergy. One of these, the so-called First Fruits, which was payable by every incumbent on his appointment to the Crown, had recently been revoked by Queen Anne. The Church of Ireland was merely seeking equity with its English counterpart. But the Whig Government would only consider such a concession if the Irish bishops removed 'the Test'.

The Test Act, first passed in England in 1673, had been extended to Ireland in 1704. It prevented any person who refused to take communion in the established Church from holding public office. Although it was principally aimed against Roman Catholics, dissenters and Presbyterians were also caught in its wake. Swift considered the Test essential to the survival of the Irish Anglican Church, and this was a line he would not cross in any negotiation, even if the cost was the continuation of the exorbitant financial constraints imposed on Irish clerics. Swift's failure to persuade the intransigent Government must have been very galling to him. And against him, as was made clear in his almanacs, was John Partridge, a staunch Whig who lambasted the Tories for supporting idolatry, popery and tyranny.

As well as religious, there were major political differences between the two men. In 1707 the Union Act between England and Scotland was enacted. For his 1708 Almanac, *Merlinus Liberatus*, Partridge wrote a poem titled 'On the Glorious Union of the Two Kingdoms'. Swift opposed the Union as it appeared to reward Scottish dissent ahead of Irish loyalty. Another divergence was in the continuance of the War of Spanish Succession. Partridge was against any peace overtures while the Catholic Philip V remained on the Spanish throne. As he was the grandson of Louis XIV, it meant Spain was effectively a satellite state of France. Partridge stated his own position in his 1708 Almanac, although in doing so he hid behind familiar ambiguities. In February of that year he predicted that there would be endeavours to attain peace, but that he would rather have no peace than one that didn't endure. In June, he hinted that a general peace is in the air 'but not on a sudden'. Swift was unequivocal in wanting the war to finish. He felt that the Whigs were pursuing the fighting for their own ends, either for prestige, as in the case of the Duke of Marlborough, or for financial gain. Two years later he would be actively involved in producing propaganda pamphlets to persuade politicians and noblemen to accept a peace treaty, while still allowing Philip V to remain as king.

One can easily imagine, therefore, how Swift, effectively side-lined by the English Government in his overtures to help the Irish clerics, would have been tempted to turn his anger on someone who was his polar opposite in religious and political beliefs. And, on top of that, here was a person successfully peddling those opinions through the fulcrum of some sort of scientific rationalisation which, in Swift's view, was superstitious nonsense. In contemplating his retribution, Swift wanted to do more than merely 'send up' astrology and cause maximum mirth. He was seeking several ambitious goals. He needed to warn the public about Partridge's dangerous and inflammatory opinions, show the logical absurdity of his prognostications and – perhaps hardest of all, given Partridge's capacity to absorb criticism and relish debate – genuinely needle him. As we will discover, Swift succeeded in all these aims.

II

It was in early February 1708 that *Predictions for the Year 1708* [Fig. 5] by Isaac Bickerstaff was published. Swift chose the pen-name because he had observed the name Bickerstaff on a locksmith's house. It was just one of many almanacs published for that year. Apart from those by Partridge and Parker, there were others authored by George Rose, Thomas Trigge, John Woodhouse, John Goldsmith, Richard Gibson, John Wing and Francis Moore. Many buying *Predictions* might have taken it at face value as a new addition to this popular genre. The main oddity was the date it came out. Most almanacs for the following year's predictions were sold in the three months leading up to the beginning of that year. However they normally remained on sale until March, so it is conceivable that a late purchaser might think that it was a standard almanac. A quick flick-through would have disillusioned them. Unlike most almanacs this one included no list of kings and queens, no table of sunrises, sunsets, tides and interest charts – and no explanation of how Bickerstaff had arrived at his predictions by reference to the planetary placements and movements

PREDICTIONS

FOR THE

YEAR 1708.

Wherein the Month and Day of the
Month are set down, the Persons
named, and the great Actions and
Events of next Year particularly
related, as they will come to pass.

Written to prevent the People of England *from
being further impos'd on by vulgar Almanack-
makers.*

By ISAAC BICKERSTAFF *Esq;*

Fig. 5. Title page of *Predictions for the Year 1708*,
by Isaac Bickerstaff, alias Jonathan Swift.

for each month.

Instead, Bickerstaff begins his almanac with an overview of the
current consensus about astrology. He acknowledges that there are
some who are sceptical about the subject, with several learned men
contending that it is absurd and ridiculous to imagine the stars can
have any impact on human actions, thoughts or inclinations. This,
of course, was Swift's own position. Scientists were coming to the
realisation, given that neither the sun nor the earth was at the centre
of the universe, and knowing about the vast distances to the stars, that
it was not possible to identify any planetary influence. Bickerstaff
admits that there are charlatans around who, rather than inspecting
the stars for their information, look no higher than their own brains.
Bickerstaff is not like that. Indeed he intends to publish 'a large and

rational Defence' of astrology. And if anyone condemns it, clearly they don't understand it.

He then turns on the best-known astrologers of the day. He expresses surprise that any Member of Parliament should bother to consult Partridge's almanacs to find out events of the year both home and abroad. Similarly, why does anyone bother to look at Gadbury to check the weather before going hunting? He mocks them for their grammar, spelling and lack of ability to write common sense. He gives examples of generalised predictions that can't fail – for instance, forecasting that in a specific month, deliberately choosing 'the sickliest Season of the Year', a great person will be threatened with death or sickness. There is no month, Bickerstaff argues, where someone of note doesn't die. And there are those that work either way: 'God preserve King William from all his open and secret Enemies', plainly predicts his death. But, if he survives, then it could be taken as a pious statement of a loyal subject. After he lambasts his rivals, including having a dig at their advertisements selling quack medicine to combat venereal disease, Bickerstaff lays out his own credentials. He had previously foretold the inconclusive nature of the naval siege of Toulon and the death of Admiral Shovell in the Scilly Isle maritime disaster, together with another Allied defeat at the Battle of Almanza. He had, moreover, shown these forecasts to friends many months before they happened.

Bickerstaff confidently asserts that he is prepared to be judged on the accuracy of his prognostications. Partridge and his colleagues can call him a cheat and impostor if he fails. He does say that he will concentrate his predictions on overseas events, hinting that it would be dangerous to disclose state secrets. But for those occurrences that are not of public consequence he will matter-of-factly predict them. He reprises the standard 'get-out', should he fail in any of his predictions, that the stars only incline. He elaborates further by saying that man's free will can overcome a planetary influence. One final explanation is required before turning to the predictions themselves. Why is he starting from the end of March, as opposed to January? Bickerstaff ingeniously claims that he is going by the 'natural Year', which is from when 'the *Sun* enters into *Aries*'. This was a throwback to when many countries used 25 March, the feast of the Annunciation, as New Year's Day.

Bickerstaff's introduction, as written by Swift, is a wonderful satirical pastiche. He jeers at astrology generally but argues that his own methodology works. He gives examples of why most prognostications are mere guesses but says his own are verifiable. He states that he is happy to be appraised on the basis of his predictions but explains why circumstances might produce different results. And yet, while readers would have doubtless immensely enjoyed the send-up of the ambiguities and contradictions which were a feature of all almanacs, Swift wasn't bringing anything new to the table. He rectifies this with his very first prediction, even though he dismisses it as 'but a Trifle'. He writes that he has consulted Partridge's nativity and concludes that he will definitely die on 29 March, about eleven at night, 'of a raging Feaver'.

The ingenuity of Bickerstaff's statement is that it confronts Partridge with a double-edged sword. First, Bickerstaff is positioning himself as a rival astrologer who has devised a system that is absolutely certain in its predictions – not just in the actual name of the person but even down to the exact time of the day the event will take place. No astrologer had previously dared to be so specific. Even though he doesn't elaborate on how he has arrived at his conclusion, merely saying he is using his chosen rules, it is a direct threat to Partridge's own methodology. Second, he is taunting Partridge with his own death, which he implies Partridge had himself anticipated. In his 1708 *Merlinus Liberatus*, Partridge had forecast in the month of April for the City of London 'a Tertian Ague and Fever'. Partridge, dying from a 'raging Feaver', seems to be verifying his own prognostication.

Partridge was faced with the dilemma of whether and how to respond. One solution was to ignore it. The problem was that the *Predictions* quickly came a bestseller. Swift wrote about the printing of 'thousands' of copies and complained that Grub Street printers were selling rip-offs at half price. There was an advertisement in *The Daily Courant* for the pamphlet for 30 March, still selling two months after its publication. Could Partridge therefore afford to take no notice of such a widely disseminated attack on his own integrity as an astrologer, particularly one that was forecasting his own death?

All of Partridge's instincts must have been to reply, as that was how he had always previously dealt with criticisms from rival astrologers. The author of pamphlets such as *The Black Life of John Gadbury* and *The Whipper Whipp'd* surely could not stand meekly aside from this fray, saying nothing. One aspect that remains unanswered is whether Partridge at this time knew Bickerstaff's almanac was a spoof. Pamphlets were more often than not written under a pseudonym, so just because he didn't recognise the name would not have assisted him in clearing up the mystery of whether Bickerstaff was a genuine astrologer. The evidence either way is conflicted because of the response that did emerge, *Mr Partridge's Answer to Esquire Bickerstaff's Strange and Wonderful Predictions for the Year 1708.*

Scholars are still unsure whether Partridge wrote this himself. Those who think he did base that judgement on the content and tone, which catch exactly his belligerent style of writing. My own instinct is that Partridge would at least have waited until after his predicted death on 29 March before responding. Nevertheless, because the parody is so good, anybody reading *Mr Partridge's Answer* at the time would have considered Partridge the author. The writer of the pamphlet takes Bickerstaff seriously as an astrologer. So his response is exactly what you would expect in those circumstances. He argues that if he survives beyond his predicted death, this proves that Bickerstaff is a liar, and therefore Bickerstaff's conjecture that the whole art of astrology is a cheat must be wrong. He makes the obvious point that Bickerstaff does not provide any evidence of who his friends are that apparently confirmed the accuracy of his previous predictions. He then goes through Bickerstaff's own monthly prognostications, beginning with his own demise. He derides him, rather unconvincingly, by saying that it seems 'odd' that the stars can't find anybody better to kill than a poor publishers of almanacs.

Besides his foretelling of Partridge's death, in his *Predictions* Bickerstaff made many other forecasts for the six months from April to September 1708, the majority of a grisly nature. They included the demise of the Pope, the destruction of the French navy caused by a storm, and the deaths of Louis XIV of France, his son and great grandson. However he 'saved' the French monarch's grandson, Philip V of Spain, who was one of the stumbling blocks to end the on-going War of Spanish Succession. As already noted, the Whigs, with Partridge prominent among them, were not prepared to consider a peace treaty without the Spanish King stepping down, a position encapsulated in the slogan 'No peace without Spain'. Bickerstaff had therefore tantalisingly fulfilled many of Partridge's anti-French and anti-Catholic sentiments, except the one that really mattered to him. When it came to domestic matters, Bickerstaff kept to his promise to talk 'sparingly of Home Affairs'. His predictions were suitably frivolous. A peer of the realm will die at his country house, a famous buffoon of the playhouse will suffer a ridiculous death and mischief will be done at Bartholomew Fair caused by the collapse of a booth. *Mr Partridge's Answer* ridicules and mocks all of these. But given they were not meant to be taken seriously in the first place, it is rather a redundant exercise.

For Swift, *Mr Partridge's Answer* was an irrelevant distraction — although he would doubtless have been pleased that it kept his own publication in the limelight. He had already planned his follow-up, which was to focus on the death of Partridge. This came in two parts. The first was an elegy in rhyming couplets '*on the supposed Death of Partridge, the Almanack-Maker*'. It wittily links Partridge's previous occupation as a cobbler to his present profession of an astrologer, showing 'how the Art of Cobbling bears / A near Resemblance to the Spheres'. It concludes with Partridge's Epitaph, of which these are the best-known four lines:

Here, five Feet deep, lies on his Back,
A Cobbler, Starmonger, and Quack;
...
Weep, all you Customers that use
His Pills, his Almanacks, or Shoes;

The second was in prose and was called *The Accomplishment of the First of Mr Bickerstaff's Predictions*. It was in the form of a letter from a tax collector to a nobleman. Allegedly the Revenue official was an acquaintance of Partridge, as the astrologer used to present him with a copy of his almanac each year in exchange for a financial favour. Hearing that his former colleague is seriously ill he decides to visit him on his sickbed. After commiserating with him he asks Partridge if he thinks Bickerstaff's prediction had adversely affected him. Partridge confesses this might well be the case, admitting that, like himself, Bickerstaff just guessed his predictions. He admits that the foretellings in his own almanacs were invented in order to make money. He had no other means of earning a living, given that mending shoes was a poor livelihood.

After half an hour's conversation, the civil servant retires to a coffee house to await the news of Partridge's inevitable death. He is informed that Partridge expired at five minutes past seven, which meant that Bickerstaff was out by four hours from his original prediction. This is a delightful touch by Swift, highlighting the inexactitude of the astrologer's art. The anonymous writer concludes by speculating as to whether Bickerstaff was both the predictor and the cause of Partridge's death, a type of self-fulfilling prophecy. He was now waiting with keen anticipation to see if Bickerstaff's next prediction – the death of a Cardinal de Noailles on 4 April – would occur.

Swift once again shows how masterly he is in manipulating the hoax by distancing the author of *The Accomplishment* from Bickerstaff himself. No one could think the letter was anything other than a work of fiction. Many would have first read it, along with the accompanying *Elegy*, on 1 April, thereby emphasising that it was an April Fool's Day joke. But that still left the possibility that the *Predictions* were genuine. It would seem, though, by 24 April 1708, that Partridge had realised they were a spoof. He wrote to his friend Isaac Manley, the Postmaster-General for Ireland, that 'there is no such Man as Isaack Bickerstaff it is a sham Name'. He speculates that the actual author is William Pittis, a high Tory churchman and pamphleteer who had previously attacked Partridge in print. Significantly, however, Partridge admits in this letter that the whole episode is getting to him, with plenty of 'Rogues' suggesting he is dead. He even has to reassure Manley that he is still alive.

Given this, it is hard to understand why Partridge decided to continue drawing attention to Bickerstaff, and the prank, in a publication indisputably written by him. His 1709 almanac, *Merlinus Liberatus*, was composed not long after this April letter when the subject matter was still very much preying on his mind. As almanacs had to be cleared for censorship, they were written well in advance of their publication in October. Another couple of months of contemplation might have alerted Partridge to the wisdom of keeping silent on the subject. Instead it was almost as if he had a vested interest in perpetuating the hoax.

On the front cover Partridge states what is to be expected from his latest almanac, including the usual astrological observations on the next twelve months. He then informs the reader that he is alive, contrary to the 'base paper' written by Bickerstaff. In his February predictions he forecasts the production of scandalous pamphlets, with the added comment that perhaps a second Bickerstaff may appear. This is as close to a joke as Partridge is capable of. At the end of the almanac Partridge reminds his readers of the pamphlet predicting his death. Moreover 'the same Villain' told the world that he had died and that he was with him at the time of his death. He reassures everybody that not only is he alive now but he was also alive on 29 March. The Bickerstaff paper was written by 'an *Impudent Lying Fellow*', for, even though he had calculated Partridge's nativity, his prediction proved to be false. It gives the impression that Partridge still believes that Bickerstaff's predictions are somehow authentic, as at least there was some sort of astrological computation used to forecast his death.

One suspects that Swift, before the publication of this almanac, had no intention of carrying on with the joke. However Partridge, in his protestations, had given him too easy a target to ignore. So in 1709 Swift published his final response, called *A Vindication of Isaac Bickerstaff*. He begins by expressing his regret at receiving such criticisms from Partridge, observing that such behaviour is ungentlemanly. Bickerstaff stresses the intellectual and class divide between the two of them by noting he had received nearly 100 honorary letters from several parts of Europe praising his work. He reproduces three testimonials, all in Latin, one of which translates that the noble Englishman Bickerstaff is easily the prince of astrologers of our time. He suggests that Partridge should have responded in like manner to his *Predictions* by producing evidence of Bickerstaff's own lack of learning, which he would have taken on board. He observes that the only prediction Partridge has disputed relates to his own death. By this, Swift seems to accept that Partridge had not written *Mr Partridge's Answer*, as in that pamphlet, many of Bickerstaff's predictions, not just of Partridge's demise, had been scorned by the author. He claims that this is the only objection he has encountered against any of his forecasts, apart from a Frenchman who said Cardinal de Noailles was still alive. But then how could you trust the word of a Gallic papist against an English Protestant?

Bickerstaff now turns to his forecast of Partridge's death on 29 March 1708. He reminds the reader that Partridge has contradicted this fact. However he will now prove that Partridge is dead, with 'Brevity, Perspicuity and Calmness', fully aware that the eyes of not just England, but Europe too, will be upon him. His first argument relates to Partridge's almanac itself. He acknowledges that thousands will have bought it, even if it is only so they can find out what he has written against Bickerstaff. But anybody reading it would have to conclude that 'no man alive' could write such nonsense. Which means that either Partridge must disown his almanac or admit that he is indeed 'no man alive'.

Bickerstaff demonstrates similar twisted logic in setting out another reason why Partridge can't be alive. He pretends to tell fortunes, but this can only be achieved by conversing with the devil and other evil spirits. Such conversation can only take place once you are dead. He directly addresses one obstacle to his supposed death, that he continues to write almanacs. Bickerstaff points out that this was a common practice in the profession, with some publishing an annual almanac even though they had been dead 'since before the *Revolution*'. Ironically, Partridge would join that select band of almanac writers whose names continued to grace publications long after they had died.

Whether or not Partridge intended to respond to this diatribe, or if he thought it best to finally let the matter drop, we will never know. Because of a financial dispute with the Company of Stationers who published his almanacs, his next edition of *Merlinus Liberatus* did not appear until 1713. In the meantime the persona of Isaac Bickerstaff was taken on by writers other than Swift, most notably by Richard Steele in *The Tatler* for its two years of existence between 1709 and 1711. It was perhaps mainly because of this that Partridge came back to confront his tormentor one final time in his 1714 *Merlinus Redivivus*. He seems by this stage, though, to be in a more forgiving, and indeed playful, mood. He admits in the foreword to the almanac, addressed directly to Isaac Bickerstaff, that he had been for some years silent or, 'in the Language of Mr *Bickerstaffe, Dead*'. He says he no longer has any quarrel with Bickerstaff because he too was abused by having his name hijacked by the 'notorious cheat', Jonathan Swift. He hopes that if Bickerstaff does seem fit to return again, in whatever capacity, that he 'will do Justice to Your Revived Friend, and Servant, John Partridge'.

Swift, though, had no intention of taking up the challenge. By 1714 he had assisted the Government in successfully concluding the Treaty of Utrecht to end the War of Spanish Succession, even though Philip V remained on the Spanish throne. In that respect he had succeeded in combating Partridge's political ideology. Unfortunately for Swift, he had upset Queen Anne by criticising one of her confidants in *The Windsor Prophecy* – written in 1711, forecasting the defeat of the Whigs – and in *A Tale of a Tub*, where she mistook its purpose for profanity. As a result he never received the English clerical living that he craved. In August 1714 he returned to Dublin, his posting as Dean of Saint Patrick's Cathedral, and a six-year publishing hiatus. Partridge died less than a year later, in June 1715. He was a wealthy man, leaving over £2,000 in his will. He passed away knowing that George I's accession to the throne meant the definite end of the hated Stuart dynasty. His legacy continued to the last decade of the eighteenth century, with almanacs still published under his name. In the immediate aftermath it was boldly claimed that the 1716 and 1717 editions were transcribed from a copy 'written with the Doctor's own Hand'.

III

Looking back on the Bickerstaff affair from the perspective of the twenty-first century, some might question whether *Predictions for the Year 1708* was a deliberate hoax, or if it was even meant to be one. Did Swift really think purchasers would believe he had written a genuine almanac? Wouldn't it have been obvious that it was set out to mock the person, profession and politics of Partridge, using a parody of an almanac to accomplish that aim? It is conceivable that some people might have been convinced that Bickerstaff was serious in his predictions; but then there were some people who thought parts of *Gulliver's Travels* were true. So that is not really an argument in support of Swift's intentions. What really converted it into a hoax was John Partridge himself. As soon as he engaged with the *Predictions*, most notably the forecast of his own death, he fell into the trap of investing the almanac with some validity. In this respect,

Swift had the measure of his opponent. Partridge had always been a man who enjoyed robust exchanges with his fellow astrologers. He made the mistake of confronting the fictional Bickerstaff in the same manner as he did the genuine John Gadbury or George Parker and, what is more, using the same types of argument to attempt to discredit him.

In so doing Partridge forgot how easy it was, as he had himself done so many times before, to find excuses for failed predictions. He swallowed the bait of thinking he could disprove his own death by the simple expedient of proclaiming he was still alive. And yet, as we have seen, twenty years earlier he had tried to convince his supporters that his forecast of King James II's death in October 1688 was correct, even though the monarch was very much living. For Swift, such verbal subterfuge was meat and drink. He effortlessly came up with no fewer than five reasons why Partridge's protestations that he still existed could be ignored. That they were all nonsense was irrelevant. The readers of Swift's pamphlets would have shared his own belief that the whole subject matter of astrology was ridiculous anyway. He was merely using the same false logic, ambiguous language and obscuration that was beloved by almanac writers. He was playing by their rules and using them against themselves.

Part of the brilliance of Swift is that throughout he remains remarkably mischievous. He obviously thinks that astrology is preposterous. However, rather than attacking existing almanac writers, he portrays himself as an expert on the subject, confident enough in his ability to make extremely specific predictions. We can also be certain, given his own religious and political beliefs, that he has nothing but contempt for Partridge. But this never emerges from his pamphlets. All he really does is predict the man's death, and mocks him when he refuses to accept his fate. By not using the obvious tactic of disputing Partridge's own forecasts, he completely wrongfoots him. Partridge flounders over how to respond. All he can do is contradict his own demise – and when that is the only way you can win an argument, you are in trouble.

From Swift's perspective, the whole scheme played out perfectly, better than he had envisaged. The original *Predictions* proved very popular and generated plenty of interest and gossip. This gave him the opportunity to publish a third-party report, with *The Accomplishment*, of Partridge's supposed death on 29 March. It should really have ended there. Instead Partridge responded in his own almanac which enabled Swift to produce his *Vindication*. The perfect one, two, three scenario: first the teasing set-up, then the entrapment, and finally the killer denouement.

Apart from the personal humiliation of Partridge, did the hoax have any further ramifications? It did not sound the death knell of astrology which, even today, as can be seen by the daily publication of horoscopes in many newspapers, is still felt by many to have some legitimacy. What it did do, though, was assist in convincing people that it had no place in the political and religious affairs of the State. The Bickerstaff papers, as they have come to be known, helped in converting astrology from a 'scientific' art, taken seriously by men and women of influence, to a faith-based craft, one that more gullible sections of the general public consulted for assistance in relatively minor personal and domestic issues.

Of all the hoaxers in this book, apart from Benjamin Franklin, Swift is by far the best known – although not, of course, for the subject matter of this chapter. He will always be most remembered as the author of *Gulliver's Travels*. But it is arguable that his role in finding the means to ridicule a profession that had managed, for many centuries, to skirt around censure and avoid attempts to expose it as a sham, was equally impressive. For a hoax to make a positive contribution to society, while simultaneously giving everybody a good laugh, is very rare. And yet somehow, with the 'trifling' inspiration to predict the death of an astrologer, Swift did precisely that.

THREE

'AN EXTRAORDINARY DELIVERY OF RABBETS'

* * *

I

In 1726 Mary Toft claimed that she was giving birth to rabbits. Her ordeal started in April of that year when she was five weeks pregnant. She was working in Godalming in the county of Surrey as a hop-picker. She and another woman had spied some rabbits which they tried to catch without success. That night Mary dreamt of rabbits and for the next three months had a strong desire to eat them. About four months after the start of this longing, Mary had a miscarriage, although she still appeared to be pregnant. At the beginning of September, milk flowed from her breast.

The date of her first unusual birth was on 27 September 1726. After being ill in the night, she brought forth what was described as the liver and guts of a pig. Mary's husband took the animal parts to John Howard, who was a surgeon at Guildford. He was reluctantly persuaded to come and see Mary for himself. Arriving at the house he found her in labour and promptly delivered the stomach, intestines and three paws of a cat. Rather than dismissing the whole matter as an absurdity, he stayed around long enough for a rabbit's head and foot to appear. With enough body parts to assemble some sort of complete creature in place, Howard was a convert. Over the next few weeks he oversaw many more deliveries of dead rabbits.

The story hit the papers on 22 October, nearly a month after Howard stepped in. It doesn't seem, at that stage, to have gained much traction – maybe because the report was truthful to the extent of not invoking much incredulity. It stated that a woman, with the help of a man-midwife, had given birth to 'something in the Form of a dissected Rabit' with the legs of a cat, and that it was now housed in Guildford. With no hint at any ongoing productions, you can see why it might not have aroused much interest. However by this stage Howard was present at almost daily births, so he was determined others should witness these miraculous conceptions. He began writing to 'Persons of Distinction in Town'. The first man with influence to appear on the scene was Henry Davenant, a courtier of George I. He visited Howard on 4 November and the surgeon subsequently updated him with two letters on 6 and 9 November, by which time Howard had delivered the components of twelve rabbits.

Henry Davenant was not a doctor though, and Howard needed a specialist from London if he was going to make his name with this case. Enter Nathanael St André, anatomist and surgeon to George I. It is easy, given his subsequent naivety, to label the Swiss-born man as incompetent. In truth he was well-respected, having pioneered the preparation of anatomical specimens by means of wax injections. He was also a proficient surgeon, his prowess as a fencing expert probably assisting him in this regard. In September 1726 Alexander Pope had asked for his services when he was wounded in a coaching accident. The fact they remained friends presupposes it was a successful consultation. Although his royal appointment in May 1723 was considered to be partly dependent on his fluency in German, his skills in medicine must have played some part. What he didn't have any experience in was childbirth. Midwifery came under the auspices of the physicians, who were considered to be the elite of the medical profession.

Howard had been neglecting his other duties with his continuous journeys to Godalming, so he had persuaded Toft to join him at his house in Guildford. St André was accompanied by Samuel Molyneux, who was Secretary to the Prince of Wales, the future George II. Two years later, St André would marry Molyneux's wealthy widow, adding to the rumours of unprofessional conduct that emanated from this period. Arriving on 15 November, they no doubt considered themselves fortunate that Mary Toft appeared to be in the throes of another happy event.

With the assistance of John Howard, St André delivered the entire trunk of a rabbit, without fur. Mary was then left alone for a couple of hours. On their return a nurse, in their absence, had delivered the lower part of the rabbit, which matched the upper section that had arrived earlier. In its rectum they found five or six pellets that had the same colour and constituency as the 'common Dung' of a rabbit. St André also discerned in its gut a slender, brittle object that had the shape of small fish bones. If he had any misgivings over how these could have got into the foetus of a rabbit, or how it could have evacuated its bowels while in the womb, these were overridden by the excitement of the next birth. He thoroughly checked her before bringing out the skin of a rabbit squeezed into a ball, followed ten minutes later by the head. His analysis was that the creatures were bred in the fallopian tubes and from there, as a result of her agitations, they ended up in the womb.

As befits an anatomist, St André examined carefully his own, and the previous, deliveries from Mary Toft. These were all faithfully preserved by John Howard, who intended to present them to the Royal Society. In describing them, St André resorted to the word 'like' rather frequently. All the animals were 'like well formed, common, natural Rabbets'; they were 'exactly like such Creatures, as must inevitably undergo the Changes that happen to adult Animals'; and three of the feet were 'like the Paws of a Cat'. However, rather than conclude that 'like' might mean 'identical to', he postulated that the animals were of a particular kind and not bred in the normal way. In other words they were preternatural, outside the ordinary course of nature. St André presented his findings before George I on 26

November, thereby obtaining the stamp of royal approval. He must have been reassured by the newspapers, which were strictly factual in their reporting. Only one raised any concerns, noting that some people were angry at the story and that, if it was true, 'a Veil should be drawn over it, as an Imperfection in humane Nature'.

On 19 November Cyriacus Ahlers, another surgeon to His Majesty, visited Mary in Guildford. Writing after her later confession, Ahlers said that he had been dubious about her from the outset. She had interrupted her supposed labour pains to join in some laughter with himself and Howard 'which I thought so extraordinary for a Woman in her Condition'. Howard refused to let him search Mary when she was in the throes of labour as St André had already done it – he told Ahlers that he ought to be satisfied with his colleague's findings. It later transpired that Howard had made this decision because when Ahlers had examined Mary earlier he had put her through a great deal of 'unnecessary Pain'. Ahlers was also surprised by the dryness of her deliveries. Hiding his suspicions, Ahlers feigned a headache so he could make an early return to London to report his conclusions. However he expressed none of this publicly at the time, admitting he 'thought fit to conceal it'.

On 26 November, the ultimate authority got involved. This was Sir Richard Manningham, considered to be the leading man-midwife of his day. He was asked by George I to investigate, doubtless confused by the conflicting statements he was receiving from his two surgeons. As a Fellow of the College of Physicians, Manningham outranked both Ahlers and St André. Arriving at Guildford he gave Mary a thorough examination. He was unconvinced by her labour motions. He extracted something which he thought was a piece of hog's bladder. In his view it had never been in the womb but had been 'artfully conveyed' direct to her vagina. On overhearing this Mary Toft began to cry, aware that Manningham thought her a cheat.

Nevertheless St André managed to persuade Manningham to hold back from any direct accusations of fraud and it was agreed that further investigations were needed. To this end St André arranged for Mary Toft to be moved to Lacy's Bagnio in Leicester-Fields in London. A bagnio was a bathing-house, complete with hot baths and appliances for sweating – the eighteenth-century equivalent of the modern-day Turkish Bath. It also doubled up as a brothel, or at least a meeting place for illicit assignations and affairs, all of which would later provide ammunition to the pamphleteers and satirical cartoonists. Mary arrived there on 29 November, attended by Manningham and St André. The latter, concerned about Manningham's initial scepticism, needed further support. He wrote to a further medical authority, James Douglas, that same day, urging him to come over, tempting him with the delightful anticipation of delivering himself a rabbit.

James Douglas, although born in Scotland, spent most of his working life in London. He was best known as an anatomist, hence, perhaps, his professional relationship with St André. However for a long period he had specialised in midwifery and was one of the first to use forceps to deliver a baby. His reputation was such that in 1734 he was sent to attend the daughter of George II when it was thought that she might be pregnant. He was therefore an ideal candidate, alongside Richard Manningham, to investigate Mary Toft. Although they did finally manage to expose her as an imposter, it took several days and a fair amount of bickering between the two of them. Furthermore it was not their combined enlightened medical knowledge that cracked the case open but rather a resort to primitive interrogation and threats of torture and imprisonment.

During their time of observing her, interest and speculation in the 'rabbit woman', as she came to be known, ratcheted up. The story, declared one pamphlet, had occupied the 'Conversation of People of all Ranks, Ages, and Conditions'. Another similarly stated that the poor woman of Godalming was 'now the Topic of every Conversation'. 'There is one thing that employs everybody's tongue at present,' wrote Lord Hervey to Henry Fox, and that was a woman 'who had brought forth seventeen rabbits'. He went on: 'Every Creature in Town both Men & Women have been to see & feel her,' and 'All the eminent physicians, Surgeons, and Men-midwives in London are there Day & Night to watch her next production.' There was a reluctance to come down on one side or the other as to her authenticity. Nobody knows, he declared, whether they are to believe their eyes or their ears. Alexander Pope noted that London was 'divided into factions about' the story. A Dr Deacon, writing to a Member of the Royal Society, John Byrom, stated that at present he could 'neither believe nor disbelieve' but would have to wait until it was 'thoroughly examined on both sides'. A newspaper report assured its readers that the whole affair was 'far from being detected; but remains, as yet, as much in the dark as ever'.

John Howard and Nathanael St André had no such doubts and were still vigorously promoting their belief in the rabbit births. Douglas tried to remonstrate with St André, in particular his belief in the formation of the animals in the fallopian tubes and their subsequent passage, somehow, through into the uterus. As Douglas put it, it was 'repugnant to the Structure of these Parts'. Similarly Howard's claim that you could hear the noise of snapping and breaking of bones of the rabbits, brought about by her contractions, was a complete 'Romance': it would be impossible to make out such a sound. St André's reply was that Douglas would soon experience it himself. Backing himself to the hilt Nathanael St André published on 3 December *A Short Narrative of an Extraordinary Delivery of Rabbets*, putting the case in writing for the genuine birth of rabbits by Mary Toft.

Unbeknown to St André, his decision to go public was about to dramatically backfire. In Godalming the authorities were unhappy about all the controversy surrounding one of their residents. Thomas, 2nd Baron Onslow, in his role as Lord Lieutenant for Surrey, began interviewing witnesses to the initial births. Onslow had earlier been a signatory to a list of thirty-eight men who had been caught with the intention of stealing fish from a local pond and who appeared at the Guildford quarter session in July 1726. One of those held in custody was Joshua Toft. The involvement of Mary's husband in such activities was not unexpected, given that Godalming was going through a recession in the wool trade and Joshua, a cloth-worker, was directly affected. The trespass suggested that there was a black economy in animal products that the Tofts were implicated in. The prosecutions reflected a general fear of the gentry that their property was increasingly violated by the labouring classes. It was hard to argue that Mary Toft's births were contributing to this threat to land ownership. Nevertheless the idea that this ignorant peasant woman and the spouse of a criminal should, through her spurious claims, be making a disruptive impact far above her social status was anathema to the likes of Onslow.

On 4 December Onslow wrote to Sir Hans Sloane (the physician and collector of antiquities who had earlier shown his scepticism about Psalmanazar's claim to be from Formosa) expressing his fear that the reports of Mary Toft had 'almost alarmed England'. Enclosed with the letter were depositions taken from six individuals over the time that Mary was in labour in Godalming and Guildford. Their testimony was pretty devastating. Four said that her husband, Joshua, had purchased rabbits from them, one even going so far as to say that Joshua had expressed regret that a dead one was thrown away as 'it would have done as well for me as a live one'. Another two confirmed that Joshua specifically said he would be going to Guildford with the rabbits. A further two witnesses affirmed that the rabbits he had delivered could not have been for Mary to eat, as they had never seen her consume any. Indeed Mary admitted herself 'that she could not eat a Bit of a Rabbit, was she to have a Thousand Pounds for so doing'. Mary Costen, who was hired as a nurse, said that while she was at Guildford she had seen no rabbits eaten but had witnessed at least seven delivered. Rather poignantly she added that she never saw Joshua in any way 'concerned for his Wife's Misfortune'. That, in all the writings during this period, is the only word of sympathy that Mary Toft receives.

If this were not bad enough for St André, the day before the publication of his pamphlet one of the porters at Lacy's Bagnio confided that Mary Toft had implored him to clandestinely procure her a rabbit. This information was withheld for twenty-four hours. Douglas said they hoped 'that more effectual Measures might be taken to come at the whole Truth'. In other words, the physicians were banking on proving Mary Toft a liar through medical observation and examination. When Mary was confronted with the porter's testimony, she at first denied it. After her own sister backed up the story, she admitted it – but said she had wanted it for eating, persisting that she still had a rabbit inside her. This plea temporarily saved her from prison. Sir Thomas Clarges, a Justice of the Peace, wanted to take her into custody. But Manningham still felt the fraud was not yet fully detected and persuaded the reluctant Clarges to let her remain at the premises for further scrutiny.

By 6 December the physicians had finally given up on employing their midwifery expertise to entrap Mary Toft. As James Douglas put it, to get to the truth 'other Arguments were necessary, than Anatomy, or any other Branch of Physick'. The outwardly sympathetic Manningham told Mary that he believed her to be an imposter and that, unless she confessed, he would try a very painful experiment on her. An incentive for her admitting her guilt was that he would speak to several of the nobility on her behalf, although to what end was not stated. She decided to sleep on it. The next day, 7 December, she began the first of her three confessions in front of not just Manningham and Douglas (who took the notes) but also the Duke of Montagu and Lord Baltimore.

The papers got wind of Mary's first confession and reported it. Readers were informed that it took up several sheets of paper, and that she refused to name her associates until she was assured of the King's pardon. There is no evidence to support her having made such a demand. It was not in her confessional notes and, in any event, she had already accused someone of assisting her: the travelling wife of a knife grinder. She had sold Mary a few rabbits and then suggested that she should put one of them into her body. Having committed herself to the scam, and once John Howard was on board as a believer, Mary was unable to back out. She was frightened that if the surgeon uncovered her deception she 'should be ruined'. She was also told that she needed to give birth to at least ten rabbits, as that was the average number in a litter.

Her interrogators did not buy the story of the knife grinder's wife. And in her second confession, the following day, she admitted that she had been assisted by her mother-in-law, the formidable Ann Toft. At the time of the hoax Mary Toft was twenty-three years old. She had married Joshua Toft when she was seventeen and he was eighteen. They had one living son, their daughter having died a few months after she was born. Joshua was the sixth of twelve children. Not only was his mother, Ann, personally experienced in childbirth, she was also an informal midwife for the community in Godalming. She must have been a dominating and imposing figure, someone whom Mary both respected and feared. We do not know why Mary changed her story. But surrounded by an exclusively male entourage of noblemen and prominent physicians, and doubtless threatened with imprisonment and worse if she didn't reveal all, she would have found it virtually impossible to sustain the pretence of the malevolent shadowy figure. At the start of the final confession, she was asked upfront who had contrived the scheme. 'Ann Tofts My husband's mother,' was her response.

The intense psychological pressure that Ann had placed on her daughter-in-law now emerged. Having persuaded her that she could make a living from the venture, she had told Mary that under no circumstances must she betray her participation. A couple of times Mary says that Ann 'ordered' her to do a task. On one occasion she was told to place in her vagina the jaw of a creature, which was so jagged that it tore her 'to pieces'. Only after Ann had left, did an assisting neighbour remove it for her. Opportunities for such humane interventions would seem to have been infrequent as she admitted that her mother-in-law was constantly by her side.

Mary Toft said she also thought Howard was a confederate, and the consensus afterwards was that he was part of the conspiracy. No one came near her apart from Howard and her mother-in-law, so they 'must have put them up' her, as she related. It would explain his enthusiastic and unchallenging endorsement of her reproductive abilities. However, understandably, at this stage Mary was trying to minimise her own involvement. Blaming the principal man-midwife was an obvious tactic in maintaining her relative innocence. Moreover, she rather contradicted herself in saying that Howard had believed the births to be genuine because of her convincing fake labour pains. Either way, Thomas Clarges now had what he wanted in the form of a confession. Mary Toft was incarcerated in Bridewell Prison to await her forthcoming trial as a 'vile Cheat and impostor'.

II

With the hoax finally revealed, the recriminations immediately started. 'The learned Gentlemen, who find themselves mistaken at last in their Judgments of that Affair, are healing their Reputations as well as they can by writing of Pamphlets,' reported one newspaper. First off the block was Nathanael St André, who made an abortive attempt at damage limitation by stating he was now thoroughly convinced it was a 'most abominable Fraud'. He also unwisely said that he intended to publish a full account of the discovery. It never appeared. No wonder one paper speculated that he had lately 'gone distracted'.

Richard Manningham, James Douglas and Cyriacus Ahlers all rushed into print their version of events, essentially implying that they had known from the start that Mary Toft was fraudulent, but for understandable reasons hadn't declared it at the time. Other doctors who had been on the periphery, of which there were plenty, were keen to distance themselves too. Dr Hempe was mentioned in St André's booklet as having been present during one of his visits to Mary. He put a notice in the paper that he had never believed in the truth of the matter.

Following quickly on from these self-serving pamphlets came those ridiculing the participants. Two of them were forensic dissections of St André's *Short Narrative*, showing how his supposed scientific explanations of the rabbit births were untenable. *The Anatomist Dissected* is reputed to have been written by Jonathan Swift, under the pseudonym Lemuel Gulliver, 'Surgeon and Anatomist' to the King of Lilliput. This was a reference to *Gulliver's Travels*, which was published in the same year. Although full of sarcastic invective, *The Anatomist Dissected* also makes telling points about St André believing the rabbits were bred in the fallopian tubes, that the lungs of the supposed foetus floated rather than sank, and that Mary Toft was able to walk normally straight after a delivery. The second pamphlet was written by Thomas Braithwaite, a surgeon himself, who doesn't seem to have examined Mary Toft. He doubtless took pleasure in parading his superior knowledge before his disgraced colleague. It is unlikely that St André would have taken comfort from the author stating he had refrained from enlarging more upon the anatomical parts of the book for, if he had done so, he would have had to contradict 'him almost in every paragraph'.

By now, with everybody aware that it was a hoax, the satirists could join in the fun. Their responses came in all forms: ballads, pamphlets, theatrical productions and satirical prints. The wittiest ballad was by Alexander Pope and William Pulteney and was titled *The Discovery: Or, the Squire turn'd Ferret*. It is scurrilous, crude and full of sexual innuendo, but far more mocking of the doctors involved than Mary Toft. For instance one verse goes as follows:

The Woman, thus being brought to Bed,
Said, to reward your Pains,
St. A--nd--re shall dissect the Head,
And thou shalt have the Brains.

One of the pamphlets, called *Much ado about Nothing*, was penned as if written by Mary Toft, imitating her speech pattern and poor spelling. Any amendments, the reader is told, would render it 'less

Genuine and Credible'. She gives her opinion of the doctors who had come to examine her, preferring best the '*pritty Gentilman*' who '*plaid swetly* on the *Fiddil*', a reference to St André's recognised abilities as a string player and dancing master. The worst doctor is '*a fine-faced long-nosed Gentilman, with a Neck lik a Crain*'. Sir Richard Manningham is described as '*an ugly old Gentilman* in a grate blak wig'. The hoax was also staged. At the Theatre Royal in Lincoln's Inn Fields an additional scene was added to the play *The Necromancer*. The harlequin, the stock comical character for such farcical pieces, mimicked a woman pretending to be in labour. She delivered four rabbits which ran around the stage 'and raised such a Laughter as perhaps has not been heard upon any other Occasion'. Later she gave birth to a large pig.

By far the most famous engraving relating to the hoax was done by a young William Hogarth, one of the most outwardly amusing of all his works. The title itself, *Cunicularii or The Wise men of Godliman in Consultation*, is funny on its own, with the crude Latin translation of a rabbit burrow juxtaposed with the religious connotation of the three Wise Men witnessing the birth of Christ [Fig. 6]. The sacred theme is maintained in the picture with Mary Toft in a martyr's pose while the figure of Richard Manningham, head turned discreetly away, is feeling inside her, resulting in what seems like an orgasmic cry of delight from the violated woman. Manningham is plotting the progress of the animal's birth: 'It Pouts it Swells, it Spreads it Comes.' Scattered around on the floor are already delivered whole, and parts of, rabbits. The fact that most of the rabbits appear to be alive might have convinced some that Mary gave birth to living, breathing creatures.

Nathanael St André is literally dancing for joy as he closely observes. He has a fiddle under his arm and is holding an anatomical drawing of a frog or toad, possibly a symbolism of some sort of monster being produced. He is crying out in delight at 'a great birth'. Meanwhile John Howard is by the door, rejecting a rabbit offered to him by a man with his finger to his nose in a conspiratorial gesture,

Fig. 6. *Cunicularii or the Wise men of Godliman in Consultation*, an engraving by William Hogarth, 1726.

as being 'too big'. Also in the etching are Joshua Toft, looking rather aghast at what is happening to his wife, while his sister, labelled as a rabbit dresser, supports her in her labour pains.

One of the striking features of Hogarth's print is the concentration of men assisting Mary Toft, noticeable in a period when midwifery was very much the preserve of women. Hogarth directly references this by giving Manningham a rather androgynous appearance with the wearing of a woman's gown. The very term 'man–midwife' shows how reluctant society was to embrace the presence of men at a birth. Part of the reason was that it was rare for physicians to examine their patients for any ailment. They would rely primarily on observation and history-taking. However, when it came to childbirth, close inspection was a necessity. This opened up questions around the motives behind male participation in the procedure.

And no one was more thoroughly inspected by men than Mary Toft. Although there is no reason to believe that any of them were getting sexual gratification from such behaviour, the satirists delighted in drawing that conclusion. The sub-title of *The Anatomist Dissected* is 'Being an Examination of the Conduct of Mr St André. Touching the late pretended Rabbit-bearer'. There was no subtlety there by the irrepressible Swift in his pun on the word 'touching'. The same play on words is used in the pamphlet *Much ado about Nothing*, when in order to hear what the poor woman has to say for herself, they will be 'touching *her in the Tenderest part*'. This turns out to be 'her Conscience', but no reader would have believed that is what the author was referring to. The confession 'in her own words' that follows is full of men trying to insert various objects inside Mary, whether it be fumbling hands, a telescope or a chimney-sweep boy. In Hogarth's *Cunicularii*, St André is holding a phallic scalpel, an obvious symbol of lust.

All of this, of course, sustained intense public interest in Mary Toft while she continued to be held in Bridewell Prison. There were even complaints that her story was monopolising the news, preventing other events being reported. Many visitors were keen to see this notorious woman. Her celebrity status was confirmed when, in January 1727, she sat for an engraving that was widely reproduced as a mezzotint print [Fig. 7]. Looking rather surly, and yet defiant, she is seated on a chair, one elbow resting on a table. In her other hand she is holding a rabbit.

The same month she was told that she would be tried at the next assizes in Surrey. A few days later, readers were informed that she was dangerously ill, a condition perhaps brought about by the knowledge that her prosecution was going ahead. Nothing more appeared in the newspapers until, out of the blue in late March, it was stated that there was 'a Difficulty in the Case'.

The problem was under 'What Statute she and her Confederates shall be try'd upon'. If she was to be tried for fraud, then there needed to be a false token that could be displayed. Somehow dead

Fig. 7. Portrait of Mary Toft, an engraving by T. Maddocks, from a painting by John Laguerre, early 1727.

pieces of rabbit did not cut the mustard. Furthermore there was no evidence of anybody being defrauded of money. The little that Mary Toft received was handed over to her voluntarily. Identifying her accomplices was also going to be a major problem. It was obvious that Mary could not have acted alone, but determining just how many others were involved, and what exactly was their role, was by no means an easy task. Finally the authorities must have reflected on the potential embarrassment that any trial would have caused, not just to the higher echelons of the medical profession but also potentially to the Royal Family. The public were well aware that it was only on the 'Order of his Majesty' that Mary was brought up to

London. All these factors contributed to her release without charge on 8 April 1726.

A month later John Howard was also discharged. He had been directly implicated in the hoax by Mary Toft's confession. He had attempted to clear his name with a statement on 15 December that he had no 'Hand in the Imposture, but did really believe the Truth of the Production of the Rabbits'. He maintained that, like others, he had been taken in by the cunning artifice of Mary and her accomplices. He was not believed and he was bound over to appear for trial at a later session, with bail set at an astronomic £800. It is presumed that his case collapsed for similar reasons to those regarding Mary Toft. He returned to his surgeon's practice in Guildford and remained there until his death on 3 March 1755, aged nearly eighty.

Nathanael St André avoided any criminal proceedings, but his standing with the Royal Family was forever tarnished: he never returned to court again. After rabbits reappeared on the menu (in London it was claimed that their consumption fell by two thirds at the height of the controversy), 'they were not at his own table'. Nor were they cooked in any recipe by his considerate friends, who were presumably sensitive about making rabbit-related jokes at his expense. Not so some others. On asking a market woman why she hadn't any more parsley to sell, she told St André that his rabbits had eaten it all. He was described as 'the famous Surgeon' in 1730 on his marriage to the extremely wealthy Lady Elizabeth, the widow of his old friend Samuel Molyneux – a match that in itself caused controversy, with a claim that St André had poisoned her husband two years earlier. '*This* famous Surgeon *shewed his extraordinary skill at the labours of* the Godamin Rabbit-breeder,' one paper reminded its readers. He lived to the remarkable age of ninety-six but, deprived of inheriting Elizabeth's money on her death, ended up in straitened circumstances.

Mary Toft returned to Godalming. Her venture into breeding rabbits did not prevent her reverting to more normal births. In early 1728 she had another daughter. However her life of crime wasn't fully over, as in April 1740 she was committed to Guildford jail for receiving stolen goods. As no more was heard about the case, the assumption must be that once again she was released without charge. She died in January 1763, outliving her husband by some eighteen years. The entry in the St Peter's Church parish register for her burial called her the 'Imposteress Rabbett Breeder'.

III

The Mary Toft case has been very well covered over the years, in both factual and fictional books, in academic treatments and in plays and documentaries. Indeed, even as I was writing this chapter, a brilliantly researched new full-length book on the subject was published (Karen Harvey's *The Imposteress Rabbit Breeder*). However, I think there are a couple of aspects of the hoax which haven't been fully delved into, ones that I find particularly intriguing and especially relevant to this volume. How did she convince the men who attended her that she really was giving birth to rabbits, and what was her motive?

There are two parts to discovering how she fooled so many eminent physicians. The first revolves around the definition of the type of birth that she produced. On 22 November 1726, when it was thought that Mary was telling the truth, John Howard weighed in about the genuineness of her 'monstrous' products. Two months later, when the game was up, she was charged with being an imposter in pretending to have had several 'monstrous' births. The epithet was not unique to Mary's offspring. Around this same period there were reports of a woman in London bringing to bed 'four Children and a Monster'; and closer to home a woman at Guildford having a 'monstrous delivery of a Child'. In both of these there were no further details of what the 'monsters' were. The use of the word 'monstrous' was significant because it placed Mary Toft's alleged offspring into a category that had been at the forefront of scientific discussion for many years.

From the middle ages onwards a monstrous birth meant any

human or animal that was in some way abnormally formed. Up to the start of the seventeenth century, they were often considered to be prodigies, a portent of God's wrath. Gradually, though, non-religious explanations were put forward and interest in them evolved from a sign of imminent disaster to one of curiosity. Alongside that, as advocated by Francis Bacon in his book *Novum Organum*, came a resolve to thoroughly research any cases of aberrant progeny. 'A compilation,' he wrote in 1620, 'must be made of all monsters and prodigious births of nature.' It needed to be done 'with a rigorous selection'. Embracing this new approach was the Royal Society, which was founded in 1660. Its papers were published in the *Philosophical Transactions*, and there were many written on monstrous births, listing names of witnesses and particulars of time, place and circumstances. When investigating, Royal Society members were instructed to use 'their *own Touch and Sight*'. It was a '*Fundamental Law*' that they should get 'to *handle* the subject'. In 1726 the editor of *Philosophical Transactions* was Sir Hans Sloane and, when Mary Toft was moved to London, St André asked him to visit. Sir Richard Manningham and James Douglas were both Fellows of the Royal Society; a paper by St André had been published in its journal; even one of the noblemen bystanders at the bagnio, the Duke of Montagu, was 'a very distinguished Member of the *Royal Society*'. It is therefore not surprising that Mary was treated more like a specimen than a human being.

One theory as to the cause of monstrous births had its roots in Greek and Roman writers and philosophers: that of maternal imagination. This proposed that the imagination of the mother, through an accident, obsession or confronting a terrifying image or event, could leave an impression on the soft and pliable material of the foetus which resulted in a possible monstrosity. Many in the medical field had accepted the concept over the years, but two were of particular significance when it came to Mary Toft: Daniel Turner, in a chapter in his book on skin diseases written in 1714 and, ten years later, John Maubray with *The Female Physician*. Neither was a member of the Royal Society, but Turner put it about that he was, and had written reports for the *Philosophical Transactions*; Maubray had sought the patronage of Sir Hans Sloane and, presumably because of that, had attended Mary Toft in London.

Turner, in particular, gave numerous examples of maternal imagination. They could vary from the relatively mild – if a baby has an unusual birthmark, it was the result of some fruit falling on the mother during pregnancy – to the horrific. He told how a woman had given birth to a child with a feline head. This was because she was startled by a cat that had climbed into her bed. In another example, a lady who had been frightened by a beggar's stump arm produced a child with a missing hand. It was not just physicians who were believers. James Paris, a servant of Samuel Pepys, recorded and illustrated various monstrosities he had seen. He recounted how his own relatives had given birth to a 'monstrous child with two heads' and 'a child in the form of a lobster'. The former, he claimed, was the result of the mother looking at a similar image in a French almanac; the latter because of her desire to eat a large lobster.

Although neither John Howard nor Nathanael St André directly allude to maternal imagination, it is clear that they endorsed it. In his pamphlet St André writes about Mary Toft weeding in a field and developing 'a longing for Rabbets'. She also dreamt about rabbits and had cravings to eat them. Mary Toft admitted in one of her confessions that John Howard had asked her about 'the story of my longings for the Rabbits'. A pamphlet on Mary Toft before she was exposed took it for granted that 'the *Imagination* has a most prevailing power in Conception'. Soon after the hoax was revealed, a newspaper speculated 'that if the Force of Imagination in the Female Sex should be able to bring about such strange Effects', just how far could the mischief spread? With Mary Toft, therefore, the two surgeons seemed to have a textbook example of a mother's unnatural desires creating impressions in her mind which were subsequently imprinted on her infants. By preserving and analysing the resulting rabbits, with the intention of presenting them to the Royal Society, they were providing the proof to substantiate the theory.

They must have realised, though, that in Mary Toft they had a quite exceptional case of apparent maternal imagination. There had been no previously recorded study with such prolific and extreme samples. Normally when a woman produced a monstrosity, it was still recognisable as human. Never before had the offspring comprised another species entirely. It was therefore vital that the observation of the actual delivery of rabbits was watertight and could stand up to scrutiny. Which brings us to the second element of how the doctors were fooled: Toft's deceptive acting. Just how skilled she was in her techniques is clear from the reports of those who examined her.

John Howard said that her labour motions had been so strong 'as to move the Bed-Clothes', and that they had lasted some twenty to thirty hours in total. One of the rabbits supposedly cavorted in her belly for eighteen hours before dying. As soon as it was removed, another took its place. An eleventh rabbit leapt for twenty-three hours in the womb before it too deceased. Howard claimed that he heard the bones of the animals snap and break through the violent motions of her uterus. Richard Manningham described her labouring as strong pulsations of the heart, with 'sudden Jerks and Risings'. At times she fell into violent convulsions with frequent contractions of her fingers, rolling of her eyes and great risings in her stomach and belly, during all of which she made whining noises. Nathanael St André was convinced that her deliveries were genuine, as no person touched her 'from the first time that I had examined her' to the time of her production. And again, when he oversaw another birth: 'I constantly stood before her, nor did any Person whatsoever touch her'. He had his hand inserted inside her and only withdrew it when he brought out some rabbit skin.

In her confessions Mary explained some of her methods. To begin with her mother-in-law carried out the insertions, but eventually she could do it herself. She placed the pieces up one at a time. After one emerged, she would wait until nobody was looking and put in another part of the animal. She would keep bits of rabbit in her pocket ready to be utilised at an opportune moment. The creatures were brought to her by her mother-in-law, either in a handkerchief or in a hog's bladder. They were skinned and broken up, each foot inserted individually. She was reminded not to forget the fur, so that always the parts of a complete rabbit would emerge.

She repeated again and again how agonising the process was, describing it once as if a 'very coarse brown Paper was tearing from within her'. The pain was clearly not faked. 'We found her in exquisite Torture', said St André. The equally unsympathetic Manningham invited others to examine her 'while her Pains were upon her'. He noted that, because of the alien insertions, her uterus expanded, producing convulsions which were observed even when she was fast asleep. In terms of duping her observers, all of her genuine suffering worked in her favour as it 'very exactly counterfeited' true labour pains.

Another factor in Mary Toft pulling off the hoax was the number of people with her during her 'rabbit' births. We don't know if she had more helpers besides her mother-in-law, but the chances are she did. It would have been easy in all the confusion of those surrounding her for somebody to slip her a piece of rabbit. Richard Manningham said that, when he examined her in Guildford, there were 'five or six Women' with him. Similarly St André noted that, when 'she fell into violent Labour-Pains', four or five people had to hold her down in a chair. Given the length of time she was in labour, and the crowded and chaotic room, you can easily see how St André's attention could have been momentarily averted at some point so that a rabbit could be inserted either by Mary herself or an accomplice – despite his recall that nobody went near her.

Tied up with this is the misconception that men of science are more likely to discover fraud. The opposite of this is true. History is littered with examples of highly intelligent men taken in by those intent on deceiving them. The reason is twofold. They assume they are clever enough to detect any nefarious activities; and they play by their own rules, assuming that the parties they are testing are behaving honestly. Another example of a prodigy from this period was Nicholas Hart, the Sleeping Man. Every year of his life, on the 5th of August, he fell 'into a Deep Sleep, and cannot be awaked till Five Days and Nights are expired'. Many members of the Royal Society claimed to have watched him and 'declared that he was no Cheat'. If someone who is completely comatose can dupe scientists, how much simpler was it for Mary Toft to do so during her violent convulsions? In the case of St André, even when he was given direct proof of Mary Toft's duplicity – when she inadvertently produced a piece of hog's bladder along with parts of a rabbit – he just wouldn't accept it was evidence of any fraudulent activity.

Once Mary Toft had been moved to the London bagnio, she was still not left alone. But her entourage now were predominantly hostile men, none of whom was part of the conspiracy. In this environment – bereft of any rabbits – she could only resort to acting out the pre-birth symptoms. It is remarkable that she kept the pretence up for so long, nearly a week in total, knowing that she had nothing to deliver. Yet during that period the leading medical men of this Georgian era were unable to prove it was all faked. Even without the theory of maternal imagination to back it up, one can well envisage Mary Toft pulling off the hoax on her abilities alone. When Richard Manningham told Mary that 'she was differently form'd from other Women', he didn't just mean physiologically. He also meant psychologically, given her ability of 'imposing upon the World'. It was a huge compliment from her nemesis.

The other question relates to Mary Toft's motivation. In one sense it is very straightforward, as she made apparent in her first confession. She was persuaded by her mother-in-law to agree to the scheme because she could give up her present work and, instead, 'get so good a living that I should never want as long as I lived'. The only catch was that Ann Toft would 'expect part of the Gain' for 'continually' supplying her with rabbits. However it was never elaborated on how this 'living' would be achieved. She was promised one lucrative source of funding from the duplicitous surgeon Cyriacus Ahlers, who visited her in Guildford. Having, in his own words, 'feigned a great Compassion for the Woman's Case', he was approached by John Howard. With the knowledge of what Mary Toft had suffered, he hoped that His Majesty would give her a pension. Howard's plea was far from altruistic, though, as he also wanted a pension for himself for his own 'pains', arguing that many who did receive pensions 'did not deserve them'.

There are no existing records of the recipients and numbers of private pensions awarded by the Crown in this period. But they were given to people in poor health, reduced circumstances or needy writers and artists. So it is possible that Mary Toft might have qualified. Whether Ahlers, even though he was surgeon to George I, had the ear of the King in this regard is unknown. It is clear, though, that he had no intention of passing on such a request. The only money we are aware of that Mary Toft received was a guinea, handed to her by Ahlers before he departed. This considerable sum, particularly given that she claimed during her confession that she was earning one penny a day working in the fields, might well have persuaded Mary to make the perilous trip to London in the hope of further financial rewards.

However, in their initial planning of the hoax, the Toft family could not remotely have forecast that the Royal Family would get involved. And obtaining money from the arbitrary payments of visiting doctors would hardly secure a living for life. Ann Toft must have had something else in mind. In my view her intention was that Mary Toft's anticipated future income stream would have come from exhibiting herself. As the playwright Oliver Goldsmith remarked, from the highest to the lowest in the land 'people seem fond of sights and monsters'. There was a plentiful supply of malformed humans to cater for the appetite, and many examples of the exhibition of a monster by a poor family generating a relative fortune. With the amount of publicity that Mary Toft had garnered, she surely would have been one of the foremost attractions for the paying public.

There was no shortage of venues for her to appear at. In London alone there were a large number of inns around Charing Cross, the Strand, Fleet Street, the City and Westminster, which had both the space for enticements of this sort and a steady stream of potential customers passing through. In 1725, at the Crown and Appletree in Pall Mall, for the price of one shilling, a woman with a horn growing out of the back of her head could be seen. According to a visitor the protuberance was solid and of yellowish colour. It was ten inches long. He at least had the decency to name her, unlike the newspaper notices. She was called Elizabeth French and was about fifty years old. Ten years later, at the Sign of the Prince and Princess of Orange in the Haymarket, the curious could have seen a boy from Suffolk who was 'cover'd all over his Body with Bristles like a Hedge Hog'. These exhibits were certainly a couple of the more quirky. The majority of unusual people on display fell into the categories of dwarfs, giants, conjoined twins, hermaphrodites and those with missing limbs or extra appendages. Price for admission varied from six pennies to two shillings and sixpence. Mary Toft would surely have been at the top end of this price range.

Particularly profitable were the annual fairs where booths of living rarities competed against numerous other more conventional performers. The best known of these was Bartholomew Fair, which ran in August for four days. Here Mary would have been up against the likes of the woman with three breasts, a human foetus passed off as a mermaid or the boy covered below his neck with fish-scales. To add authenticity, the advertisements occasionally made reference to endorsements by the Royal Society. Those intrigued by the lad 'with Bristles like a Hedge Hog' were referred to a specific issue of the *Philosophical Transactions*. There was even an extract from the minutes of a Royal Society meeting speculating whether his skin resembled the bark of tree or the hide of an elephant. Similarly a 1736 notice about a conjoined boy and girl, who could be seen at the Rummer tavern in Fleet Street, had been admired by 'Sir *Hans Sloane*, and several other Physicians'. As we know, it was certainly the intention of St André and John Howard to have the Mary Toft case presented to the Royal Society. If she had been validated, then doubtless their stamp of approval would have been used to promote her subsequent appearances.

Another lucrative engagement for Mary Toft would have been private viewings. Interested parties were informed that Elizabeth French would 'wait on any Gentleman or Ladies, if desired, at their own Houses'. Readers were told that Hedge Hog Boy had been 'view'd and greatly admired' by none other than the prime minister of the day, Sir Robert Walpole. There is even an indication that this did happen to Mary Toft, although it is hard to tell whether the suggestion was in jest or actually took place. Colonel Pelham, in accepting an invitation to dinner with the Duke of Richmond – who had a house in Godalming – in 1736, requested that 'the Rabit Woman' should be asked 'to sup with us'. Even if it was only a joke, it shows the possibilities that Mary Toft might have had to earn a considerable amount of money as a cause célèbre.

Whether she would have had a better life if this career path had been open to her is a moot point. Not that her mother-in-law, one suspects, would have cared that much. Available to be gawped at as some sort of freak for up to twelve hours a day, not to mention spectators openly talking about you and being permitted to examine and prod you, was hardly an easy life. When her horn is touched 'a little Violently she suffers Pain' was a dispassionate observation of one onlooker in observing Elizabeth French. This was nothing compared to the treatment inflicted on hermaphrodites, who had a cloth flap which could be lifted up in order to expose their genitals for inspection. The one consolation for Mary would have been that surely the public could not have been as intrusive as any of the examinations she had previously experienced during her rabbit births. Nevertheless, if this was the plan envisaged for her financial security, perhaps it was fortunate the hoax ultimately failed.

When I tell people I am writing a book on eighteenth-century hoaxes, their first question is to ask for an example. And the one I always select is Mary Toft, the rabbit woman from Godalming. It is a guaranteed laugh that I shamelessly exploit by adding further details, some of which are true – for instance, pedlars threatened to sue 'the detestable Rabbet-breeding Woman' for their financial losses resulting from the fall in the purchase of rabbits during the affair. And others I put in for my own amusement: allegedly Nathanael St André, before the surgeon was consulted on the case, was treating George I for myxomatosis. If ever a hoax seems to show the gullibility, bordering on the stupidity, of the citizens of this period, then surely this is it.

As we have seen, though, there was much more to the hoax than straightforward credulity; and good reasons therefore not to condemn too harshly those who were taken in. Perhaps harder to explain is why the theory of maternal imagination survived beyond Mary Toft. In 1727 James Blondel wrote *The Strength of Imagination in Pregnant Women*, inspired directly by 'the Occasion of the Cheat of *Godalming*', giving a rational explanation of why it was not possible for the mother's thoughts to be communicated to the child. The foetus was a salient being in its own right. However, Daniel Turner replied to that, which then sparked off a further response from each as there developed a pamphlet war over the issue. Ironically, although they were at loggerheads over the theory, both offered similar advice to pregnant women: remain calm and bear fearful sights 'with Christian Pity and Compassion'. Neither gained the upper hand, with some members of the Royal Society still believing in maternal imagination a decade later. For instance the *Philosophical Transactions*, in its report in 1734 on the Hedge Hog boy, noted that 'his Mother had received no Fright' while she was pregnant. Another later report told of a woman who produced the 'exact Resemblance of the *Foetus* to a hooded *Monkey*' after obsessively watching a tame monkey playing tricks. In the event it would take until the end of the eighteenth century before maternal imagination was completely discredited.

As a result it is hard to point to anything positive in the world of medicine that emerged from Mary Toft's case. Not that that particularly concerns me. From my perspective I salute Mary Toft because she pulled off a remarkable hoax under the harshest possible conditions and against all the odds and, in the process, ran rings around the male establishment. Nathanael St André in his pamphlet called her a 'very stupid' woman, hopefully a term that came back to haunt him. There is no grave for her in Godalming. I did ask the museum curator whether they had checked out the rabbit burrows, but he wasn't amused (that's another joke, by the way). She certainly deserves one for all the laughs she has given over the years.

FOUR

'I Had Rather Relate Your Stories Than Other Men's Truths'

* * *

I

In his influential book *A Social History of the American Family*, first published in 1917, Arthur Calhoun gave some examples of punishments inflicted on women for misdemeanours in New England during the eighteenth century. One such was Polly Baker, a resident of Connecticut, who was whipped, fined and imprisoned several times for having given birth to illegitimate children. The author commented on the harsh sentences imposed. Her final court appearance ended on a happier note. Following an impassioned speech in which Polly claimed that she had consented to get wed, but had been betrayed by her lover, the magistrates discharged her case, lawyers gave her presents and, in a remarkable turnaround, her seducer did eventually marry her. Nevertheless, the historian considered it a perfect illustration of how 'women were more sternly dealt with than men' when it came to sexual misconduct.

Calhoun had obtained his information from a book published sixty years earlier by Charles Elliott called *The New England History*. He, in turn, cited an 1804 biography of *Remarkable Female Characters*, which had given the reader a back-story about Polly. She was the daughter of a reputable mechanic and had been well educated. She had fallen in love with the son of a local magistrate who deserted her after she became pregnant. She was now a wretched outcast who became the mistress of a neighbouring trader. She had several bastard children, each one resulting in fines, whippings and prison. It was postulated that her original lover decided to marry her because he was shamed into it by her courtroom plea. After reproducing Polly's life history, Charles Elliott wrote about other women at that time in New England. In doing so he mentioned the wag and wit Benjamin Franklin. It is possible that some of his readers might have picked up on the irony of the juxtaposition, although Elliott himself would have been totally oblivious. For Polly Baker was a wholly fictitious character that had sprung from the fertile imagination of none other than Benjamin Franklin.

The Polly Baker Speech, as it is now known, first appeared over a century before Elliott's book in an English newspaper, *The General Advertiser*, on 15 April 1747. The original article was wholly devoted to her oration. The only information given as to why it was made, and who Polly Baker was, was given in a short introductory passage. This stated that it was before a Court of Judicature at Connecticut near Boston in New England and it was Polly's fifth prosecution for having a bastard child. The speech influenced the wavering of her punishment 'and induced one of her Judges to marry her the next Day'. There was no elaboration on Polly's earlier life nor any suggestion that her husband was also her first lover.

Apart from *The General Advertiser*, three other daily newspapers were published on 15 April; none of them printed the speech. But this did not prevent the thrice-weekly evening papers picking up the story. *The General Evening Post*, *The London Evening-Post* and *The St James's Evening Post*, all of which came out the following day, reproduced the article. By Saturday 18 April the two weekly papers, *The Westminster Journal* and *Old England*, had inserted it, leaving *The Penny London Post* lagging behind. It published it on the following Monday. As was the custom there was no editorial or other commentary on the piece and none of these papers referred to Polly Baker again.

Monthly magazines for April also featured the speech, including *The London Magazine* and *The British Magazine*. The most popular monthly journal of the period was *The Gentleman's Magazine*. It was launched by Edward Cave in 1731 and introduced the word 'magazine' as referring to a journal. Previously it had meant only a storehouse for arms and ammunition. Cave's publication came to pre-eminence over its rivals through running longer articles on the news and other items of general interest. In 1736 it published reports on proceedings of Parliament. It was also the first, in October 1745, to print the National Anthem, with the opening words of 'God save great George our king'. Polly Baker's Speech appeared in the April 1747 edition of *The Gentleman's Magazine*. However, when informing the reader that Polly had married one of the judges the next day, it put in the amusing detail that they subsequently had fifteen children. This insertion was made only in the initial print run; later copies of the same issue omitted this questionable statement. One likes to think that a typesetter was indulging in his own hoax, and that when the addition was discovered by the irate editor, it was swiftly deleted. It clearly caught out *The Scots Magazine* who, in copying their version verbatim from an earlier edition of *The Gentleman's Magazine*, left in the quote about the numerous offspring.

The Gentleman's Magazine was unique among all the newspapers and journals, though, in following up the story. In the May 1747 issue it published a letter from William Smith. He confirmed that he had met Polly Baker a couple of years previously. She was now about sixty years old and was married to Paul Dudley. They were indeed blessed with fifteen children. He felt the need to write as 'it has been insinuated, that the speech publish'd in her name was entirely fictitious'. This rather sensational news was retracted the following month. A letter from 'L. Americanus' pointed out that Paul Dudley had never acted in any judicial capacity in Connecticut. More significantly he had long been married to the daughter of a distinguished governor, and they had no offspring.

While all this was playing out in England, the April editions of the various British newspapers and journals were making their way by sea over to the American colonies – it would take them about a month to arrive. Polly Baker's Speech therefore did not appear in an American publication until July. We do not know when Paul Dudley, who was actually the Chief Justice of Massachusetts, had sight of the libellous letter written by William Smith. Doubtless he fired off a response after reading it, perhaps threatening to sue for damages. It is unlikely that the subsequent repudiation in the form of the letter from L. Americanus would have placated him. Eventually, over a year later, *The Gentleman's Magazine* printed a full apology. They confessed that they had unwarily published a letter signed by William Smith which had contained 'groundless, vile and injurious' imputation against both Paul Dudley and his wife. She was known for 'her great modesty, virtue, and other amiable qualities'. William Smith, whoever he was, had absconded so that he could not be punished for 'his malicious and gross abuse'. All they could do, therefore, was to ask for pardon from the maligned couple.

Of course the fact that the wrong man had been named as Polly Baker's subsequent husband did not, in itself, imply that the speech was a work of fiction. There were no hints in the American press that it was false. Nobody seems to have picked up on the words in the June 1747 issue of *The Gentleman's Magazine*, where it had regretted that the Dudleys were connected with 'a fictitious speech'. This was too obscure a reference, and made too late in the day, to prevent Polly Baker's declamation spiralling out of control and becoming, as we have seen, part of the accepted social history of New England. Ultimately this was due to the believable nature of the words put into Polly Baker's mouth. To find out how they were crafted in such an effective manner, we need to turn to the hoaxer himself.

II

Benjamin Franklin [Fig. 8] is one of those rare men who would still be famous if he had just excelled in one field of endeavour. As

Fig. 8. Portrait of Benjamin Franklin, an engraving by Johann Lorenz Rugendas.

a scientist he proved that lightning was electrical in nature; as an inventor, he designed a more efficient stove; as a diplomat he was noted for his ambassadorial duties in France; as a statesman he was the only person to sign all three of the Declaration of Independence, the 1783 peace treaty with Britain and the Constitution of the US; as a writer he gained fame through his autobiography; and he made his mark as a publisher, editor and journalist for *The Pennsylvania Gazette*.

Franklin was born in 1706. He was the fifteenth child and youngest son. He had very little schooling and worked from the age of eleven in his father's shop making candles and soap. Realising that he was not cut out for such work, he was apprenticed to his brother, James, who had set up a printing shop in Boston. In 1721 his brother started up *The New-England Courant* and Franklin was involved in all aspects of the paper, including setting the type, printing and delivering it. Unbeknown to his brother he would soon start writing for it too.

Franklin's series of essays that appeared in the *Courant* in 1722 have all the hallmarks that would later feed into Polly Baker's Speech. They were written under a female persona, they were full of humour and wit, they show a fondness for rhetorical declarations and burlesquing logic and they were satirising social issues that were prevalent at the time, including feminism, the clergy and religion. In all there were fourteen articles supposedly penned by Silence Dogood, a minister's widow. They were inspired by Joseph Addison's *The Spectator* and Richard Steele's *The Tatler*, which were published in England between 1709 and 1712. Franklin had been an avid reader of these and at times mimicked both their style and intent.

Franklin was sixteen when he wrote the essays, but already mastering his style of humour. In the seventh Silence Dogood issue, he quotes an elegy written by a New England poet, John Herrick, on the death of 'a Wife, a Daughter, and a Sister'. He compares it with a poem by Isaac Watts about the death of Thomas Gunston, described as 'the Just, the Generous, and the Young'. Franklin writes that the latter:

> ...only mentions three Qualifications of *one* Person who was deceased, which therefore could raise Grief and Compassion but for *One*. Whereas the former, (*our most excellent Poet*) gives his Reader a Sort of an Idea of the Death of *Three Persons*, viz. *a Wife, a Daughter, and a Sister,* which is *Three times* as great a Loss as the Death of *One*, and consequently must raise *Three Times* as much Grief and Compassion in the Reader.

Franklin initially got his Silence Dogood articles into his brother's newspaper by slipping them under the door of the printing shop at night. When eventually Benjamin confessed that he was the author, James wasn't best pleased. Although Benjamin had taken over the running of the newspaper while James was imprisoned for accusing the authorities of failing to tackle pirates, it was clear that in the long term the two could not work together. Franklin sailed from Boston to New York without telling his family. He informed the ship's captain that his departure needed to be kept secret as he had got a 'naughty girl' pregnant, and her friends were insisting that he married her. A rather prescient confession, even if it wasn't true, in the light of Polly Baker's Speech. Over the next few years, Franklin gained further experience of the printing trade and journalism, both in England and his homeland, before purchasing the failing *Pennsylvania Gazette* in 1729. As owner and editor of this paper, together with publishing other books, pamphlets and periodicals – not to mention securing printing contracts in his role as clerk to the Pennsylvania Assembly – he became a wealthy and influential citizen in New England.

The essays by Silence Dogood are not hoaxes. The pseudonym was too absurd to be taken seriously and the satirical objective of the writing would have been obvious to the reader. But one suspects that this is when Franklin first got caught up in the possibilities and thrills of this type of deception – after all, his own brother had not worked out that he was the author. He therefore started putting such pieces into his own publication. It might seem odd that a respectable newspaper would resort to subterfuge of this sort, but the object was always to entertain as well as inform. It was because *The Pennsylvania Gazette* embraced skits, essays and satires, as well as news coverage, that it became the leading paper of its day. Making up the occasional story when copy was short sat comfortably with this format.

One of Franklin's most imaginative articles related to an apparent witch trial that took place at Mount Holly in New Jersey. Some citizens had allegedly conjured up dancing sheep and caused hogs to speak and sing psalms. To discover if they were indeed witches they would be weighed on scales with a Bible. If the holy book proved to be heavier, they must be guilty. The accused agreed to undergo the ordeal only if the most vehement claimers of their satanic deeds were tried with them. To the astonishment of the spectators, the two men and two women all passed the test: 'Flesh and Bones ... outweighed that great good Book by abundance.' This outcome not having been deemed satisfactory, it was decided the couples should be undressed, bound and thrown into the river. If they floated, this was proof of witchcraft. In the event they all kept their buoyancy. It was concluded that because the women, unlike the men, were allowed to retain their undergarments, the outcome was flawed. The trial would therefore be postponed until warmer weather when the women would be stripped 'naked'.

For many of the puritanical readers of Franklin's paper, rounding off what was clearly a farcical article with such a sexually charged image of decadence must have been close to their threshold of tolerance. The mischievous journalist was keen to push to the edge of public taste, but the cautious editor appreciated that to do so would be professional suicide for his proprietorship. Franklin therefore indulged in his propensity to provoke by circulating private papers exclusively among his friends. One of these, produced not long before the Polly Baker Speech, was called 'Old Mistresses Apologue'.

It was written in the form of an epistle to a young friend and began by recommending marriage in order to 'diminish the violent natural Inclinations you mention'. Franklin went on to say that, if that was not an option, and the man was forced to look for women outside wedlock, he should choose older, rather than younger, ones. Franklin then sets out his eight reasons in what one recent critic has called 'a small masterpiece of eighteenth-century bawdry'. But it makes for rather uncomfortable reading now, given that among his recommendations for elderly ladies are that they will be 'so grateful' and that, in the dark, all women are the same below the waist.

It is hard to know whether the 'Apologue' was a joke, in the sense of Franklin not expecting his small coterie of readers to believe he meant what he had written. The best example of an obvious hoax that Franklin undertook before the Polly Baker Speech was unveiled, was a rip-off of one that has been covered in an earlier chapter. In December 1732 Franklin began writing annual almanacs under the pseudonym of a character he created called Richard Saunders. They were known as *Poor Richard's Almanacks*. They included all the usual information that people expected from such books – the times of sunrise and sunset, high and low tides, important dates, lists of kings and queens, weather forecasts. However when it came to predictions he openly acknowledged the absurdity that any accuracy could be guaranteed by consulting astrological data. In one almanac he reassured his readers that even if his prognostications were wayward, at least he *'always hit the Day of the Month'*.

Poor Richard's eventually became the second best-selling almanac in America, surpassing 10,000 copies a year at its peak. One reason for its success was the amusing prologue, supposedly written by the eponymous author. But Franklin needed something more than mere humour to hook the potential purchaser. And he achieved it in his first almanac by copying what Jonathan Swift had done in his guise as Isaac Bickerstaff. He predicted the death of a rival almanac publisher, the Philadelphian Titan Leeds. Franklin's approach was less confrontational than Swift had been in forecasting the demise of John Partridge. Richard Saunders claimed to be a good friend of Leeds. The only reason he was entering the market now, apart from his nagging wife insisting he made money from his stargazing, was precisely because Leeds's death was imminent. This left a gap that he was reluctantly forced to fill.

The scenario played out very much like Swift's own hoax, with Leeds replying, in his 1734 almanac, that he was very much alive. This enabled Franklin to replicate Swift's response that no man alive could possibly write such nonsense. He also used Richard's supposed friendship with Leeds against him, arguing that it couldn't be Leeds writing that he was a fool and a liar as 'his Esteem and Affection for me was extraordinary'. Franklin is gentler in his teasing of Leeds than Swift was in attacking Partridge. But then the Irish satirist genuinely despised his rival, whereas Franklin was simply trying to sell almanacs.

In some ways the best, and funniest, prologue that Franklin produced for *Poor Richard* had echoes of Polly Baker's Speech, in that it was written by a woman, Richard's wife, Bridget Saunders. In her spouse's absence 'to visit an old Stargazer of his Acquaintance' she had opened up the 1738 almanac. Her husband had finished it and had asked her to send it to the publishers. Having read some critical remarks about herself, including that she had lately taken a fancy to drinking tea, she scratched out the preface as it 'was not worth a printing'. She also altered some of the weather predictions, as there was an overabundance of rain forecast. She substituted more sunshine so that women like herself could dry their washing. She had wanted to make other corrections, particularly to change some verses she didn't like, but had been unable to do so as she had unluckily broken her glasses.

Franklin's antennae as to what was suitable for publication was finely tuned. Most of the time he got it right. Occasionally he did overstep the mark, normally when it came to the sensitive area of people's faith. On 23 April 1730 he published a letter in *The Pennsylvania Gazette*, purporting to be from a clergyman who had experienced a strange drumming noise in a house, which he believed to be the Devil at work. It mocked both the gullibility and naivety of the minister involved in such a way that no one could doubt that it was a spoof missive. Nevertheless one can only presume Franklin received some complaints, because two weeks later he published a response stating that bringing into contempt the clergy, who are 'the Teachers and Supporters of Virtue and Morality', was unjustifiable. This epistle concluded by stating that, if it were published, that must mean the editor didn't approve of the intended cynicism as expressed in the first letter. As the author of both letters, Franklin was playing a delicate balancing act in satirising religion.

Although the Polly Baker Speech was written over a decade later, Franklin would not have forgotten the fallout from the 'Letter of the Drum'. But his relentless search into the pursuit of truth and his desire to systematically test out religious tenets, combined with a love of playfulness in his writings, overcame any qualms he might have had in offending anyone. However, given its controversial theological content, the questioning of the prevailing law in New England, and a dose of sex thrown in for good measure, he would this time make certain it could not be traced back to him. Not only would it not be published by his own newspaper, it would not even be published in his own country.

III

The Polly Baker Speech [Fig. 9] is made before a Court of Judicature, at Connecticut near Boston in New England. She is being prosecuted for her fifth bastard child. On the previous four occasions of giving birth to children outside wedlock, she had either been fined or received corporal punishment. A discerning reader would have spotted a legal inconsistency. In the mid-eighteenth century there was no law against having an illegitimate baby in Connecticut; the actual offence was that of fornication. In practice it was hard to prove the latter without the evidence of a child, which was why the two were often tied together in the eyes of the public. But it is notable that all of Polly's persuasive arguments are based on the unfairness of having children. If this really had been a court of law, they would have been ruled out of order as being irrelevant to her case. Although it is the first clue that it is a hoax, it is not one that most British readers would have detected.

Nor, one suspects, would many of them have picked up on Polly Baker's profession, which is never specifically stated. A couple of modern writers, in their analysis of the speech, say there is no doubt Polly is a prostitute. This, again, would have made the joke more obvious, in that how could a whore have the education and intellect to produce such an articulate broadside? However the most comprehensive book on the literary deception, *Benjamin Franklin & Polly Baker* by Max Hall (1960), never discusses her job. Those that discern evidence of her occupation find it primarily based on puns

The SPEECH of Miſs POLLY BAKER,
before a Court of Judicature, at *Connecticut* near
Boſton in *New-England* ; where ſhe was proſecuted
the Fifth Time, for having a Baſtard Child : Which
influenced the Court to diſpenſe with her Puniſhment,
and induced one of her Judges to marry her the next
Day.

MAY it pleaſe the Honourable Bench to indulge me
in a few Words : I am a poor unhappy Woman,
who have no Money to fee Lawyers to plead for me, being
hard put to it to get a tolerable Living. I ſhall not trouble your Honours with long Speeches ; for I have not the
Preſumption to expect, that you may, by any Means, be
prevailed on to deviate in your Sentence from the Law, in
my Favour. All I humbly hope is, That your Honours
would charitably move the Governor's Goodneſs on my
Behalf, that my Fine may be remitted. This is the Fifth
Time, Gentlemen, that I have been dragg'd before your
Court on the ſame Account ; twice I have paid heavy
Fines, and twice have been brought to Public Puniſhment, for want of Money to pay thoſe Fines. This may
have been agreeable to the Laws, and I don't diſpute it ;
but ſince Laws are ſometimes unreaſonable in themſelves,
and therefore repealed, and others bear too hard on the
Subject in particular Circumſtances ; and therefore there is
left a Power ſomewhat to diſpenſe with the Execution of
them ; I take the Liberty to ſay, That I think this Law,
by which I am puniſhed, is both unreaſonable in itſelf,
and particularly ſevere with regard to me, who have always
lived an inoffenſive Life in the Neighbourhood where I
was born, and defy my Enimies (if I have any) to ſay I
ever wrong'd Man, Woman, or Child. Abſtracted from
the Law, I cannot conceive (may it pleaſe your Honours)
what the Nature of my Offence is. I have brought Five
fine Children into the World, at the Riſque of my Life ;
I have maintain'd them well by my own Induſtry, without
burthening the Townſhip, and would have done it better,
if it had not been for the heavy Charges and Fines I have
paid. Can it be a Crime (in the Nature of Things I mean)
to add to the Number of the King's Subjects, in a new
Country that really wants People ? I own it, I ſhould
think it a Praiſe-worthy, rather then a puniſhable Action.
I have debauched no other Woman's Huſband, nor enticed
any Youth ; theſe Things I never was charg'd with, nor
has any one the leaſt Cauſe of Complaint againſt me, un-
leſs, perhaps, the Miniſter, or Juſtice, becauſe I have had
Children without being married, by which they have

Fig. 9. The start of the Speech of Miss Polly Baker, as
it was first published in *The General Advertiser*, 15 April
1747.

of a sexual nature. In her opening statement Polly says she is 'hard put' to earn a living; later, emphasis is placed to highlight the double meaning in the words 'conceive' and 'miscarriage'; complaining about her 'want of money' could read as 'wanton money'; custom forbids her to 'solicit' men; and she concludes her speech by saying she wants a statue 'erected'. Perhaps this tells us more about the minds of some readers than necessarily the intentions of the writer.

Polly makes it clear that she has all the characteristics of a woman that would make a good wife. Along with frugality, hard work and skill in managing money, she also includes 'fertility'. Despite having all these attributes, she is still unable to gain a husband. She would be more than willing to accept the hand in marriage of any man, but no one has been forthcoming. The only person who did propose used it as a snare to dishonour her. He promptly abandoned her after he had taken away her virginity. He is now a magistrate himself.

Having forcefully made the point that women are totally reliant on the integrity of men to get wed, she then changes her tack to argue the case why having children, whether in or out of wedlock, is undeserving of punishment. From a practical viewpoint she had never burdened anybody by seeking financial help; the children had been brought up entirely through her own industry. Indeed she could have done even better for them if it were not for the heavy fines she was previously forced to pay. In becoming pregnant she had 'debauched no other Woman's Husband, nor enticed any Youth'. The only people who had any justifiable cause for complaint were the clergymen, but only because they missed out on their wedding fees. Finally, in the relatively new country in which she is living, increasing the population is important for its long-term prosperity. Her contribution to this trend is therefore deserving of praise rather than retribution.

From defending her position through secular arguments, Polly turns to religious ones. She is aware that she has committed a biblical sin and therefore must suffer 'eternal Fire'. She asks, isn't that enough? Why should the magistrates want to add to her perpetual damnation by fining and whipping her? She questions, though, whether she has in fact committed any wrongdoing. If God was genuinely angry, would he have created her children with such 'admirable Workmanship' and 'with rational and immortal Souls'? Here she is confronting one of the central tenets of the existence of God: that only a supreme being has the ability to design man. As God appears to think she has done no wrong, as evidenced by her unsullied offspring, then on what basis are the magistrates punishing her?

She offers a final convincer that having children is no transgression. She quotes the Bible at her accusers, saying that, according to God's own command, it is man's duty to increase and multiply. In a concluding flourish, Polly gets carried away by her own oratory. If having children is the primary religious goal, then bachelors who fail to reproduce are effectively committing murder. At the very least they should be forced to get married or, failing that, pay double the fornication fine for each year they remain single. As for herself, rather than being punished for fulfilling God's 'Command of Nature', she should have a statue built in her memory.

It seems likely that the complexities and intricacies of the religious analysis inherent in the speech might have been overlooked by many readers. This is especially so in England, where there was no law at the time against fornication, and when bastards were commonplace. What English readers would have come away with, though, was the knowledge that many men failed to face up to their responsibilities by refusing to get married; that punishing somebody for having children out of wedlock was counterproductive and unjust; and that the laws in New England dealt far more harshly with women than they did with men.

Was Franklin reflecting his own convictions in Polly Baker's Speech? Or was he merely mocking those who had more liberal views by taking them to an absurd conclusion? It is sometimes hard to tell what Franklin truly thought. But it does seem that he was generally egalitarian in his treatment of women – his frequent adoption of a female persona in his writing supports this – and that he didn't condemn those who had children outside marriage. His personal life backs this up. In 1724, Franklin was courting Deborah Read. Her parents would not let them wed. The following year, after Franklin sailed to London, she married John Rogers. It later transpired that Rogers was a bigamist. Deborah left him and, on 1 September 1730, she and Benjamin joined in a common-law marriage. Sometime before this formal arrangement, Franklin had had an illegitimate son called William. The mother is unknown, but he was brought up by Benjamin and Deborah. It would be hard to accuse Franklin of being in any way hypocritical.

Franklin clearly believed in marriage, although his personal reason seemed to be as much to do with ensuring that he wouldn't contract any venereal disease as it was with his affection for Deborah. A year before the Polly Baker Speech was published he wrote an anonymous pamphlet titled *Reflections on Courtship and Marriage*, in which he put forward the case for matrimony. He acknowledged that the prevailing law gave man arbitrary power over his wife, but he didn't think this arose from reason or nature. He thought they should be equal partners in marriage. 'One good Husband is worth two good Wives,' wrote Franklin in his *Poor Richard's Almanack* of 1742. But he followed that up with: 'for the scarcer things are the more they're valued.'

One justifiable accusation that could be made against Franklin is that he was not prepared to air his view. At the end of her speech Polly Baker says she merits a valedictory statue. This could be seen as an echo of Jonathan Swift's *A Modest Proposal*, written some fifteen years earlier. The Irishman wrote that someone who could solve the problem of the overabundance of children deserved a similar memorial. Swift's satire was far more biting, given that his solution to depopulate was for the youngsters to be eaten. Nevertheless, risking the potential wrath and backlash of those who might take it seriously, Swift was prepared to put his name on the cover of the pamphlet. By contrast Franklin, who admired Swift perhaps more than any other author, hid behind anonymity in his, arguably, less contentious and inflammatory piece.

The difference though was that Franklin was a respectable member of the Philadelphia community and the publisher and editor of a prominent newspaper with a predominantly Puritan readership. He couldn't risk the Polly Baker Speech being in any way associated with him, hence its initial publication in another country. It is not known if it appeared in *The General Advertiser* in England at his instigation. It is possible that he forwarded it to one of his friends or contacts requesting that it should be inserted. Equally it could have started off as an article written to amuse a select few, and somebody decided to submit it to the paper without his knowledge or permission.

As noted above, having been reproduced in most of the English papers and journals, it made its way over to the US. In 1747 there were twelve weekly newspapers in the thirteen colonies. Daily newspapers were not yet in circulation. At least four of those published the speech, although Franklin's *Pennsylvania Gazette* was not one of them. The most interesting version appeared in *The Maryland Gazette* on 11 August 1747. This is because it differed in a few ways from that published in *The General Advertiser*. The reason for this was made clear in the introduction to the speech, presumably written by its editor, Jonas Green. He wrote that the British papers had printed it incorrectly owing to errors in transcribing from its original. Fortunately for his readers he had the correct copy, which he was pleased to reproduce.

Modern critics seem to accept that *The Maryland Gazette* version is more authentic. Jonas Green was friendly with Franklin, and a couple of months before had reprinted his 'Verses on the Virginia Capitol Fire'. On 30 January 1747 a fire broke out in the state's capital building and Sir William Gooch, the Governor, claimed that it must have been arson because a fire started by accident could not have spread so fast. Franklin mocked both this statement ('And that Fires kindled by Accident *always burn slow* / And not with half the Fury as when they *burn on purpose* you know') together with the Governor's assertion that Virginians were not capable of such wickedness. On 25 July Jonas Green wrote to Franklin saying that his parody had caused a great deal of laughter. Their relationship suggests that Green had Franklin's blessing in the variant of Polly Baker's Speech that he published.

The main addition comes near the end when Polly Baker expands on the consequences of it being considered a sin to have an illegitimate child. She conjures up an image of abortions, and worse – of mothers scooping out their own offspring from their wombs. It is the law, she says, that is responsible for these outrages. She appeals to the court that it should be repealed and 'expung'd for ever from your Books'. It has been suggested that this incendiary passage was omitted from the English papers as Franklin did not want the British public to realise how barbaric the consequence of the fornication laws might be. It would just give too much ammunition to anyone intent on reinforcing the stereotype of how uncivilised were the colonies.

If the likes of Jonas Green knew that Polly Baker was the *nom de plume* of Franklin, they were not confessing it. It would be another thirty years before his authorship was revealed. The catalyst for this was the publication of a six-volume book on history by the former French Jesuit priest Abbé Raynal in 1770. It is a rambling account of European infiltration into many parts of the world, including North America. Its success was principally due to its tirade against religion and government, enlivened by colourful anecdotes. So how better to illustrate the severity of the laws in New England than to reproduce Polly Baker's Speech as historical fact? It is noteworthy that Raynal omitted Polly's plea for a statue, realising that this flippant appeal might detract from the gravitas of his contention.

Raynal's take on American history was not popular in the colonies. For instance he wrote, 'it must be a matter of astonishment to find that America has not yet produced a good poet, an able mathematician, or a man of genius in any single art of science'. Both George Washington and Thomas Jefferson refuted this and, in so doing, chose each other as examples of great men! Besides being sceptical about Raynal's grasp of historical fact, Jefferson was well aware of Franklin's love of playful writing. It is said that Jefferson explained that Franklin was not asked to contribute to the Declaration of Independence because he could not have refrained from putting a joke into it. It is therefore apt that it was Jefferson who related how Franklin confessed to Raynal himself that the Polly Baker Speech was a hoax.

In 1777 or 1778 Franklin and Silas Deane, an American politician and diplomat, were at Franklin's house in France discussing the numerous mistakes in Raynal's *Histoire*. Coincidentally the Abbé called by and Deane explained what they had been talking about. The French historian retorted: 'I took the greatest care not to insert a single fact for which I had not the most unquestionable authority.' Deane mentioned the speech of Polly Baker as a counter-example. He knew it couldn't be true because in 'Massachusetts' there was no law against having a bastard child. Raynal resorted to the common defence that he couldn't immediately recollect where he had heard it from, but was positive it came from a verifiable source. It was here that a smirking Franklin intervened. He told the Abbé that, when he was the printer and editor of a newspaper, they were sometimes short of copy. So, to amuse his readers, he would fill up the vacant columns with anecdotes and fanciful fables. The Polly Baker Speech was 'a story of my making, on one of those occasions'. Raynal's response to this showed great magnanimity, informing Franklin that he 'had rather relate your stories than other men's truths'.

Jefferson's telling of the anecdote is wrong in at least two respects. Massachusetts was not mentioned by Raynal in his *Histoire*, and Franklin never published the Polly Baker Speech in his own newspaper. But those mistakes can be excused by Jefferson having recalled the story long after the encounter took place. There is, though, other evidence that Franklin was the author. John Adams, a Founding Father and second President of the United States, was not a fan of Franklin. In 1783 he wrote that his 'whole Life has been one continued Insult to good Manners and to Decency', adding that the Polly Baker Speech was an example of an outrage to 'Morality and Decorum'. In this same letter he had a dig at him for producing an illegitimate son, William. The latter also confirmed the hoax in 1807, noting that his father had 'wrote and printed a Piece called the Speech of *Polly Baker*'.

Although Franklin's confession had taken place in the late 1770s, it only became universally known some forty years later. And so, as in America, the speech was frequently reprised in publications in England, with the assumption that it was genuine, following its initial debut in *The General Advertiser*. In 1771, *The Gentleman's and London Magazine* – not to be confused with the better-known *The Gentleman's Magazine* – reproduced the speech for no particular reason. The same was true three years later when *The Covent-Garden Magazine* did the same: it had been submitted by a contributor 'for the entertainment of your Readers'. A novel excuse was invented to reprint it in 1799 in the *Evening Mail*. A race horse owner had named one of his mares 'Polly Baker', so the paper thought it might be 'amusing to some curious and inquisitive persons to know something of this wonderful Lady, to whom the compliment is paid'.

More significantly, the biographical elaboration of Polly Baker's life which, as noted at the start of this chapter, was reproduced in *Remarkable Female Characters*, had first appeared in the April 1794 edition of *The Edinburgh Magazine* in 'Interesting Reflections on the Life of Miss Polly Baker'. Part of the reason for the article was to highlight the excessive legal punishment inflicted on such women for their wayward actions 'in New England, which has been called the Land of Saints, the Hot-house of Calvinistic Puritanism'. The fleshing out of her back-story convinced the editors of *Remarkable Female Characters* that she was a real person eligible to be included with such luminaries as Joan of Arc, Mary Queen of Scots, Cleopatra and, an important character in Chapter 6, Mary Squires. The book was published in England in 1803. It was the 1804 American edition that instigated Polly Baker's eventual inclusion in Arthur Calhoun's *A Social History of the American Family* some 100 years later.

It is therefore from England that both the start of, and the further colourful addition to, the Polly Baker Speech arose. Franklin clearly realised that the reputation of the English press, compared with its American counterpart, meant that any hoax targeted in England had greater influence than in his home country. Many of his subsequent jests appeared in English newspapers. Some of them had serious intent, despite the seemingly frivolous nature in which they were expressed. In 1761 he wanted to prevent England making peace with France to end the Seven Years' War. He was concerned that otherwise France would be free to concentrate on expanding their presence in his own country. To this end he wrote a chapter that appeared in *The London Chronicle*, allegedly from the translation of a 1629 Spanish book *Of the Means of extending the Greatnesse of the* Spanish *Monarchie*. It was suggested that 'France' was substituted for 'Spain' in reading it. In 1773, shortly before the American War of Independence, he produced an edict in the same paper, supposedly from Frederick II (the Great) of Prussia, claiming territorial and financial rights from England due to its early Germanic settlements. The latter was a dig at the taxes inflicted on the American colonies at that time.

In 1782 he published a *Supplement to the Boston Independent Chronicle*, which he clearly hoped would be picked up by the British press, as it was intended to highlight the cruelties inflicted on American citizens during the revolutionary war. It comprised a series of letters relating to 1,062 scalps extracted in the previous three years by the 'Senneka Indians' from the men, women, children and babies of New England. They had been given as a present to the Governor of Canada with the request that they should be sent to England to demonstrate their support in killing their mutual enemies. It was hoped they could be secretly hanged on the trees in St James's Park at night, therefore providing a pleasing spectacle for King George and Queen Charlotte when they woke up the next morning. However, fixing them to trees was not approved so, instead, it was now proposed that they should be sealed in packets and samples given to all members of the Royal Family. Any left over should be distributed to both Houses of Parliament, with a double quantity to the Bishops.

Others were more playful. In 1765, in *The Public Advertiser*, he satirised inane reports that appeared in the English press about America by making up a few of his own ('the grand Leap of the Whale in that Chace up the Fall of Niagara is esteemed by all who have seen it, as one of the finest Spectacles in Nature'); and mocking those that might dispute them ('the next Step might be a Disbelief in the well-vouch'd Accounts of Ghosts and Witches'). The year before, *The London Chronicle* published a parable against persecution, supposedly from *Genesis* and written in the style of the King James Version of the Bible. Franklin enjoyed reading it out loud at dinner parties, delighted if any of his listeners thought it was authentic. In 1768, in two issues of *The London Chronicle*, there appeared extracts from *An Account of the Captivity of William Henry in 1755, and of his Residence among the Senneka Indians six Years and seven Months till he made his Escape from them*, published in Boston in 1766. Needless to say, no such work existed.

None of these, though, or indeed any of Benjamin Franklin's other hoaxes, was as successful and as enduring as the Polly Baker Speech. There is something very seductive about this poor unfortunate woman, with her five infant children, pleading in such an articulate manner for her punishment to be waived. Facing down a courtroom full of elderly male magistrates and, by sheer force of oratory, overcoming their prejudices and winning them over to pardon her, would surely have had readers at the time mentally cheering her victory. It is the emotional impact of the speech that drives it forward, so that the logical inconsistencies and the absurd conclusions of her arguments are somehow lost, or at least pushed to one side as irrelevant. Even if your head is telling you that much of it is nonsensical, your heart wants it to be true. Who cares that she is questioning religious beliefs and denouncing the laws of the land, when the end result is that she marries one of her judges? She may not deserve a statue for her ability to procreate, but she deserves it for winning through against all the odds.

Of all the hoaxes in this book, this is the one that seems most in tune with twenty-first-century sentiments. This is not just in the way it spread, albeit rather more slowly, in the manner of a contemporary social media posting going viral — even to the extent of a reliable statement that it was fictitious being completely ignored. But it also resonates in the issues it raises about sexual and financial inequality. The religious themes may no longer be pertinent to most. However, questions over men deserting the mothers of their children, and being impoverished as a result, are still as prevalent as they were in the eighteenth century. Sometimes it is not just the reasons why 300-year-old hoaxes work that remain relevant to our times: it is the subject matter itself.

FIVE

'A Common Tavern Bottle'

* * *

I

Of all the hoaxes in this book, the Bottle Conjurer is my favourite. It was disarmingly simple in concept, it was done without malice or for personal gain and it took many years for the perpetrator to be uncovered. Even now we cannot be totally certain that we have the right man. Try as I might I haven't been able to find a smoking gun. But I like to think that I have collated sufficient circumstantial evidence for a jury to find him guilty. I also hope that the judge would be lenient in its sentencing. It was not exactly the hoaxer's fault that extensive damage was done to a theatre, that the brother of the heir to the throne was humiliated, and that the words 'Bottle Conjurer' became a derogatory term for an opportunistic imposter.

It started with a prominently placed advertisement in two daily papers, *The General Advertiser* and *The Daily Advertiser*. The latter had begun in 1730 as a two-sided single sheet, subsequently increased to two sheets. It adopted the use of three columns per page and was the first to permanently establish the word 'Advertiser' as part of its title. Its successful format was wholly copied by *The London Daily Post and General Advertiser* four years later, which dropped all pretence of being different in 1744 when it rebranded as *The General Advertiser*. These were the only two London daily newspapers in 1749 that listed upcoming theatre shows – such an important source of information for many readers that newspapers sometimes paid the theatres for the privilege of inserting their event.

The estimate of the weekly sale of newspapers in London was around 100,000, resulting in nearly half a million readers. Many of these were read in the 500-plus coffee shops which stocked papers and journals in order to attract customers. The advertisement ran for five consecutive days, excluding Sunday, so anybody who regularly attended the theatre would have seen it. According to one pamphlet written after the hoax it was 'the Conversation of every public Place'. Its first appearance was on Wednesday 11 January 1749. It began: 'At the New Theatre in the Hay-Market, on Monday next, to be seen a Person who performs the several most surprising Things'. Calling it the 'New Theatre' was to differentiate it from the much larger King's Theatre, also in the Haymarket, that featured operas. The notice followed up with a description of what this anonymous entertainer would do. First, he borrows a walking cane and plays the music of every instrument. Second, he displays a wine bottle which, after it is examined, he enters and sings inside. In addition he will identify anybody sitting on the stage or in the boxes who is wearing a mask. It was common in popular productions for benches and boxes to be situated on the stage, even thought it restricted the actors' performance area. Gentlemen chose to pay for this privilege so they could converse with the actresses.

Ticket prices were comparable with the rival Drury Lane and Covent Garden theatres. However the advertised programme did not appear to be a particularly long show. Georgians liked to get their money's worth at the theatre, with a typical evening lasting in excess of four hours. This is because they featured not just the main play but also a prologue, music and dancing interludes and an 'afterpiece', often a farce or a pantomime. So the inclusion of the words 'The Performance continues about Two Hours and an Half' was doubtless to reassure potential audience members. Other useful information was that the show would begin at half past six and that people needed to pay for their seats at the theatre. The advertisement concluded with a rather drawn-out footnote. It stated that for an additional fee, in a separate room after the main show, the performer would bring to life any dead relative or friend so that patrons could see and chat to them for a few minutes. It also offered a private booking in somebody's house for £5, while simultaneously triumphing that 'most of the Crown'd Heads of *Asia*, *Africa*, and *Europe*' had seen the performances.

A complete reading of the advertisement gives the impression that it was not well thought through. It was almost as if there had been a brainstorming session to determine what were the most incredible exploits a person could achieve if he had supernatural powers: play any music on a walking cane; climb inside a wine bottle; identify people who had their faces hidden; and bring back to life, and speak to, the dead. They were then all thrown into the mix with no preconceived idea that one of them would stand out and connect with the readers. If it had been anticipated that someone getting inside a bottle would become the main talking point, then it surely would have been the lead item in the advertisement. It is only in hindsight that it seems obvious that this part of the programme would have the most appeal. Proof that it did is demonstrated by the insertion of a spoof advertisement in *The Daily Advertiser* three days before the hoax. Readers were informed that on the same bill at the New Theatre, Jumpedo, 'a *surprising Dwarf*, no taller than a common Tavern Tobacco-Pipe' would 'open his Mouth wide, and jump down his own Throat'.

A more generalised indication that interest in the show was gaining traction was a statement added to the advertisements from 13 January onwards: 'There will be a proper Guard to keep the House in due Decorum'. The hoaxer, knowing that the whole performance was a sham, was concerned about crowd control on the night. And he was right to be worried, for the combination of the advertisements, and the hype around them, resulted in a near packed-out theatre. What is not known is why the theatre management let everybody into the auditorium, given they must have known that the show wasn't going ahead. Maybe they were optimistically hoping that the performer would arrive at the last minute, rushing onto the stage without rehearsal. They would also have weighed up the likely consequences of refusing entry. A riot was probably inevitable at some point during the evening. It was just a question of when it would occur.

According to newspaper reports the following day, the theatre was fully lit up at seven o'clock. As was typical, candles and oil lamps were everywhere, illuminating the audience as much as the stage. Before most shows begun, music was played. But on this occasion there was not 'a single Fiddle to keep the Audience in a good Humour'. Growing impatient the audience exhibited their frustration by 'a Chorus of Catcalls, heightened by loud Vociferations, and beating with Sticks'. Eventually a spokesman emerged 'from behind the Curtain'. Attempting to be as obsequious as possible to forestall further trouble, he bowed and said that 'if the Performer did not appear, the Money should be return'd'.

This promise of recompense did not have the desired effect. Immediately a 'Wag' in the pit proclaimed what must rank as one of the all-time great heckles. Picking up on the advertised claim of the performer to climb into a two-pint bottle, he shouted: 'if the Ladies and Gentlemen would give double Prices, the Conjurer would get into a Pint Bottle'. A call to arms was then made when 'a young Gentleman in one of the Boxes seized a lighted Candle, and threw it upon the Stage'.

In the rush to the exit, many were pickpocketed of their hats, snuffboxes, wigs, cloaks and swords. Some remained inside and, augmented by an outside mob who entered the premises, they dismantled the theatre by tearing down the benches, boxes, scenery and drapes. These were taken outside and burnt on 'a mighty Bonfire'. With a theatrical touch, the curtain was 'hoisted on a Pole, by way of Flag'. Remarkably nobody was reported injured, although a 'young Nobleman's Chin' was hurt when he fell into the pit. He brought this upon himself by breaking up, with his foot, the box in which he was sitting. During the melee the takings disappeared. One report stated that about £100 was carried off by the 'Principals', while the remaining £15 'fell into the Hands of the Audience'. Others speculated that the non-existent Conjurer or the theatre proprietors stole it all.

After the newspapers gleefully reported the events of that evening, it was the turn of the pamphleteers and the cartoonists. The first satirical print relating to the hoax was published eight days after. Given the work required to produce such an engraving – the initial drawing, the etching of the copper plate and the complex and time-consuming process of printing each individual copy – this was a fast turnaround. It is called *The Bottle Conjurer, from Head to Foot, without Equivocation* [Fig. 10] and it was based on the newspaper reports. The scene is set outside the theatre with people looking out of the windows at the rioting below. There is a bonfire in full blaze, with the stage curtain on top of the flagpole. People are dancing and celebrating. A group of soldiers approach the scene from the rear, one of them holding his hands out towards the fire. This ties in with the information in the papers that a 'large Party of the Guards were sent for, but came Time enough only to warm themselves round the Fire'. In the absence of any formal policing in this period, they would have come from a nearby army garrison. In the top right-hand corner of the print the supposed perpetrators are sitting in a tavern laughing at those caught up in the hoax. They are holding a bottle with a man inside. Underneath the etching is a poem published three days before in *The London Evening-Post*, another example of the caricaturist borrowing from the papers.

The day before the print appeared, the first pamphlet went on sale for the same price of six pennies. It was called *A Letter to The Town, concerning The Man and the Bottle*, and it mocked those who had been caught out by the hoax. A follow up was *A Modest Apology for the Man in the Bottle*, 'By Himself', the most amusing part being the title. Rather funnier were the spoof notices inserted in the papers in the following days. A companion to the Bottle Conjurer promised to exhibit at the same theatre that 'which never was heretofore, nor

Fig. 10. *The Bottle Conjurer, from Head to Foot, without Equivocation*, an engraving published 24 January 1749.

ever will be hereafter seen'. Anybody who paid for the original performance would be admitted for free. The wittiest included an explanation of why the Bottle Conjurer didn't turn up. A gentleman had persuaded him to give a prior performance for a fee of £5. As soon as he had squeezed himself into the bottle, the spoilsport had corked it up and kept him trapped. This prevented his appearance 'for he never advertised he would go into two Bottles at one and the same time'.

With so many having fun at the expense of those caught out by the Bottle Conjurer, rival theatres to the New Theatre in the Haymarket were not going to be left out. The first to take up the challenge was John Rich. Rich had risen to fame with his performance, under the name Lin, as a Harlequin in pantomimes and farces in the early eighteenth century at the Lincoln's Inn Theatre. Having made a fortune staging John Gay's *Beggar's Opera*, he built the Covent Garden Theatre, which opened in December 1732. On 25 January 1749 the afterpiece at his new establishment was *Apollo and Daphne*, with William Phillips playing the part of the Harlequin. This was an ongoing role for Phillips, who had first appeared in this production the previous year. The following day an additional scene was introduced into the Greek mythological setting of 'the Escape of Harlequin into a Quart Bottle'.

The only description of how it played out is from a print called *An Apology to the Town, for Himself and the Bottle* [Fig. 11]. This shows a theatrical setting of a table and chair and two chandeliers lit by candles. On top of the table is a bottle with a large funnel coming out of it. A black-faced Harlequin is inside the funnel holding onto the sides with his hands. It must be presumed that he is about to disappear completely inside, thereby creating the illusion that he has gone into the bottle. The reader is informed that this is 'an exact Representation of Harlequin's Escape into the Bottle' as enacted at the Covent Garden theatre 'to crouded and polite Audiences'.

In March an additional sequence was added to a different afterpiece, *The Royal Chace*: 'Don Jumpedo in the Character of *Harlequin, will* Jump down his Own Throat.' Jumpedo was the nickname for the Bottle Conjurer, which was first touted in the spoof advertisement, mentioned earlier, about the forthcoming hoax. Once again there is no reportage of how it was staged apart from another print, titled *A Companion to the Bottle*. In this the Harlequin is precariously balanced on a pedestal, his arms in the air and his feet stuck into his mouth. This is an indication of the contortional skills necessitated by the performer in reproducing the comical sight for the audience. It was obviously a success as, when *Apollo and Daphne* was reprised on 23 March, the audience were treated to both the Harlequin leaping inside a bottle and down his own throat. And the following month yet another variation was added, with Don Jumpedo not only jumping down his own throat but jumping up again afterwards. Not to be outdone there was a one-off performance at the Drury Lane Theatre where Jumpedo entertained the audience by dancing a hornpipe and swallowing himself.

As time passed, and memories of the actual events of the night

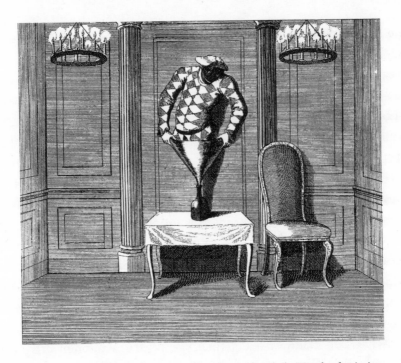

Fig. 11. *An Apology to the Town, for Himself and the Bottle*, depicting the theatrical representation of a harlequin climbing inside a bottle, published 8 February 1749.

began to fade, the Bottle Conjurer came to symbolise in prints an opportunistic, or impudent, impostor. In 1774 John Wilkes, the radical journalist and controversial politician, is depicted inside a funnel in a bottle. In 1805 a cartoon by Isaac Cruikshank shows Napoleon, called the *Corsican Bottle Conjurer*, being spiked out of a bottle by Britannia. Isaac's more famous son, George, sends up an absurdly inflammatory speech by the Lord Mayor of London by featuring a bottle blowing out smoke. In 1820 there is the *Italian Bottle-Conjurer*, a reference to an Italian valet called Theodore Majocchi who lied under oath at the trial for adultery of Queen Caroline of Brunswick. In this case the bottle has 'urinal' written on it. In 1823 an Irish print called *The Bottle Conjurers Arms* shows the stand-off between Protestants and Catholics.

An exception was James Gillray, who made a direct reference to the hoax itself in an 1805 print called *The Theatrical Bubble*. It features Richard Brinsley Sheridan – the author in his younger days of three great comedic plays, *The Rivals*, *The School for Scandal* and *The Critic* – as a Harlequin. By now he was equally known as a Whig politician, the right-hand man to Charles James Fox, and as the owner of the Drury Lane Theatre. This was rebuilt in 1794 with a massive auditorium of over 3,500 people, saddling Sheridan with debts that would remain with him for the rest of his life. As a result he was always looking for innovative productions to recoup his losses, and for Sheridan anything would go. Pantomimes, processions and performing animals made frequent appearances at his theatre. In the last chapter there will be another example of a dubious production staged by Sheridan.

Sheridan was sensitive about how he was depicted by Gillray, and this image shows why. He is obese; he has a red nose, to represent his excessive drinking; and an empty pocket indicates that he is broke. He is blowing bubbles out of a pipe and inside a giant one is the child prodigy actor William Betty. Sheridan had booked him at vast cost, even though he didn't have much regard for his acting ability. The message of the print is that this is another money-making scheme that is about to burst. As part of the myriad extra details that Gillray includes, there is on a table behind Sheridan a bottle with a funnel in the top. Written on the funnel are the words 'Bottle Conjurer' and stuck inside, up to his waist, is a podgy man. There is a label attached to the bottle with the words 'To be repeated the first opportunity'. Sheridan is being advised to perhaps revive the hoax if he wishes to make a quick buck.

II

Although there were many people caught out by the hoax, there was one man who was especially embarrassed by the incident. On 17 January it was reported that 'a great General lost his Sword in the Quarrel'. This was confirmed by an advertisement inserted the same day. It stated that on the previous night at the Haymarket theatre a sword with a gold hilt was lost. Tied around the hilt was a crimson and gold sword-knot. Whoever found it was instructed to bring it to Mrs Chenevix's Toy-Shop near Charing Cross, where they would receive a reward of 15 guineas 'and no Questions asked'. The shop was regularly used to return lost or, more likely, stolen valuables. The thief could collect a reward without fear of prosecution. Fifteen guineas, worth over £3,000 in today's money, was a generous amount, three times the normal going rate for a recovered item. The same offer was repeated for the next two days. On 20 January it was doubled to 30 guineas.

Once the news had broken, there was no lack of writers and caricaturists determined to make the most of it. A short poem was published on 21 January about the hoax which ended with the lines 'Peace was well restored / Before the G—L lost his *Cutting Sword*.' A spoof advertisement stated that a *'Gold-hilted Sword'* had been *'Found entangled in the Slit of a Lady's demolish'd Smock-Petticoat'*. It was *'supposed to have been stolen from the Plump-Side of a great General'*. Any enquires should be made at *'the* Quart-Bottle *and* Musical Cane *in* Potter's-Row'. Three of the surviving prints about the hoax reference the missing sword. In *The Bottle Conjurer, from Head to Foot, without Equivocation*, there is a figure of a headless man exclaiming 'I have lost my Head' with an empty sword scabbard. The next day a much cruder print came out called *The Bottl'd Heroes*. The most striking feature is a winged devil carrying in one hand a man trapped inside a bottle. In the other, he holds a sword with a piece of paper attached. It reads 'At the Theatre in the Hay Market. Ha Ha', implying that was where the weapon was found.

The best print relating to the hoax appeared on 30 January, with the title *English Credulity; or Ye're all Bottled* [Fig. 12]. This is the first time that the phrase 'English Credulity' is used in the sense of suggesting that it is some sort of disease which rendered the English especially susceptible. In the print the people caught up in the hoax are being dragged in by a length of rope held by the figure of the Fool. They are led towards a Satyr with a bag of money and a bottle in one hand. He is saying in Latin 'if people want to be deceived, let

Fig. 12. *English Credulity; or Ye're All Bottled*, an engraving published 30 January 1749.

them be deceived'. The artist is paying homage to two of Hogarth's prints, *The Beggar's Opera* and *Masquerades and Operas*. The people entrapped are asking for further miracles – for instance wanting to bring famous people back from the dead – while Britannia has her head in her hands in despair, muttering 'O! my Sons!' At the top of the engraving, there is an angelic nymph chasing after a flying sword, while crying out 'Stop or I loose 30 Guineas'. A label is attached to the sword with the words 'Thirty Guineas reward'.

None of the references name to whom the lost sword belongs. But anyone looking at the *English Credulity* print would have recognised a strutting corpulent figure, arrogantly poised with one hand inside his tunic, the other resting on his hip. He wears a tricorn hat and the speech bubble emanating from his mouth says 'Shew me Alexander Caesar Marlbro'. He is asking for great generals to be brought back from the dead, in line with the claims of the original hoaxer to resurrect the departed. This is William Augustus, the second son of

George II, otherwise known as the Duke of Cumberland. Three
years earlier he had been hailed as an all-conquering hero, having
defeated the Jacobites at the Battle of Culloden on 16 April 1746.
This ended once and for all any attempt by the Stuarts to reclaim the
throne. He had returned to England to great acclaim. A thanksgiving
service was held at St Paul's Cathedral with the first performance of
Handel's *The Conquering Hero*, composed especially for him. He was
voted an income of £25,000 per annum over and above his money
from the Civil List.

Three years later, though, his standing had deteriorated. It had
started with rumours about his treatment of the Jacobites in the
aftermath of Culloden, both in slaughtering them on the battlefield
and tracking down and killing anybody remotely connected with the
rebellion. Soon after he incurs the derogatory title of the Butcher of
Culloden. He had followed that up with an inglorious re-entry into
military combat in the continuing War of Austrian Succession, when
he was defeated for a second time by Marshal Saxe. By January 1749
the war was over but he was still Commander in Chief of the English
armies. An obsession with army reform and discipline added to his
reputation as a sadistic taskmaster. Furthermore there were rumours
about his private life, not enhanced by his unattractive, overweight
appearance. The Duke was considered fair game for satirical attacks.

A letter written on 23 January purported to explain how the
Duke lost his sword at the New Theatre. It was claimed that, when
the event was known to be a hoax, he was the first who flew into a
rage. He drew his weapon, commanding that the house should be
torn down in vengeance. But someone slipped in behind him and
'pulled the sword out of his hand'. The female writer was not a fan of
the Duke, calling him a 'Monster of Nature!', so the anecdote ought
to be treated with some caution. While later retrospective accounts
also postulated that the Duke was the instigator of the rioting, there
was nothing else written *at the time* to collaborate that he was so
directly involved.

The ridicule of the Duke was confined to the satirical pamphlets, spoof insertions and prints. His involvement in the hoax was never publicly stated as a news item in the papers. There is also no private correspondence in existence giving an indication of what he thought about the episode. The closest he comes to it is a letter sent to a friend in April where the Duke writes about escaping to the country to 'purify me after the bad air and humour I contracted in London'. The following month it is recorded that he made a return visit to the New Theatre, when he attended an opera. Maybe by now he had put the humiliating event behind him. However if the Duke thought he could avoid further derision in relation to his leisure activities, he was much mistaken. For in July 1749 gossip emerged about the Duke attempting to seduce a Savoyard girl who he had met on his travels. He ordered her to go to Windsor and offered her £100 for her 'services'. She refused the money, so he sent her packing.

A Savoyard girl was a wandering minstrel who strolled around the country playing a hybrid of a violin and an accordion, called a hurdy-gurdy. Marian was the name of the girl that caught the eye of the Duke, and she was described as 'a poor mean-dressed wench, but pretty enough if she was dressed out'. An amusing print appeared of the attempted seduction. It was called *John of Gant in Love*, a throwback to John of Gaunt, the younger son of the fourteenth-century King Edward III, who had aspirations for seizing power. It depicts a fat Duke of Cumberland, hands clasped, knees bent, staring lovingly into the eyes of a Savoyard woman, his sword thrusting towards her. She is cranking the shaft, and toying with the keyboard, of an extremely phallic-looking hurdy-gurdy. In the background a Scotsman is staring angrily at a great fat hog saying 'No Swines for me'. The sexually predatory nature of the Duke, the continued antipathy by the Scots to his victory at Culloden, his excessive weight and his designs on the throne are all encapsulated in this print. No wonder Horace Walpole observed that it had 'more humour than I almost ever saw in one of that sort'.

Other prints followed which were even more scurrilous and suggestive regarding the incident and, by showing support for the

Jacobite rebellion, potentially traitorous. So much so that prosecutions were instigated against the publishers for seditious libel, contempt for King and Government, as well as obscenity. It is possible that William Hogarth would have met a similar fate if a painting that he executed in this year had been reproduced as a print. It was called *The Savoyard Girl* [Fig. 13]. A young woman is standing and singing, while gazing upwards. She is playing her hurdy-gurdy. She is wearing a rounded hat with strings tied under her chin. Her dress is full-length and of simple design. She looks a picture of innocence.

However what jars is that she is indoors, outside her natural working habitat. There are no obvious signs of furniture, although there is the hint of some sort of chair or small table immediately behind her. She is standing next to an unlit fire hearth decorated with Dutch tiles. Leaning against it is a sword. Here is the Duke's missing weapon, pointing upwards to depict the most erotic of the five senses, that of touch. The only ornament is a plain, broken, mirror which is standing on the mantelpiece. The lack of reflection depicts the shattered illusion of those who attended the theatre that night. Hanging on the wall is the type of tricorn hat worn by the General. Hogarth has cleverly juxtaposed Cumberland's attempted seduction of the Savoyard girl with the Bottle Conjurer hoax. These were dangerous allusions to be making in these litigious times. So it was as well that Hogarth sold the painting privately to a friend, George Hay, and it never appeared in public view until some fifty years later.

III

One aspect of the hoax that was never thoroughly investigated at the time was the question of who had perpetrated it. Indeed no one seemed that interested in even raising the question, at least publicly. The papers were more concerned with describing what had happened and then mocking those who had fallen for it. A reference was made to David Hume's recently published *An Enquiry*

Fig. 13. *The Savoyard Girl*, a later engraving by G. Sherlock from a 1749 painting by William Hogarth.

Concerning Human Understanding, in which he questions the existence of miracles. It was claimed that many enemies of this book were 'greatly disappointed by the Conjurer's Non-Appearance in the Bottle'. If he had succeeded in jumping into it, it would have been convincing proof that miracles still occurred. If there was speculation about the hoaxer it was far from incisive. One pamphlet did declare that 'you are doubtless impatient to know how all this came about', but concluded that they were unable to say anything with certainty.

The most obvious suspect was the owner of the New Theatre in the Haymarket, John Potter. He was originally a carpenter by trade and had built the establishment in 1720. It had taken some time to get going but eventually flourished in the 1730s, principally due to the satirical plays written by Henry Fielding. The 1737 Licensing Act put an end to its staging legitimate drama. Only the Drury Lane and Covent Garden theatres were given the requisite permits for such productions. The New Theatre managed to survive by creatively putting on shows that circumnavigated the Act. These included running a teaching class and charging for people to see the students' output; getting the audience to pay for a concert, which also included a play for free; or coming up with pieces that had no script and therefore did not need to be submitted in advance to the Lord Chancellor for clearance.

The man who perfected skirting with the law was Samuel Foote, now recognised as one of the first stand-up comedians. In 1747 he advertised taking chocolate with himself at twelve o'clock in the morning. He later changed this to drinking a dish of tea at 6.30 in the evening. This evolved into his long-running hit *Mr Foote Gives Tea*. It was a parody about plays and bad acting, using cardboard cut-outs to represent the various personalities that Foote gave voice to and interacted with. His subterfuge of charging the audience for drinks, and throwing in the show for nothing, didn't fool the authorities for long. But they allowed him, and the New Theatre, leeway because the entertainment was popular and it was on only two or three times a week.

In 1748 he came up with a new production, which was *A Sale at his Auction Room*, again staged at the New Theatre. In this, with the help of giant picture frames on stage, Foote brought various characters in the art world to life. By the start of 1749, his *Auction Room* had reached its fiftieth performance. Foote was performing it twice a week, on a Monday and Saturday. Except, that is, for Monday 16

January, when it was replaced by the Bottle Conjurer. That decision, to substitute an on-going successful run with a controversial one-off and unproven production, was made by John Potter. It was therefore natural that he should be considered to be the man behind it.

Potter was forced to quickly explain his side of the story. On 18 January a notice appeared in both *The Daily Advertiser* and *The General Advertiser* stating that Potter had initially been sceptical about the proposed performance. He had only agreed to hire out his theatre on condition that the ticket money was returned if the show didn't go ahead. As this was readily agreed to, and payment was made up front for the 'Rent of the House', he strongly believed 'no real Imposition' was intended. He related how, on the night of the rioting, the office where the takings were kept was broken into. His staff were 'obliged to fly to save their Lives'. Finally he said the damage caused by the rioting was 'upwards of Four hundred Pounds', and he hoped that the gentlemen who had injured him would 'make me a reasonable Satisfaction'. Perhaps there were still those who distrusted Potter, as the same insertion was made the following day with a N.B. added. The person who had leased the theatre was called William Nicholls.

If it wasn't Potter, then perhaps it might be Samuel Foote, either drumming up some publicity for his *Auction Room*, or in order to renege on his promise to put on a performance as a bonus pay-out to his actor's company. He was just as swift to pronounce his innocence in the papers. He wrote that, when he heard from Potter that his show was to be replaced that night, he advised that he considered it a fraud and that the doors should not be opened. He was informed that, because money had been paid upfront, it had to go ahead. Foote himself attended the performance and therefore would have witnessed for himself the destruction of the theatre. As one observer wrote, 'so ruinate a Place never did my eyes behold'. Foote's next *Auction Room* didn't occur until 25 January, after the theatre was repaired, so both he, and Potter, would have been out of pocket. The conclusion must be that there was no reason for the two men to have played any part in the hoax.

With the proprietor and principal performer of the New Theatre out of the reckoning, suspicion fell on the owners of the Drury Lane and Covent Garden theatres. As one correspondent put it, some supposed that the 'Managers of both Play Houses contriv'd it to hinder Foote's going on'. Mention has already been made of John Rich at the Covent Garden theatre. David Garrick, the famous actor, was in charge of the Drury Lane theatre, having purchased it two years before. The possibility of his involvement is hinted at in the first print that came out about the hoax, *The Bottle Conjurer, from Head to Foot, without Equivocation*. Directly under the three men laughing at the antics of those caught up in the fracas has been written Gr—k. This implicates Garrick as one of the trio.

However it makes no sense for either Garrick or Rich to have carried out such a stunt. If their names had emerged, it would have seriously backfired on them. Their theatres were both doing good business, so they had no need to try to shut down the New Theatre. Furthermore Foote was coming to the end of his run, so the timing made no sense. There is no other contemporary reference where either of the two men is accused of any involvement in the hoax. In my view they, too, are firmly in the clear.

For the next six years, all went quiet about a possible suspect. Then in 1755, a confession was made in a book called *The Life and Uncommon Adventures of Capt. Dudley Bradstreet*. The eponymous author claimed his reason for carrying out the hoax was to make money. Bradstreet had led an extremely adventurous life, culminating in infiltrating the Jacobites' camp, during the 1745 uprising, as a spy for the Duke of Cumberland. Given the rest of his hyperbolic narrative, it would be easy to dismiss this as another fantasy tale. But it appears to be true. He was recruited by the Duke of Newcastle who, together with his brother Henry Pelham, dominated the political landscape in this period. On 5 December 1745, posing as an English Lord, he rode into Derby, where the Stuart Prince was planning his next move. He informed the rebels that there was an army of several thousand men waiting for them if they chose to march on London. In reality 'there was not nine Men'. This false information contributed to the fatal decision of the Jacobites to retreat to Scotland. If they had carried on to the capital, they might well have achieved their aim of overthrowing the throne.

Bradstreet received some monetary rewards for his endeavours, but not the compensation he expected. A venture into a lottery scheme didn't work out either. Desperate for cash, he wrote his book. In doing so, he 'introduced the noisy and famed Bottle Conjurer to the World, in *January* one thousand, seven hundred and forty seven-eight'. Getting the wrong year in which it occurred was not a good start to claiming ownership of the hoax. In order to demonstrate to the reader that he had a track record in this type of stunt, he mentioned a couple of other schemes he had come up with previously. One was to 'fly to the Moon in the People's Presence'. Another was to 'teach *French* and Cooking perfectly well in an Hour'. Although he writes that the reasons why these sure-fire, money-making schemes were abandoned would be 'hereafter explained', they never were.

It is hard to grasp the actual details of the hoax, as related by Bradstreet, because inserted into the book is a play called *The Magician; Or, The Bottle-Conjurer*, which recreates the story in a dramatic setting. According to Bradstreet it is necessary to refer both to his autobiographical prose and his script in order to piece together how the complete scenario unfolds. It is only if he turns it into 'an Historical Comedy', every part of which, we are assured, is true, that people will believe the 'extraordinary Oddities'. Bradstreet had aspirations for the play to stand in its own right. He said that the actress Peg Woffington had praised it and that it had played with 'great Success' for four nights before the Westminster Magistrates shut it down. There is, though, no existing record of any performances.

Most of Bradstreet's description of how the hoax was planned and implemented comes from the papers at the time, with facts occasionally muddled. For instance he claims that the original advertisement stated that the performer promised to 'restore Youth to old Age', which it never did. His principal new information is that he had the assistance of confederates: a nineteen-year-old youth, a half-pay officer who supplemented his wages by practising as a 'Lawyer in *London* in a low Way', and the madam of a brothel. According to Bradstreet, having come up with the scheme, they looked into potential venues. Drury Lane and Covent Garden theatres were ruled out because they needed to be 'paid before-hand'. So they opted for the New Theatre in the Haymarket. This contradicts with what we know – that the hirer of the premises did pay for the rental upfront.

Bradstreet's friends go to the coffee houses to publicise the show and to listen to what others are saying about the forthcoming performance. They hear one man say that he 'shall send this Afternoon to all my Friends in *Cumberland*, to hasten to Town', a dig at the Duke of Cumberland and the only joke in what is meant to be a comical play. Bradstreet says that a day or so before the performance he arranges for a child to take a parcel of tickets to the theatre, presumably to sell them at the door. The plan is that they will 'receive the Money for Tickets, and take it away when the House is full'. The details of how they achieve this is scant. The men guarding the takings are distracted while one of the confederates makes off with the loot. According to Bradstreet they end up with 300 guineas, which is three times the amount of receipts as reported in the papers.

Bradstreet claims that, soon after the hoax, he publicly confessed. But nowhere is there any verification of this. More incriminatingly, he admits that he paid for the publication of the book by travelling around Ireland in order to entice backers to contribute to the cost. Being introduced 'as the real *Bottle-Conjurer*' yielded him 'a vast many Subscribers'. Bradstreet saw an opportunity to make money by claiming to be the hoaxer. As he writes himself, 'I hope my *Magician* or *Bottle-Conjurer* will please, for it has neither Nature nor Reason to support it.'

I am unconvinced of Bradstreet's role in the Bottle Conjurer affair. Much of what he tells us could be derived from a cursory reading of the newspaper reports at the time – and, even then, he gets many of the basic facts wrong. He fails to tell us the names of his accomplices, although there is no reason to hide their identities; he has no history of being a hoaxer, his supposed examples of previous and post schemes being just too fanciful to be believable; there is no third-party evidence to substantiate any of his outlandish claims, some of which are consequential enough to have been recorded in the press; his involvement in spying activities demonstrates that he is a man who is comfortable with lying; key parts of the narrative, such as whom he contacted to arrange the booking of the theatre, how he paid for the advertisements and the theatre, how he stole the takings and how it was discovered he was the culprit, are missed out; and finally, and perhaps most significantly, he gives us no credible motive why he wanted to enact the hoax.

So if Bradstreet is not the culprit, then who was? Ironically Bradstreet himself gives us a clue when he writes disparagingly that, at the time of the Bottle Conjurer, 'the reports of the Town and the three Kingdoms, was that a certain Duke contrived it'.

IV

The idea that a nobleman might have been involved first emerged a few days after the hoax when it was announced in *The Daily Advertiser* that the 'Presence of some Noble Contributors' would ensure the New Theatre in the Haymarket was 'put into neat Order'. In other words a prestigious person had coughed up for the repair of the theatre damaged by the rioting. Who that might be was not announced until another twenty-three years had passed. The revelation was made in *The Town and Country*, a magazine that started publication in January 1769. Its success owed much to its 'Tête-à-Têtes' column which each month, in an article of some two to three pages long, gossiped about the sexual liaison between a man of distinction with, normally, a less privileged woman. They were distinguished by featuring a double oval engraving of the couple with the placement alongside of incomplete but instantly recognisable names. In September 1772 the two exposed to public shaming were Mrs O–b–n and L—d G—, otherwise the commoner Mrs Osbern, who at one time had been a milkmaid, and Granville Leveson-Gower, also known as Viscount Trentham.

Back in November 1749 Viscount Trentham had been a controversial figure. Due to his promotion to the Admiralty Board, he had had to resign his seat for Westminster and offer himself for re-election. This was bitterly fought with his opponent Sir George Vandeput, the final outcome not determined until May of the following year. On 14 November, Trentham had attended a performance by a troupe of French actors at the New Theatre in the Haymarket. Anti-French feeling was rife and a group attempted to disrupt the play. It was claimed that Trentham had led an attack against these unarmed patriots, an allegation that he vehemently denied, but which did immense damage to his campaign. The Tête-à-Têtes succeeded in conflating this riot with the Bottle Conjurer fracas that had taken place ten months earlier. It stated that Lord Trentham had attended both events – in fact there is no evidence that he was at the earlier show – and that at the November performance a bonfire was made of the scenery and benches, which was not true. It is fortunate, however, that these errors were made, as it enabled the author to enlarge on the January hoax by stating it was 'a scheme planned by the late duke of Montagu, in company with the duke of Richmond'. The former offered a wager of 100 guineas that 'if an advertisement was published, setting forth that on such a day a man would get into a quart bottle, the inhabitants of this metropolis would flock to pay for being spectators of an impossibility'. For the first time, therefore, John Montagu, 2nd Duke of Montagu, becomes the prime suspect.

Two questions that immediately arise are how reliable is the article and whether it's backed up by other authorities. All the Tête-à-Têtes were written anonymously and mainly came from correspondents who attended coffee houses gathering gossip, anecdotes and amusing stories. On the whole, though, they were considered to be remarkably accurate, the publishers doubtless aware of the potential for libel if falsehoods were put in print. When it comes to another, independent, source, the closest that can be found is dated seven years later in an article on J. J. Heidegger, a leading impresario of masquerades. Here it refers to 'the late facetious Duke of Montague (the memorable author of the scheme of the bottle-conjuror, at the Theatre in the Hay-market)...' However it is impossible to know whether the provenance for this quote came from the earlier reference in *The Town and Country Magazine*. With no positive proof of the Duke of Montagu's involvement, it is necessary to turn to circumstantial evidence.

John Montagu [Fig. 14] was born on 29 March 1690, the only surviving son of Ralph Montagu, the first Duke, who died in 1709. He married Mary Churchill in 1705, when he was aged fourteen and she was a year older. She was the daughter to the Duke of Marlborough, the great general during the War of Spanish Succession, and Sarah Churchill, the confidante and favourite of Queen Anne. Perhaps wishing to ingratiate himself with his father-in-law, Montagu volunteered for active service in 1706. He did not enjoy the 'carnage' and returned home soon after, never again to be involved in any active fighting. This might have been part of the reason why Sarah Churchill never warmed to him. However the Duke of Marlborough never held it against him, admiring Montagu's honesty and appointing him a trustee of his will. The respect was mutual, with Montagu always standing up when the general was eating. He was the chief mourner at the Duke's funeral when he died in 1722.

Montagu owned Boughton House in Northampton and Montagu House in London, which later would become the British Museum, together with other property. With these huge estates, an income in excess of £17,000 a year and a wayward wife, Montagu could choose his own lifestyle. Although he contributed to public service – including being Governor of the Isle of Wight, captain of the gentlemen pensioners and Master-General of the Ordnance – it could be said that, compared with some of his illustrious contemporaries, he led a life rather more devoted to personal pleasures. Exactly the

Fig. 14. Portrait of John, 2nd Duke of Montagu by Thomas
Hudson, painted in 1749.

type of person, in other words, who would have the inclination, the
means and the time to mastermind the Bottle Conjurer hoax.

In February 1721 Montagu signed a two-year lease with John
Potter, the owner of the New Theatre in the Haymarket. He brought
over a company calling themselves French comedians, although they
included in their repertoire a number of tragedies. In the event they
performed for only five months between December 1721 and April
1722. However it demonstrates Montagu's fondness of the theatre
– he even named his dog Harlequin – and a working relationship
with John Potter. His love of playfulness and the curious, though,

extended outside the confines of a dramatic venue. Montagu was a serial practical joker, which was another reason that Sarah Churchill did not approve of her son-in-law. She wrote that he behaved more like a fifteen-year-old than someone aged fifty, commenting further that he invited people into his garden and squirted them with water, put itching powder in their beds, 'and twenty such pretty fancies like these'.

There are so many anecdotes about the Duke of Montagu and his jests that it is hard to know whether they were all carried out by him, or whether his name was just conveniently attached to some, as he was the best known prankster of this period. He had wonky mirrors installed outside his drawing room. Gentlemen who used the reflection to adjust their wigs and cravats then entered with them all askew. He invited a group of people who stammered and stuttered to dinner and, because they all thought everybody else was mimicking them, a fight broke out. The French political philosopher Montesquieu visited the Duke at his country residence. Before the two gentlemen had even been properly acquainted, he was drenched with a tub of cold water poured over his head. The Duke took the Mayor and his aldermen from Windsor on a water trip and deliberately left the boat plug behind so they all sank. The whole corporation had to splash their way back to the shore. He and a friend dumped sewage from 'a couple of great earthen pots' onto the favourite garden seat of Dr John Misaubin, a French expatriate who was much mocked as a quack. A gourmet was given a very tough steak to consume, having been informed that he was late for dinner and everybody else had already eaten. The Duke, with a couple of friends, on arriving at their destination in a hackney-coach, stepped out. They then immediately rushed around to the opposite side to re-enter and exit the vehicle again. The coachman ran into the first public house he saw convinced 'he had been carrying a legion of devils, for he had counted eighteen of them, and they were coming out still.'

Perhaps his most elaborate hoax involved the aforementioned

J. J. Heidegger. The Swiss masquerade impresario was invited to a function with a few hard drinkers and ended up drunk, dead to the world. A plaster-of-paris cast was taken of his face and a mask was constructed to make someone look exactly like him. At the next Royal Ball, as the King entered, Heidegger arranged for *God save the King* to be played. When he exited the room, the fake Heidegger ordered the musicians to strike up *Charley over the Water*, a Jacobite anthem. An enraged Heidegger came rushing back to change the music. No sooner had he left than the lookalike repeated his directive. The Duke arranged it that both men should apologise to the King at the same time, at which point Heidegger discovered the deception. There is no date for when this event took place but it might well have been around the time that the Duke was present at the confessions of Mary Toft, as mentioned in Chapter 3. Maybe she inspired him to be equally creative in his own hoaxes.

On first reading, some of these pranks appear to have an element of cruelty about them. But Montagu is eager to make up for any indignity caused to his victims. Both the Mayor and the aldermen, and the inedible steak consumer, were given a lavish meal afterwards. While Montesquieu said that he thought his ducking was 'odd', Montagu's 'great goodness to me, and his incomparable understanding, far overpaid me for all the inconveniences'. For all the stories there are about his jests, there are an equal number about his kindness and generosity. He paid out nearly £3,000 a year in private pensions to individuals. He used to ride out into the country with his pockets full of money, which he would away give to anybody whom he met that was deserving. He helped with patronage a black man called Ignatius Sancho, who had been born on a slave ship before coming to England. He pardoned a man sentenced to death for stealing from him. He bought books from all kinds of authors, often paying over the odds, and gave them away to his friends. Meeting an impoverished curate who had the same name as him, he promised him a living on the death of an incumbent parson: Montagu honoured the commitment. He found a half-pay officer in dire circumstances, separated from his wife and children. He reunited the family at a surprise dinner informing the officer that he had obtained him another commission in the army. Finally he presented the man with a bank note of £500 before sitting down to dinner 'as composedly as if he had done nothing'. 'He was your friend and the friend of mankind,' wrote one correspondent on his death; while another noted that 'as his grace's humanity and benevolence was universal, so his loss is irreparable'. Horace Walpole said 'he was a most amiable man, and one of the most feeling I ever knew.'

This combination of being a benevolent hoaxer matches him up with the nobleman paying for the repairs for the damage done to the New Theatre in the Haymarket, following the non-appearance of the Bottle Conjurer. Montagu, having had his fun, didn't want anyone to come away the worse for it. One man who did suffer, as we have seen, was the Duke of Cumberland. Montagu was good friends with him. This indeed is confirmed by the two of them standing next to each other in *English Credulity; or Ye're all Bottled* [Fig. 12]. Montagu is the tall lean man with the cane on the Duke of Cumberland's left. He is saying 'Raise the Infernals to teach me Fireworks'. This is a reference to the well-known fact that Montagu was in charge of organising the fireworks, which were to take place in April 1749, to celebrate the treaty of Aix-la-Chapelle ending the War of Austrian Succession: the two men attended the event together. One suspects it is just an amusing coincidence that the perpetrator of the hoax is included in this print. In any event, confessing to have caused such embarrassment to a prominent member of the Royal Family would not have been a good career move; and probably explains partly why he never admitted publicly that he was the man behind it. That Montagu was able to conceal his involvement from his friend is confirmed by his ability 'to keep a very grave Face, when he was not in the most serious Earnest'. After a suitable time had lapsed maybe he could have admitted his part. But on 5 July 1749, less than seven months after the hoax, the Duke of Montagu died of pneumonia.

There is one intriguing coda to the affair. In John Potter's disclaimer about being involved in the hoax he stated that the man he dealt with in negotiating the rental of the theatre was called William Nicholls. It has been assumed that the name was a pseudonym. No attempt has previously been made to track him down. There was though a William Nicholls who had a strong connection with the Duke. He was a curate at Scaldwell and rector at Little Oakley, both parishes in Northampton near the Duke's main estate at Boughton. These livings, as they were called, were bestowed by the Duke and were among many such lifetime appointments that were in his hands. From the two posts Nicholls earned sufficient to sustain a career in the Church and have six daughters. As a curate, Nicholls would have reported to Scaldwell's rector who, until his death in 1742, was Charles Lamotte. In 1728 they had a falling out and Lamotte made it clear that he hadn't been in favour of giving Nicholls the living, suggesting that he had been overruled by the Duke. In 1730 a parsonage house was built in Little Oakley for Nicholls, with stone and timber provided from the Duke's estate.

William Nicholls went to Oxford University, but only at the lowest order of undergraduate. So he was not of a class that would have mixed with the likes of the Duke. It is not known why Montagu favoured Nicholls with the two livings. It is possible that he saw in him a talented young scholar whom he felt deserving of reward. When it came to the Little Oakley appointment, the Duke seemed to keep his options open as Nicholls was requested to sign a bond of resignation. Although in canon law such bonds were technically illegal, they meant that, if requested, the clergyman had to promise to resign – or forfeit a punitively large sum of money.

William Nicholls still held the same two positions in 1749 and was clearly indebted to the Duke for them. It is conceivable therefore that the Duke could have sent him to London to negotiate the rental of the New Theatre in the Haymarket. As against that supposition, John Potter said Nicholls was 'a Man of genteel Appearance' who 'directed Letters to be left for him at the Bedford Coffee-house'. You wouldn't have thought a lowly cleric from Northampton would be mistaken as belonging to the gentry or that he would know his way around the London coffee houses. What is more plausible is that someone close to the Duke, and acting on the latter's instructions to book the theatre for the night of 16 January, had appropriated the name of William Nicholls. One likely candidate is Philip Sone. He succeeded Lamotte as rector of Scaldwell, and therefore Nicholls was directly answerable to him. Like his predecessor Sone was one of the chaplains to Frederick Prince of Wales, the heir apparent to the throne in 1749. He moved in higher circles than Nicholls and would have matched Potter's description.

All this is speculation but, even without Nicholls in the picture, it is my view that there is sufficient evidence to implicate the Duke of Montagu. It was stated in *The Town and Country Magazine* that he acted in conjunction with Lord Richmond. This also rings true. They were friends, had residences close to each other and both were fond of practical jokes. And the fact that a wager was involved fits into the climate of the times where ridiculous bets were commonplace among noblemen. It was all done for the best possible motive – in order to test the credulity of the English public at the time. I am sure that more serious historians might despair that the Duke of Montagu is best remembered for carrying out an audacious jest, when he partook in matters far more important and significant. But for me there is something life-affirming about human nature in our preference for the undiluted pleasure of a good laugh at a sublimely constructed hoax.

SIX

'THIS RESOLUTELY-VIRTUOUS CREATURE'

* * *

I

It is paradoxical that one of the most famous hoaxes of the eighteenth century might not even have been a hoax at all. If this is so, then what you are about to read is the forthright account of somebody who was horribly exploited and abused. Look at it in a different light, though, and you have someone who was able to spin and sustain a fabricated tale so convincingly that no less a personage than the eminent writer Henry Fielding, among many others, was deceived. If you are expecting a neat tie-up at the end of this chapter, prepare to be disappointed. What I can promise you, though, is an enthralling tale of kidnapping, perjury, death sentences, bribery, corruption and court trials, all of which were extensively covered and analysed at the time. Any lack of resolution is therefore more than compensated for by a surfeit of information. Certainly enough, you would have thought, to determine whether a simple maidservant was, or was not, perhaps the greatest hoaxer of them all.

The first public notice of the story was in a newspaper on 31 January 1753. It reported that a young woman had been mugged on the evening of New Year's Day, in Moorfields in the City of London, by two men. They had knocked her unconscious, stolen her money and some of her clothes and then forcibly taken her to a house in Enfield Wash, a distance of around ten miles. Here she had been confronted by the owner of the house who had cut off her stays – a stiff undergarment which is laced and worn from the waist upwards. She had been imprisoned upstairs in a loft with just bread and water. After twenty-eight days she had managed to break out and return home to her widowed mother in what was described as a 'wretched Condition'. The article ended by implying she had narrowly avoided becoming a prostitute, unlike other women who remained on the premises.

The next day an update was provided. A warrant had been obtained from a Guildhall Alderman, subsequently named as Thomas Chitty, to apprehend the parties who had locked her up. More significantly she had 'no more than a Quartern [quarter of a] Loaf and about a Gallon of Water' to survive on during the time of her imprisonment. In a follow-up bulletin readers learnt that an officer went to the Enfield Wash house accompanied by the accuser, her friends and neighbours. At the premises eight people were arrested. They were taken to a Justice of Peace, Merry Tyshmaker, who discharged six of them. The owner of the property, Madam Wells, was committed to Clerkenwell, Bridewell, while an old Gypsy woman was sent to New Prison.

It would be a week later before further information came out in the public domain. The source involved one of the most famous novelists of the eighteenth century, Henry Fielding, author of *The History of Tom Jones, a Foundling*. This though was near the end of his career, and indeed his life, when he was primarily earning a living as a magistrate. Fielding was taking tea with his wife on the upper floor of his rooms in Bow Street, Covent Garden, when he was interrupted by his clerk to be informed that a Mr Salt was requesting some legal assistance. The attorney wanted Fielding to hear his client's statement and agree it was an accurate representation of the events leading up to the arrests at the Enfield Wash property.

On 7 February Fielding was introduced to Elizabeth Canning

[Fig. 15]. She was eighteen years of age and was described as 'plain, and short of stature', her face marred by her having suffered from smallpox as a child. She no longer lived with her widowed mother but worked, as a maid, for a prosperous carpenter called John Lyon. He was married and lived in Aldermanbury in the City of London. The Lyons were very happy with Elizabeth's work, unsurprisingly perhaps, given that New Year's Day was her first day off for about ten weeks. She chose to have a meal with her aunt and uncle, and afterwards they walked with her as far as Aldgate, before leaving her to make her own way back to her employer's house. What happened after that was recorded in the affidavit, taken down by Mr Salt and signed, with a mark, by Elizabeth Canning in the presence of Fielding.

Walking through Moorfields, her account tells us, she was set upon by two men. She could not identify her attackers but recalled that they wore bob-wigs – a short wig that imitated the natural hair – and drab-coloured greatcoats. They stole from her half a guinea in gold, and three shillings in silver, along with her apron and gown. After recovering from what she described as a fit, brought about by the blows she received, she was forced to walk to a disorderly 'Bawdy-house'. In the kitchen she encountered an old woman and two younger ones, one of whom she later discovered was called Virtue Hall. The eldest, a Gypsy, promised Canning some fine clothes if she would 'go their Way', by which she meant to become a prostitute. On her refusal the Gypsy took a knife out of a drawer, cut the laces off her stays and removed them. One of the original assailants stole her cap.

Canning was forced up some stairs into a back room resembling a hayloft and informed if she made any noise she would have her throat cut. When it grew light she discovered 'a large black Jug with the Neck much broken, wherein was some Water'. On the floor were several pieces of bread to make up a quarter loaf. From that moment on, a total of four weeks, she had no other sustenance, apart from a small mince pie – an intended gift for her brother – which she had in her pocket. During her stay, although she never saw her, she

Fig. 15. Portrait of Elizabeth Canning, an engraving by L. P. Boitard, published 27 May 1754.

often heard the name of Mrs, or Mother, Wells, who she understood was the mistress of the house. By 26 January she had consumed all the bread and water. She continued without any provision until 29 January when she broke out of a window and jumped down to safety. This was about half past four in the afternoon. She then made her way back to her mother's house, arriving there at quarter past ten that same night.

The main difference between Elizabeth Canning's statement and the information in the first newspaper article was that the woman who had cut off her stays was not the owner of the house in Enfield Wash – i.e. not Susannah Wells, otherwise known as Mother Wells.

Instead it was an itinerant traveller called, as the public would soon discover, Mary Squires. It was also noteworthy that she hadn't had a continuous supply of bread and water throughout her ordeal, as was initially implied. She had apparently survived the full four weeks on a quarter loaf of bread and a pitcher of water. Although it didn't appear in her statement, a newspaper article three days later pointed out that, although Canning had no idea where she had been held captive, she did know the premises were in Hertfordshire. This was because she recognised the coach, one on which her previous mistress used to travel, pass by her window. The exact house was identified by one of the neighbours, Robert Scarrat, who was among many who had gone to see her at her mother's house on Canning's return.

Following Canning's affidavit, Fielding ordered that anybody still living at Mother Wells's property should be brought to him. Most had disappeared from the scene, but two women were fetched. The younger was Virtue Hall. She was in a very emotional state when questioned by Fielding, trembling and crying. Fielding tried to calm her down, telling her that no harm would come to her if she told the truth. She continued to prevaricate. Fielding had finally had enough. Unless she told him what she knew, Fielding would commit her to prison. That did it. She agreed to make a full statement, which was subsequently written up, again with the assistance of the not-entirely-neutral Mr Salt.

Virtue Hall's story supported Elizabeth Canning's own version of events. The only significant discrepancy was that Hall said that the broken jug of water and bread had been carried up the stairs after Elizabeth Canning was locked away – whereas Canning claimed it was already in the loft when she was first incarcerated. A major breakthrough was that she named one of the captors who had brought Canning to the house. This was John Squires, the son of Mary. Hall had been the first to notice that Canning had gone, a full two days after she had escaped. She also swore that Susannah Wells's daughter had nailed up the boards that Canning had prised open in order to make her exit. By giving the impression they had never been broken, the kidnappers could dispute the maid servant's account of her leap to freedom.

The other woman from the house, Judith Natus, contradicted all of this. She said that she and her husband had been sleeping in the very same loft where Elizabeth Canning claimed she had been held. She had never seen or heard of the maidservant. Virtue Hall's retort was that Judith was part of a conspiracy instigated by Susannah Wells in order to nullify her own involvement. She said that the couple had moved upstairs once Canning had gone, in order to give the impression that they had slept there all the time. Fielding was tempted to prosecute Judith for perjury. He let her off with a warning that, if she intended to give evidence at the forthcoming trial, she ought to be very certain of what she was saying.

If Fielding wasn't wholly convinced of the guilt of Mary Squires and Susannah Wells by this stage, he was a few days later. The four prisoners and accusers were all brought together to confront each other in his room. Susannah Wells protested her innocence in a manner that demonstrated she had been schooled in evading justice. Mary Squires resorted to religious histrionics, behaving 'as a Person traditionally and hereditarily versed in the ancient Egyptian Cunning'. Nevertheless it didn't prevent her showing her real feelings when she said about Canning, *'Damn the young Bitch!'* This contrasted with the measured evidence proffered by the two young women.

The friends of Elizabeth Canning now had all they needed for a successful conviction. But they weren't taking any chances. Articles were dropped into the newspapers emphasising the deplorable condition in which Elizabeth Canning was held and how she was still suffering from the after-effects of her confinement. This ensured that any potential member of a jury would know in advance about the heinous crime that had taken place. A reward was offered for the capture of John Squires, the son of Mary Squires, now that he had been identified by Virtue Hall. Appeals were made for money, which would be used both for the forthcoming prosecution and to recompense Canning for the ordeal she had gone through.

The trial of Mary Squires and Susannah Wells took place on 21 February 1753 at the Old Bailey. The request for donations clearly worked, as Elizabeth Canning had a prosecuting counsel called Mr Stow representing her. He began by taking Elizabeth Canning through her story. It was essentially a reinstatement of what she had already told Henry Fielding. When it came to the cross-examination, Canning dealt with any tricky questions posed with calm assurance. How could she remember everybody who had been in the room at the time that her stays had been cut off – given that, on her own admittance, she had been terrified? Her fear had made her look around at the company, she answered. Why hadn't she tried to get out of the house earlier? Because she had hoped her kidnappers might release her. Why, on making her way back home, had she not asked for help along the way? Because she had thought she might meet someone who was friendly with the captors. Where applicable, her testimony was confirmed by other witnesses: those who had spoken to her when she arrived back at her mother's house and accompanied her to Enfield Wash, and Virtue Hall.

Mary Squires did not speak in her own defence. However, three witnesses were called who said they had seen the Gypsy in Abbotsbury in Dorset during the time of the supposed kidnapping. Although there was nothing to suggest they were lying, Mr Stow raised the possibility that they might have been confused about the dates on which they saw her. The reliability of their testimony was undercut when, straight after, the Crown produced another witness, called John Iniser. He sold fish and oysters close to Enfield Wash. He said he knew Mary Squires very well by sight and had seen her in that area during Canning's incarceration. Susannah Wells failed to produce anybody to support her testimony.

It is unlikely that the jury would even have left the courtroom in considering their verdict. It was common practice for the all-male jurors to huddle together, have a quick discussion and then make their decision. The result was inevitable. Mary Squires was found guilty of assault, putting Elizabeth Canning's life in danger and of stealing one pair of stays to a value of ten shillings. The reason Mary Squires was accused of theft, rather than kidnapping, was because the latter was considered only a misdemeanour, which had a lesser penalty attached. Susannah Wells was condemned for being an accessory to the felony. Her punishment was to be branded on the thumb, which was 'immediately inflicted, with an uncommon Severity, to the great Satisfaction, and with the loud Applause, of a numerous Crowd of incensed Spectators', and, in addition, to serve six months in Newgate Prison.

Before Mary Squires was given her sentence, she was asked if she had anything to say in mitigation. She gave a rather confused summary of where she had been before arriving at Enfield Wash, which conflicted with much of the evidence given by her own witnesses when it came to places and dates. It wouldn't have made any difference: the sentence was mandatory. Mary Squires, for the crime of grand larceny – that is, the theft of goods of the value of one shilling or more – was to be hanged.

There was no doubt at this stage that most believed Elizabeth Canning's story: there was no talk about it being some sort of hoax. The vitriol against the Gypsy Mary Squires was extensive before the trial, and it did not lessen after the verdict was passed on 22 February. The three men who had spoken for her in court, claiming she was in Abbotsbury, were beaten up on emerging from the Old Bailey. And it was pointed out in one paper how Mary Squires's alibi must have been at fault, given she had contradicted the statements of her own supporters. A warrant was issued for George Squires's arrest, now that his mother was convicted. From this point on he would be referred to as George, rather than John – the name that Virtue Hall had unaccountably called him. A story of a poor street merchant 'in a most cruel manner' being attacked by two Gypsy men, was generalised into accusing all people from this ethnic group of their 'Barbarity' and the necessity of 'rooting these Villains out of their Dens'. In contrast Elizabeth Canning 'who was so cruelly confined and almost starved' had £30 collected on her behalf from White's Chocolate House.

Fig. 16. *Elizabeth Canning At the House of Mother Wells at Enfield Wash*,
an engraving published 3 March 1753.

On 5 March both a print and a pamphlet were advertised for sale in *The Public Advertiser*. The former was titled *Elizabeth Canning At the House of Mother Wells at Enfield Wash* [Fig. 16]. It shows a rather manic-looking maidservant, her breasts exposed after having had her stays removed by a knife-wielding Mary Squires. There is also Susannah Wells, hovering in the background observing the scene – the only known portrait of her. The wording underneath reflects the popular viewpoint in titillatingly provocative language, stating that Canning was *'stripp'd'* by the Gypsy and that when she got home she was *'almost naked'*. Although the engraver considered her to be *'in a condition too deplorable to be described'*, he obviously didn't feel it was too deplorable to be depicted. The pamphlet was similarly inflammatory against that 'notorious old bawd Susannah Wells' and 'an old travelling Gipsey'. Readers were informed that Canning had only 'mouldy Crusts and stinking Water' to support her for twenty-nine days.

But matters were about to take a dramatic turn, shifting the sympathy, at least for some, from the young woman to the older one. In the process, the general level of interest from the public in the case would rise exponentially, with the knowledge that perhaps playing out before them was the most audacious and cruellest hoax imaginable.

II

Two men were instrumental in changing the certain belief in Mary Squires's guilt. The first was the Lord Mayor of London, who had been present, in a non-official capacity, at her trial. His name was Sir Crisp Gascoyne. Apart from his involvement in this case, his fame rests on his being the first occupant of the Lord Mayor's residency, Mansion House, which was completed in 1753. Gascoyne was convinced that Mary Squires's three proponents in court had been telling the truth. To confirm this, he instructed that a letter should be sent to the vicar of Abbotsbury to obtain character references for two of them, John Gibbons and William Clarke. The clergyman's reply was that they were 'too honest Men to give a false Evidence'. Word clearly got around about this as other people came forward stating they had also seen her in this region at this time. Gascoyne started to compile a dossier of potential witnesses.

The second man was Dr John Hill. Posterity hasn't really been fair to Hill, a self-made man who made a major contribution to botany. He was also a quack doctor, an unsuccessful playwright and a polemical newspaper columnist, writing under the name of 'The Inspector' in *The London Daily Advertiser*. He made many enemies with his acerbic wit. One of those was a man called Mountefort Brown, who physically attacked Hill after he was insulted in the Inspector column. Hill wanted to prosecute Brown, so the latter went to see Henry Fielding to seek his advice. The magistrate exonerated Brown's behaviour stating, in Fielding's own newspaper, that Hill had exaggerated his injuries and 'that nothing against the Honour of Mr Brown appeared before the Justice'. In retaliation Hill called Fielding's final book, *Amelia*, 'unworthy of its author' while Fielding, in his *The Covent-Garden Journal*, wrote that Hill was a 'paultry Dunghill, and had long been levelled with the Dirt'.

Knowing of Fielding's investment in the integrity of Canning's exploits, Hill's sympathies automatically aligned with Mary Squires. Having heard about Gascoyne's initial enquires, he decided to question Virtue Hall again. Ironically she was easy to find, as Canning's own supporters had paid for her to be confined in the Gatehouse Prison. They were keen that she should identify George Squires when he was eventually captured, and didn't want to lose track of her whereabouts. One can imagine Hill's delight when the young prostitute agreed to revisit her testimony. She admitted that everything she had sworn at the trial of Susannah Wells and Mary Squires was false. She no longer corroborated Elizabeth Canning's story. Hill informed Sir Crisp Gascoyne, who also interviewed the girl. This was done privately, in the presence of only one other gentleman. But then the Mayor allowed a more public examination which anybody, including Elizabeth Canning and her supporters, could attend.

Virtue Hall appeared to answer two key questions satisfactorily. First, how had she heard Elizabeth Canning's story in order to repeat it verbatim in her affidavit and in court? She said that had happened when everybody first arrived at Mrs Wells's house to arrest the occupants, and again when they were all bound over to see Justice Tyshmaker. Also, at the trial, she had been standing close to Elizabeth Canning when giving her evidence. As to why she had lied to begin with, this was because she had been terrified at Fielding's threat to send her to Newgate Prison. She had 'therefore swore falsely to save her own Life'. Hill gleefully reported all of this in his paper the day after, teasing the reader with the reason behind her retraction, saying it was not yet the time to declare the true cause: revenge is a dish best served cold.

Five days later Hill was still playing coy, writing again that what had induced Virtue Hall to originally lie would soon be made public. He reported that Crisp Gascoyne had visited Susannah Wells in prison, although nothing new was learnt from that interrogation. She merely repeated that she and Mary Squires were innocent of any wrongdoing. The Lord Mayor could not see the Gypsy as she was dangerously ill with 'jail fever'. But he was confidently moving forward in obtaining her release. Virtue Hall's public statement, alongside the affidavits from numerous people in the Dorset area who asserted that they had seen Mary Squires during the month of January, secured a stay of execution from the King. This was granted on 10 April.

Elizabeth Canning's supporters, known as the Canningites, were not taking this lying down. An attorney called John Myles was put in charge of orchestrating both the legal proceedings and ensuring that public support remained with the maidservant. On 19 March it was confidently stated in the papers that, despite the assertions of the innocence of the Gypsy woman, 'we are assured that there is very strong Evidence of the contrary discovered within these few Days', and the identity of the 'King of the Gypsies' would be revealed. The campaign deliberately aligned Sir Crisp Gascoyne with Mary Squires, both of whom apparently shared the same cavalier disregard for common decency. On 3 April it was claimed that 'Egyptians commonly called Gypsies', under the pretence of telling fortunes and curing diseases, steal and pilfer with impunity.

We don't know whether John Myles was responsible for that racist slur. But he put his name to the claim that somebody who had been mistaken for John Iniser, the final witness who had spoken in favour of Elizabeth Canning at Mary Squires's trial, had been severely beaten up by a tall lusty man dressed in a great rug coat. And also that several men on horseback had been seen near Mother Wells's house threatening to set people's homes on fire if the Gypsy were hanged. Such was the scepticism of some readers to this supposed 'news' story, perhaps, that Myles was forced to publicly state that, as several persons had doubted its truth, '*Affidavits* of the Facts are in my Hands, and may be *seen*.'

Sir Crisp Gascoyne was equally relentless, though, and an indictment was obtained against Canning for perjury. The Canningites retorted by indicting the three witnesses who had spoken against her at Mary Squires's trial. A Grand Jury needed to consider the bills and determine whether there was sufficient evidence to proceed. As it was, they threw them all out. From all this, the only inference that could be drawn, as one newspaper laconically commented, was 'that the Gipsey was neither at Abbotsbury or Endfield'. An engraving cleverly picked up on that. It depicted Mary Squires as a witch riding on a broomstick with a speech bubble emerging from her mouth: 'I can be at Abbotsbury & Enfield-Wash, both at one Time.'

All of this upped the widespread fascination in the case. There was a newspaper report of a great concourse of people, both on horseback and in carriages, visiting Mother Wells's house to see the room where Elizabeth Canning was confined. One barometer for measuring public interest in the eighteenth century is the number of pamphlets produced about a subject matter. And with regard to the maidservant it was unprecedented, far more than any other hoax of this period. The nearest rival was that of Mary Toft, with around twenty; there were comfortably double that number concerning Canning and Squires. Once word leaked out that Virtue Hall had retracted her testimony, the floodgates opened. The first one, published post-trial, was *The Case of Elizabeth Canning Fairly Stated*, concluding that the truth was 'too much eclipsed to be rightly discern'd'. *The Monthly Review* briefly reviewed it and accurately predicted that 'we are threatened with an inundation of pamphlets on this subject'. Many of those that followed were not so balanced, merely repeating information previously stated, promising what they couldn't deliver or displaying little objectivity.

One of the earliest, coming out on 20 March 1753, is undoubtedly the most famous as it was penned by Henry Fielding himself. And far from being persuaded by the recent revelations that Canning might have been economical with the truth, Fielding is even more convinced that he has backed the right person. He begins, though, by setting out all the reasons why somebody might think her story implausible. What was the motive of the men for dragging her some ten miles, given they had already robbed her? Why didn't anybody detect them on the busy roads to Mother Wells's house? What was the reason for Mary Squires starving Canning? – it was not a sensible way of persuading her to prostitution. How did Elizabeth Canning survive with such meagre fare? Why did she keep back parts of her supplies only to consume them two days before she escaped? Why didn't she try to break out earlier? And how did she have the strength to walk back home after such an ordeal?

Fielding then responds to his own points, stating upfront that, although what happened to her is improbable, it is not impossible. When it comes to why the ruffians, or indeed Mary Squires and Susannah Wells, acted in the way they did, how can one empathise with 'Wretches very little removed, either in their Sensations or Understandings, from wild Beasts'? In explaining Canning's survival, despite her lack of sustenance, and her ability to make the journey back home, Fielding leaves that to the physicians. He argues that Canning initially felt too ill to eat anything and generally had a lack of appetite – hence her delay in consuming all her food and drinking all her water until towards the end of her imprisonment. As to why she waited so many days before escaping, he postulates that eventually her despair overcame her previous lack of courage.

Having dealt satisfactorily, at least in his own mind, with all the objections, Fielding turns to the evidence that supports Elizabeth Canning's story. What is incontestable is that she returned to her mother on 29 January 1753 in a deplorable condition, which in itself is proof of having being held against her will. Given that, what possible advantage could she gain from concealing the identity of her true kidnappers and falsely accusing complete strangers instead? It couldn't have been for financial gain, as she had no means of ascertaining in advance that she would receive any monetary support.

Other factors which Fielding feels give credence to Canning's tale include her straightforward telling of it, alongside an inability, given her age and intelligence, to have the 'wit' to invent a fictitious story. He further believes that the description Canning gives of the hayloft is too accurate for her not to have been there in person. For Fielding, though, it is the collaborative evidence of Virtue Hall that is the crux of the matter. He believes that the two young women never had the chance to speak to each other. Therefore, by unanswerable logic, if two witnesses come up with the same fact, and there is no way the two could have consorted together, that fact is self-evidently true. For good measure Fielding also queries why Mr and Mrs Natus, the couple who said they were sleeping in the hayloft at the time Canning was there, didn't give evidence at the trial. Why, if she was making everything up, didn't Canning accuse the owner of the house, rather than the itinerant Gypsy, of cutting off her stays? Finally, Fielding asserts that the fact that, when she was attacked, she was carrying a mince pie to give to her younger brother, demonstrates the innate goodness of Canning's character.

It was inevitable that Dr John Hill would come back with

a rejoinder. The speed of his response was impressive. Some nine days after Fielding's, Hill's own pamphlet hits the bookshops. Hill insinuates that everybody should have been suspicious about the case from the moment Mrs Canning placed a notice on 6 January 1753 seeking information of the whereabouts of her daughter. He can't think of any reason why anyone would want to abduct her given she is neither attractive nor wealthy. His conclusion is that the advertisement was all part of a pre-planned scheme to divert attention from the actual motive behind Elizabeth Canning's disappearance. As for Canning's 'ridiculous Story', the only reason it was believed at the trial was because Virtue Hall backed it up. He can't think of any rational reason why either Mary Squires or Susannah Wells would want to imprison her.

Hill is also suspicious about just how ill she was on her return on 29 January, given that she was fit enough to travel to Enfield Wash on 1 February. He questions the differences between Canning's initial description of the hayloft and its contents compared with how it actually looked and what was found inside it. He takes issue with Fielding's logic as to why Canning is telling the truth. He agrees that Canning is not 'witty' enough to invent a good story, but this one is so absurd it is quite within her imaginative powers. His most devastating point, however, is to reiterate that Virtue Hall had plenty of opportunities to hear Canning's chain of events before she gave her own. Even so, some of the finer details she related differed from Elizabeth Canning's own telling – for instance the place where the stays were cut off and when the pitcher of water was put into the loft.

Others weighed in with their misgivings over Elizabeth Canning's story. One of them was the painter Allan Ramsay, who composed his pamphlet in the form of a letter from a clergyman to an earl. He cites the lack of information, including 'persons, places, or particularities', that Canning is able to provide about the time when she was captured, her stay in the house and the period when she made her escape; this, he maintains, is evidence of her lying. He also queries why the culprits, if indeed that is who they were, would remain at Mother Wells's property after Elizabeth Canning had escaped. Surely they would have anticipated the alarm being raised, and their subsequent seizure by the officers of justice. Ramsay suggests that Canning, if she wasn't in Mother Wells's hayloft, had disappeared for a 'lie-in', the period before giving birth.

A pro-Canningite pamphlet written by a medical practitioner addresses this. Daniel Cox MD had Canning thoroughly examined by a midwife, who concluded that she had never had a child. He also states that in his opinion she did not suffer from syphilis. A contrary pamphlet notes that pregnancy had not been ruled out, so it is possible she had undergone an abortion. Indeed, even Dr Cox accepts that she had missed her periods for at least four months. Rather less gallantly it was pointed out that none of those who examined her were claiming she was still a virgin, thereby implying she might have absconded with a lover. As to Fielding's query over Canning's fasting, which he had left to the experts, another pamphlet concluded that she could have survived.

Such pro-Canning sentiment was ignored by the authorities. As indeed was a visit to Mary Squires by twenty-one witnesses from Enfield Wash confirming that they had seen her in the neighbourhood at the beginning of January. For on exactly that same day, 21 May 1753, the Gypsy was granted a full pardon. Susannah Wells was not so lucky. She served out her complete sentence and was released from prison only on 21 August. Redemption for Mary Squires didn't automatically mean prosecution for Elizabeth Canning. And every means at their disposal was used by the maidservant's supporters to keep her out of the courtroom. When a bill for indictment was made against her, in the same ploy as before, counter bills were raised against the three original Abbotsbury witnesses. This time both were found to be true bills, which meant that all four were now charged with perjury.

The men's trial took place in September 1753, but turned into a non-event. The reason for this was that Elizabeth Canning was in hiding, her friends intent on not letting her resurface until Sir Crisp Gascoyne was no longer Mayor of London. They did not think she would get a fair hearing if he had any part in her prosecution. With the principal witness absent, the others – and there were no fewer than fifty on the original indictments – were unprepared, or perhaps hadn't been instructed, to attend. As John Davy for the defendants put it, they had all 'wisely withdraw[n] themselves from a trial which would involve them in ruin'. The three were duly acquitted for want of evidence. Sadly one of those men, Thomas Greville, did not survive long after, succumbing to smallpox which he contracted in the courtroom.

Even though Sir Crisp Gascoyne's term of office expired in November, Elizabeth Canning was still absent. Proclamations were issued in January and February 1754 at both the Guildhall and her Parish Church requiring her to surrender herself at the next sessions at the Old Bailey. Eventually the law prevailed. At the end of February she appeared in court. Bail was at £400, with four men providing sureties. The trial of Elizabeth Canning for wilful and corrupt perjury was set for April 1754. 'By which Means,' one newspaper optimistically asserted, 'this most stupendous Scene of Darkness will now, in all probability, be brought to light, to the Honour of the Innocent, to the Terror of the Guilty, and to the Satisfaction of the Public in general'.

III

Elizabeth Canning's trial lasted six days. The main reason for its length was the number of witnesses each side called, half of them swearing that Mary Squires was in Dorset at the time of the alleged kidnapping, the other half stating she was in Enfield Wash. One of the key testifiers was George Squires, the son of Mary. Now that the statement by Virtue Hall that he was one of the kidnappers had been discredited, he was safe to testify. George had apparently stayed in Abbotsbury with his sister and mother from 1 to 9 January before travelling to Enfield Wash. So the details of their journey were important.

George had a very poor memory of the itinerary and had a tough time recollecting the names of towns and villages he had passed through, yet alone any dates. And this was even before Elizabeth Canning's counsel, Mr Morton, got to cross-examine him. George plaintively complained that he was not expecting such a grilling. 'I shall ask you a great many questions you have not heard yet,' came the unsympathetic response. It is unlikely the jury would have been impressed with his testimony. The prosecutors originally intended to swear-in his sister next. They decided that this would only make matters worse as she was 'rather more stupid than her brother'. However, the sheer volume of witnesses, forty-one in total, who were called confirming Mary Squires's presence in Dorset in early January built up a strong case for the prosecution. It was not until the third day that the defence had their turn. Despite a number stating that they had seen Mary Squires around Enfield Wash when Elizabeth Canning was initially kidnapped, they were less convincing. None of them had seen Mary Squires go in or out of Mother Wells's house; few of them ever spoke to her; and no two people ever saw her at the same time.

With the seemingly endless supply of people taking the stand, there were a few moments of levity. When questioning Canning's uncle, Thomas Colley, about the last meal his niece had taken before returning to her employer – an important consideration given her subsequent starvation – the prosecution asked whether she had butter with her toast. Mr Morton sarcastically asked if the toast was buttered on both sides. Hannah Fensham claimed she knew on which day she had supposedly seen Mary Squires in Enfield Wash because she had checked her almanac to verify it. She was asked to confirm her skills at reading the astrological calendar by stating on which day of the month a Sunday fell. Hannah opted for the seventh, which turned out to be a Tuesday, provoking great merriment in the court. Her aggrieved response was to cry out, 'Why, is not *Sunday* the seventh Day?' John Ford, in contrast, maintained that the Gypsy was in Abbotsbury. He said he knew her as well as his own mother. It would seem that he was not altogether a reliable witness as 'he was so intolerably drunk, when he appeared to give his Evidence, that he was bid to go about his Business'.

Any advantage Elizabeth Canning's defence might have had in putting their case last was undone by Recorder William Moreton, the presiding judge, whose function was to put the defence's case to the jury. However he had long concluded that Canning was guilty and biased his speech to that effect. Unusually the jury actually withdrew from the court, at twenty minutes after midnight, to consider their verdict. Harassed by the court to make a swift decision, they returned at two fifteen in the morning. They found Canning guilty of perjury, but not wilful and corrupt. The Recorder would not accept a partial verdict: 'they must either find her guilty of the whole indictment, or else acquit her'. This was not true, an incorrect interpretation of the law as it stood. But Elizabeth Canning's counsel were not in court at the time to argue the legal point. The jury returned some thirty minutes later to find her guilty of wilful and corrupt perjury.

When it came to sentencing, eight Aldermen recommended her for mercy, as they believed there were other, unnamed, conspirators involved. They advocated six months' imprisonment instead. But another judge pointed out that so much money had been collected on her behalf that if Canning were sent to prison it would be 'rather a diversion than a punishment'. This assumption that you could buy yourself a luxurious life behind bars was later wittily represented in a satirical print titled *Jumpedo and Canning in Newgate, or the Bottle and the Pitcher met* [Fig. 17]. It imagines that Elizabeth is in Newgate prison along with the non-existent Bottle Conjurer, who is known facetiously as Jumpedo. They are toasting their successful respective hoaxes, a plentiful meal in front of them. Canning is seated on top of a Bible, demonstrating her willingness to lie on oath. She points to a dog which is shredding Crisp Gascoyne's dossier. On a table are cheques made out in her name and a letter of thanks to Henry

Fig. 17. *Jumpedo and Canning in Newgate, or the Bottle and the Pitcher met*, an engraving published July 1754.

Fielding. The pictures on the wall are of the bottle, with Jumpedo entering through a funnel, juxtaposed with 'The Miraculous Pitcher' that had provided enough water for Canning to survive for twenty-nine days.

Support for a harsher sentence was secured by a majority of one. When asked if she had anything to say before hearing it, Canning spoke in a low voice, saying that she desired to be considered as unfortunate. She had never intended to swear away the Gypsy's life, she was just defending herself. This plea for compassion was wasted on the Recorder. He observed that other countries inflicted the death penalty for this type of offence, clearly regretting that England was behind the times in this respect. He said that he had attended Mary Squires's trial, as well as this one, and that throughout both he had thought Canning's evidence was false. He sanctimoniously told her that, even though he was going to inflict the most severe punishment he could, she would soon be convinced that it was in no degree adequate to the greatness of her offence. With that he imprisoned her for one month in Newgate, after which she would be transported to the American colonies for the term of seven years.

If the verdict and sentence were popular with the authorities, they were not with the masses. Sir Crisp Gascoyne had attended the trial throughout, but had needed to be escorted off the premises to save him from the ubiquitous mob who threatened his life. A reward of £20 was offered to anybody who could successfully bring about a conviction for any person involved in such outrages against the ex-Lord Mayor. It seemed that a successful prosecution was about to be achieved when John Jones, a porter in Moorfields, was committed to prison for indeed 'threatening the life of Sir Crisp Gascoyne, in relation to Canning's Affair'. Three days later, the same paper had to admit it was a mistake. The unfortunate Mr Jones had been sent to Bedlam instead as he was delirious.

Nor had the judicial outcome convinced the Canningites that their champion had lied. They continued to be strident in defending her at every opportunity. When a notice in the papers appeared saying that a principal witness supporting Canning had herself been prosecuted for theft, they responded by pointing out that the woman had never actually given any evidence at the trial. Delaying tactics were used to postpone her transportation. This was normally done on a slave ship, with unthinkable consequences befalling a young woman. A petition to pardon her was rejected. More money was requested to alleviate her suffering, while Canning herself put her name to an article saying that rumours that she was about to confess to her perjury were false. A news item reported that she was dangerously ill with little hope of recovery. One reason postulated for that was because she was denied having a particular friend of hers to travel with her overseas. Her state of health was successful in deferring her enforced voyage. Doubtless aided by some serious lobbying, in July 1754 a motion was passed at the Old Bailey that she could organise her own crossing: Mr Stewart, in charge of transportation of felons, waived his right to the contract. Canning was released from Newgate to make her own arrangements. The authorities appeared to have lost track of her for a while, until eventually it was confirmed that she had sailed from the Downs (a merchant shipping anchorage near Deal in Kent) on board the *Myrtilla,* under Captain Budden, bound for Philadelphia.

IV

It is not hard to understand why this case gripped the public's imagination. There was the stark contrast between Elizabeth Canning, described by Fielding as 'a poor, honest, innocent, simple Girl', and Mary Squires who was at least seventy, having a stooping gait, a long and meagre face, a large nose and an 'under-lip of a prodigious size' [Fig. 18]. The latter had the obvious look of a witch and was depicted as such in at least three prints. In one of them she is flying on a broomstick, in another consorting with John Hill and, in a third, Crisp Gascoyne and Mary Squires are holding hands while being carried triumphantly on a platform by four other witches. In early 1753, England was gripped by controversy over the passage of the Jewish Naturalisation Act, which allowed Jews to be naturalised by applying to Parliament. There were protests and riots from Christians against the bill. Gypsies and Jews were linked together in the minds of many, as illustrated in yet another offensively xenophobic caricature. This depicts Crisp Gascoyne and his fellow aldermen supporting both groups. Elizabeth Canning is hovering in the background decrying that she has been outcast 'not by the Truth but by your Might'. All in all, Mary Squires was an easy figure for her contemporaries to hate.

Leaving aside whether people took sides purely on the basis of the two protagonists' respective perceived religion, ethnicity or appearance, there was the intriguing question as to which of them was telling the truth. In other words, was it a hoax? One journal called it 'the knotty Case of *Squires* and *Canning,* and the Pleadings of their respective Advocates', while simultaneously complaining

Fig. 18. Portrait of Mary Squires, an engraving by unknown artist.

that other stories couldn't get one 'Fortieth' as much publicity. The conclusion that Canning was making it up rests on some of the contradictions between her earlier and later statements. According to Thomas Chitty's notes, which were taken before she had had the opportunity to inspect the house and see its occupants, Canning said that, in the room where she was imprisoned, there was some furniture and no hay; that she did not know the name of the mistress of the house; and that she had not seen anyone resembling the distinctive-looking Mary Squires. Yet according to her affidavit to Fielding, which took place after her visit to Enfield Wash, she was incarcerated in a hayloft without any furniture; she had often heard the name

Mother Wells; and in the kitchen when she first arrived there was an old Gypsy woman. There were other discrepancies relating to the room in which her stays were cut off, when she received her meagre provisions, and the exact manner of her escape.

The major flaw, though, was her apparent incarceration for nearly a month with such a small quantity of bread and a pitcher of water. Even if Canning had managed to survive on such meagre fare, she would not have had the strength to travel the ten miles on foot back to her mother's house. Furthermore she is unsure about how many pieces of bread she had, the number fluctuating from five or six pieces to twenty-four (although it was never more than a quarter loaf). She was also inconsistent with when she drank the last of her water. Her testimony varied from three days before she escaped, in her statement to Henry Fielding; to the day of her flight, at the trial of Mary Squires; and there is even a claim that she left a little behind, made when talking to Chitty.

None of this looks good for those who believe Elizabeth Canning was telling the truth. But the counter argument is that, if she was deprived of sustenance, she might well have had memory lapses and started hallucinating. At Mary Squires's trial she admitted to having been 'subject to convulsion-fits' for four years. The blow to her head, which she received when first set upon, threw her directly into such a seizure. Not surprising, therefore, that she got many of the details wrong about her imprisonment.

From my perspective, the most telling indicator that Elizabeth Canning might be making up the story is that Mary Squires was still at Mother Wells's house when the officer arrived to arrest her. Why, given she was an itinerant Gypsy and also that she didn't seem to have any particular ties with Mother Wells, would she have stayed around once Elizabeth Canning had escaped? She surely would have gone on the run, knowing that it was likely the authorities would be alerted by the maidservant. It is also noteworthy that Elizabeth Canning initially confuses Mother Wells with Mary Squires. She originally accuses the owner of the house of cutting off her stays.

When she visits the house, she immediately incriminates Mary Squires with being her assailant. This would be consistent with her never having been there before: making the false assumption that the Gypsy was the proprietor. To a certain extent this undid her, assuming she was telling fibs. If, instead, she had maintained that Mother Wells was the knife-wielder, then Mary Squires's disputed alibi would have been irrelevant.

Set against this, though, is finding a motive for Elizabeth Canning's actions. The one that has the most plausibility is that she was pregnant and went away to have an abortion. This would be in keeping with the stoppage in her menstrual cycle. Determined that no one should know about it, she came up with this fictitious kidnapping. In this scenario she might have sold her stays to pay for the operation. The prolonged absence may have arisen from gynaecological complications or from having to earn additional money for the medical services. It would also explain why she might have returned in such an emaciated state to her mother's house. The apothecary, who saw her the following day, said 'she was extremely low and weak'. He could scarcely hear her speak and she had cold sweats.

The most likely candidate as her lover was Robert Scarrat. He was the neighbour who first made the suggestion as to where Elizabeth Canning was after she returned to her mother: 'I'll lay a guinea to a farthing, she has been at Mother Wells's,' he said. Scarrat admitted at Canning's trial that he had gone to Mother Wells's house on several occasions – although he claimed he had never been there with a woman, an unlikely occurrence given that it was a brothel. So was he also lying when he swore that he hadn't met Elizabeth before? Mary Squires's defence lawyer clearly thought so as, in cross-examining Scarrat, he asked why he had gone around to see the family if he was a stranger. He noted that he had talked to Elizabeth 'very familiarly'. When Scarrat interrogated her about Mother Wells's property, he put forward 'a String of leading Questions to the Girl'. All she had to do was to say 'yes', which confirmed to those listening that she knew more about the house than she actually did. As Scarrat had recently married, you can see why the pair would have wanted to keep their relationship under wraps.

Judith Moore, in the most recently written full-length book on the case, *The Appearance of Truth* (1994), does not buy into this theory. She says that, in her long career of dealing with adolescents, she had never encountered the phenomenon of a young woman claiming to have been abducted in order to conceal any sexual misconduct. This taps into present sensibilities of the laudable tendency to believe someone who tells a story of abuse, rather than dismissing it as make-believe. She surmises that Mary Squires and her son and daughter had plenty of time to concoct their version of their supposed trip from Abbotsbury. That journey had been made, but earlier than January 1753. As for all the Dorset witnesses, either they were in error or they were happy to accept bribes from Sir Crisp Gascoyne and just repeat back whatever he wanted to hear. Moore thinks there was a chauvinistic consensus among the men in authority to discount the word of a working-class servant, which led to her prosecution. She writes that 'an honest eighteen-year-old girl was virtually a contradiction in terms', with credibility residing in the ranks of gentlemen and holders of public office.

Even if you do go with the abortion theory, which at least is consistent with all the facts as we know them, it is still remarkable that Elizabeth Canning would take it to the point of having a woman wrongfully hanged; and that, once she had come up with her concocted story, she never admitted her guilt through all the questioning, trials and deportation. At every point during the proceedings her sincerity seems to shine through. It is tempting to think that, if a similar trial occurred in the twenty-first century, the verdict would be just as elusive. The same points would be discussed, and argued about, in today's newspaper editorials, television discussion programmes and internet forums, as they were in eighteenth-century pamphlets. Only perhaps modern technology – DNA used to ascertain whether Canning was incarcerated in the hayloft, CCTV cameras to check

Fig. 19. *The Conjurers 1753*, an engraving depicting the difficulty of knowing whether Elizabeth Canning was telling the truth.

out her journey from Moorfields to Enfield Wash – would crack the case. What is certain is that we are no better at determining whether someone is telling the truth or a lie on a witness stand; and that is, fundamentally, what the case of Elizabeth Canning comes down to.

At least in one sense it was an honourable draw. Both the main protagonists seemed to have survived the ordeal. Mary Squires lived for another nine years after she was released, although she was forced to adopt a fictitious name. It was speculated that she was worth a considerable sum at her death in January 1762. Elizabeth Canning settled in America, married and had several children. Despite newspaper reports to the contrary she never returned to England. She died suddenly on 22 June 1773, aged thirty-nine. She went to her grave proclaiming her innocence. *The Gentleman's Magazine* doubtless expressed the disappointment of many of its reader when it regretted that she never confessed 'where she had concealed herself during the time she had invariably declared she was at the house of Mother Wells'.

I have in my possession a print titled *The Conjurers 1753* [Fig. 19] It shows John Hill, Sir Crisp Gascoyne and Henry Fielding standing inside a zodiac-emblazoned circle. John Hill has his arm stretched out towards Mary Squires, while Fielding, in a similar gesture, is offering his endorsement of Elizabeth Canning. The maidservant is supported by a shadowy woman. The Lord Mayor appears to be deciding between the two parties. In the foreground there is a bottle, with a label attached stating 'Another Bottle'. This is a reference to the Bottle Conjurer, subtly inserted, hinting that there might be a hoax involved but by no means explicitly stating it. This engraving is the only one relating to this case which is non-judgemental. The fact that, unusually, it was drawn by a woman, the Right Honourable Lady Fanny Killigrew, perhaps explains this. It seems to be suggesting that the chances are that Elizabeth Canning is a hoaxer. But if we could only uncover her motive, she would provoke our sympathy and not our condemnation.

SEVEN

'MISS FANNY'S THEATRE IN COCK LANE'

* * *

I

Maria Hayden sailed across the Atlantic in October 1852, carrying with her an export that up to then was confined to the US: that of Spiritualism. It was George W. Stone who had persuaded her and her husband to make the crossing. Some three years earlier he had discovered the potential market in England for incorporeal remedies, using Electro-Biology to supposedly alleviate various ailments. He rightly assessed that the nation's citizens were now ready to directly communicate with the souls of those who had passed over to the other side.

Mr Stone and Mr and Mrs Hayden rented out a property in London at 26 Upper Seymour, Portman Square, a respectable address near Oxford Street. George Stone wasted no time in reminding his potential patients that he had returned from America and was eager to 'be consulted for the Cure of Diseases', with an insertion in *The Illustrated London News* on 23 October. A week later, the same journal had him promoting his protégé who would demonstrate 'the wonderful Phenomena' of 'Spiritual Manifestations, or Rappings'.

Maria had yet to fully accustom herself to her new environment when she began her first séances. She had been pregnant when she left America and had suffered a miscarriage either en route or soon after she disembarked – hardly the ideal conditions to deal with potentially sceptical clients. And it was bad luck for her that two of the most cynical wasted no time in responding to the advertisement. That they also turned out to be the Victorian equivalent of tabloid journalists, entrapping their victim in a finely orchestrated sting, made it considerably worse.

It was in early November that Henry Morley and William Wills 'rapped at the door of the house in which the knocker lived'. They were greeted by George Stone, who extolled in highfalutin language the remarkable abilities of Mrs Hayden and why she had the nervous disposition conducive to attracting the spirits who were present in the atmosphere. The listeners cut to the chase: 'Your Medium sits at the table, and the ghosts rap on it?' This indeed turned out to be the case as, having handed over their one guinea a head ('five guineas for a party of ten'), they were taken to the back drawing room and were seated opposite Mrs Hayden at a round table.

Mrs Hayden was twenty-eight years old and described in various accounts as 'a pleasant, intelligent, and well mannered woman' with a 'mobile, not undesirable face' and 'a quiet smile'. Her charisma was obvious, given those who were convinced by her abilities, but underneath there was a steely resolve. At one séance the opening word 'spoken' by the spirit was 'Silence', a command to quell the buzz of conversation from the excited participants. At another, an attendee didn't want to join the circle but Mrs Hayden insisted on it. To the participant's astonishment (but perhaps not the reader's) the first spirit that made contact was a dead relative of that very person. Maria's no-nonsense approach was again demonstrated when she was asked to conduct a sitting even though she was in a hurry to catch a train. On this occasion the spirits, who sometimes would hide away in the ether for over an hour before exposing themselves, made an appearance immediately after she sat down.

These, though, were future séances when perhaps she had perfected the art of seductively dominating her clients. Furthermore those who attended were mostly firm believers in an afterlife. By contrast Morley and Wills had come with an agenda to discredit someone whom they perceived to be a fraud, and they were immune to such authoritative charms. In their subsequent article, they described Maria Hayden's technique of answering questions posed to the spirits. Using a piece of card with the alphabet and numerals zero to nine written out, they were asked to tap each letter or number in sequence. On certain symbols a rap could be heard, and this was noted on a piece of paper. Gradually a word, or series of words, would emerge.

This worked fine so long as Maria knew, or could guess, the answer. When she didn't, she was reliant on the men to telegraph their response by slightly pausing on the appropriate character, giving her the opportunity to produce the knock. Morley and Wills were determined to give nothing away and they moved their respective fingers along the card with metronomic precision. Gleefully they recorded that the spirits thought one of them had a mother with the first name Timock ('an odd Christian name for an English lady'); the other's only sister, who was alive and well, had been dead for two years; and that this same gentleman was to have no fewer than 136 children.

All of this was written up in *Household Words* on 20 November 1852. *Household Words* was a weekly journal edited (although he used the term 'conducted') by Charles Dickens. Its first number came out on 30 March 1850. In its rather dull format of two columns a page with no illustrations could be read a mixture of factual articles and high-class fiction. The circulation was over 35,000 a week selling for two pennies a copy. Dickens was especially interested in satirical critiques of fashionable follies, and Wills's and Morley's hatchet dissection of Maria Hayden's unsuccessful séance met that criterion.

As an experienced editor, Dickens knew the importance of titles to hook in his readers. Three weeks before the paper was published he wrote to Wills suggesting that a good heading would be 'The Ghost of the Cock Lane Ghost'. For Dickens it was not so much

Maria Hayden's skill in picking up on sitters subconsciously relaying information back to her, so that they inadvertently answered their own questions – it was rather her ability to produce raps or knockings 'who make it their peculiar habit to live always under a table'. And in this respect Dickens was reminded of an incident that had caused a sensation in London ninety years earlier.

II

The rappings in the eighteenth-century episode, rather than relaying banal information from those who had died in unsuspicious circumstances, came from the ghost of a woman claiming she had been poisoned. If the spirit was found to be correct in its assertion, the accused man would hang. Ironically the first time knockings were heard in the household of Richard Parsons and his family in Cock Lane, it was in the presence of the very person who would later insist, in her ethereal state, that she had been unlawfully killed.

With her partner away on business Fanny Lynes was lying in bed with the young daughter of the household when she was awakened by loud noises. She was told by Richard's wife that the cause of the disturbance was probably an 'industrious Shoemaker'. Fanny was unconvinced, particularly when the violent sound was repeated on a Sunday. Fortunately she did not have sleepless nights for much longer, as soon after she moved out of the premises.

It was a complex series of events that had led William Kent and Fanny Lynes to be lodgers at Cock Lane. William was first attached to Fanny's sister, Elizabeth. They were forced into a quick wedding owing to her pregnancy. Elizabeth died following complications after the birth of their son. Two months later the young infant also succumbed. The desolate William was comforted by Fanny, who had been living with the family as a companion to Elizabeth since they had set up house in Stoke Ferry in Norfolk. A year later, at the end of 1758, the couple had fallen in love and wanted to get married.

There were, though, a couple of obstacles. First, Fanny's family objected. Her parents were dead but her two brothers were very protective of their five sisters. They had not been happy at William's relationship with Elizabeth and were equally against any carrying on with Fanny. This was manageable. William, following the death of his mother, was a relatively wealthy man and did not require any monies from the Lynes family to support himself and his future wife. The second hurdle was impossible to surmount. Canon law forbade a man to marry his deceased wife's sister, if they produced offspring. Even though William's and Elizabeth's son had lived only a short time, this prevented the marriage legally going ahead.

Distraught at this news, they agreed to separate. William Kent moved to London, leaving a grieving Fanny back in Norfolk with her relieved siblings. Fanny could not cope with the enforced separation and, in the summer of 1759, she cut off all ties with her protective brothers and travelled south to join William. She was assisted in this escape from her family home by John Leavy, a friend of William's. It was he who had earlier confirmed the unforgiving canon law. As he lived in Greenwich, that is where the couple temporarily resided. Leavy helped them draw up their wills. Given they could not be married, the lovers wanted to formally endorse their relationship in this manner.

Their next lodgings were near Mansion House. This did not work out well. William lent his landlord £20 and had to sue him to recover his money. Word had somehow got around that the two were living in sin and, with the other residents 'not altogether approving their Conduct', they were forced to move on. William had taken on a lease for a house in Bartlett Court in Clerkenwell, but it still needed work before it was habitable. Quite how they ended up in St Sepulchre's Church, which was situated on Snow Hill adjacent to Cock Lane in the City of London, is not known. It was there that they met the officiating clerk, Richard Parsons, who had a spare room in his leased house in Cock Lane. Parsons lived with his wife Elizabeth and his two daughters. The older girl was called Betty and she was then eleven years old. It was Betty whom Fanny shared her bed with when the knockings were first heard.

William's relationship with his new landlord began on good terms. He confided in him about his matrimonial situation and lent him £12. Most of this was probably spent on alcohol as Richard Parsons was described as a 'very drunken man'. By January 1760 Parsons had fallen behind with his repayments and Fanny was eight months pregnant. Realising that they would have to find new premises given her condition, William sought recovery of his loan from Parsons, threatening legal action. Parsons ejected them from his house. They found a single room above a jeweller's shop. Fanny, however, now complained of back pain and, when Dr Cooper visited, he was so concerned that he advised she needed better accommodation for her treatment. William arranged an earlier than anticipated move to Bartlett Court. It was there that the Doctor 'prognosticated a confluent small-pox, of a very virulent nature'. Fanny did not survive long and she died on 2 February 1760.

Despite Fanny's remaining siblings' antipathy towards William – he had now apparently killed off two of them – he seemed to have acted with propriety as far as one member of the family was concerned. Fanny's sister, Anne, had visited her when she was ill. Anne had found Fanny in comparatively good spirits so was understandably shocked when she died soon after. She attended the funeral and 'wept for some time over the body' before the coffin was screwed down. It was placed in the vault at St John's Church in Clerkenwell. According to William she seemed well satisfied with the way her sister had been treated, even turning down his inviting her to take any of Fanny's clothes. Anne said that she thought his behaviour was the same 'as if they had been actually married'. William's only lapse was that he didn't put Fanny's name on the coffin. This was understandable, given that he was wary of facing prosecution for his deceit in pretending to be married to her.

William was unaware that, while his partner lay dying, the strange knockings which Fanny had previously heard had returned to the Parsons residence in Cock Lane. It was probably soon after Richard

Parsons had ejected William and Fanny that he hatched a plan to carry out some sort of vengeance on his former tenant. It is unlikely that he had thought the consequences through, or that he even knew what his ultimate aim was. But it couldn't do his cause any harm to somehow link the supernatural noises with William Kent. To kick things off, he needed somebody outside the immediate family circle to support the contention that his house was haunted.

Parsons had the perfect candidate in his friend James Franzen, who ran a pub called the Wheat Sheaf, also situated in Cock Lane. Parsons was a frequent drinker there and he told Franzen about all the knocking and scratchings that could be heard in his house. He claimed he had no idea where they came from. He invited the publican to come around one night after hours to witness the noises for himself. He then concocted a well-rehearsed plan with his wife and daughter. When Franzen arrived he was told that Parsons was out. As the nervous publican sat with Elizabeth and Betty in the kitchen, rappings could be heard. He said they 'seemed to him like knuckles knocking against the wainscot'. That they sounded like that precisely because they were that, didn't seem to occur to him.

Franzen had suffered enough and wanted to leave. He opened the kitchen door and 'saw pass by him something in white, seemingly in a sheet'. He tried to follow it but Betty advised against it – possibly because, if he had, he would have found her father enveloped in a sheet. Franzen fled back to his pub too frightened to go to bed. To reinforce the gullible man's conviction of what he had experienced, a supposedly terrified Parsons ran into the pub a little later, demanding a drink. He said he had seen a ghost at his house. 'So did I,' declared the naive landlord, as together they tried to determine what its meaning was. Franzen would later say he was informed it was the ghost of the first Mrs Kent, 'for the second Mrs Kent he heard lay at that time dying'.

There is no evidence that Parsons was trying to frame William Kent for the demise of Fanny's sister. It was widely known she had died in childbirth. The activities of the ghost therefore receded, making only periodic rappings. In the interim William Kent found a new life, and wife. However, although he might have forgotten about the Lynes family, they had not forgotten about him. Fanny's brother, John, was seeking to recover some monies from William that the latter had received as part of Fanny's estate. It turned out that she had been overpaid on the sale of some property which had been leased, rather than owned outright. A friend of John Lynes, a man called Robert Browne, began making enquiries about William's past to see if he could dig up some dirt on him to assist in their intended legal case against him. Richard Parsons was happy to provide some, especially as William had now successfully sued him to recover his debt.

Learning in December 1761 that somebody else had a grudge against William must have encouraged Richard Parsons to escalate his own personal vendetta. He now had the motive to bring back the ghost in earnest. And what better reason for a spirit to communicate with the living than to correct some egregious wrongdoing? The family had now refined its means of communication. Whereas before the noises happened at random, from now on, when witnesses were present, they would take place only in the presence of Betty. She had proved herself adept at producing the knockings undetected, a relatively simple task given that she was lying in bed, her hands and feet hidden from view. The rappings began to ratchet up, becoming familiar to the other residents of Cock Lane who accepted that the house was haunted. Parsons though needed somebody rather more substantial and influential than a credulous publican and a few susceptible neighbours if he really wanted to make William Kent suffer.

The Reverend John Moore provided regular preaching at the St Sepulchre Church where Parsons was the clerk. He was twenty-seven years old and a man of strong faith and high morals. Unusually he was responsible for the education of two African students into the Anglican faith. Philip Quaque and William Cudjoe were the sons of local rulers in Cape Coast Castle, now part of Ghana, who had been brought over to England to potentially return as missionaries. Moore had strong affiliations with the Methodists. And the Methodists, thanks largely to the preaching of their leader John Wesley, embraced the supernatural and witchcraft. John Wesley's beliefs also impact on a later hoax discussed in Chapter 8.

Moore first witnessed the rapping spirit for himself around the beginning of January 1762. He was convinced that it was genuine. He was keen to instigate some means of talking directly with the ghost, which was amusingly encapsulated in verse by David Garrick in his playlet *The Farmer's Return*: 'With her nails, and her knuckles, she answer'd so noice! For yes she knock'd once, for no she knock'd *twoice!*' And so began the means of obtaining responses to any yes/ no questions, with the occasional reply requiring additional knocks when it involved a numbered answer.

Quite how the subject of William Kent's involvement in the death of Fanny was raised is not known. But John Moore was convinced of his guilt when he received positive answers that the ghost was a woman, her name was Fanny, she had lived with Mr Kent 'in a familiar manner', two years ago she had been taken sick with small pox, and during her illness she was poisoned. Subsequent interrogation revealed more details. The poison had been given when she drank some purl (a type of beer) supplied by her partner; she had lived for three hours after drinking it and she had told her servant, Carrots, about the nefarious deed. For good measure Fanny rapped that she 'would be pleased' if William Kent was hanged.

Even John Moore appreciated that the word of a rapping spirit was insufficient to condemn Kent to the gallows. So he brought Carrots to the house hoping she would be able to confirm Fanny's story. The real name of Carrots was Esther Carlisle; she had received her nickname because of her red hair. She had begun her employment with William and Fanny while they lived at Cock Lane and remained with them until Fanny's death. Before chatting to the ghost, Moore put to her what her late mistress had apparently said. Carrots denied being told about the poisoning, pointing out that Fanny 'could not speak some days before she died' owing to the virulence of her fever. Moore would have none of it, accusing Carrots of not understanding what Fanny had said. Annoyed by this absurd conjecture, Carrots asked to leave. The clergyman's response was to offer her money if she would just 'tell the truth'.

Moore persuaded her at least to go upstairs. His first question to Fanny was to ask whether Carrots was in the room. Having received an affirmative answer, he reiterated his questions to establish that Fanny had told her servant she had been poisoned. On Carrots again stating this was not true, Moore asked if she would confess if 'carried before a magistrate'. Carrots replied with her own questions. 'Are you my mistress?' she asked. The answer was one knock but also some scratching. 'Are you angry with me, madam?' Again one rap. 'I am sure, Madam, you may be ashamed of yourself, for I never hurt you in my life.' None of these exchanges altered Moore's belief in the spirit's version of events.

Moore had invested so much in his belief in Fanny's ghost that he was prepared to dismiss whatever evidence was offered that she might not exist. It was he, after all, who had taught her to communicate. 'You must observe one knock is an affirmative and two a negative, for so Parsons and I have settled it,' he said at one point. Another time he boasted he had 'long made her the Object of my Attention and Study, and have such an influence and Command over her, as to be obeyed in almost every Thing I can propose.' He almost seems to have fallen in love, claiming that he had 'caused her to flutter and clap her Wings like a Dove' and made her trip 'round the Bed like a Kitten'.

Plenty of others, besides John Moore, conversed with the ghost. Some of the questions were banal: How many clergymen are in the room? Is the colour of a watch [held up by one of the clergy] white, yellow, blue or black? Can you distinctly see and hear all the persons present? But they ranged right through to the existential: Could she visibly appear to anyone? Would she follow the child everywhere? Was she pleased to be asked questions? Would this knocking cease if they should go to prayers? Would the taking up and opening of Fanny's body lead to any material discovery? One clergyman enquired if the spirit was clothed in a body of air, light or flesh. When told this at the later trial the judge, Lord Mansfield, asked whether the reverend 'thought he had puzzled the ghost or the ghost had puzzled him'.

William Kent was alerted about the Cock Lane Ghost by his friend John Leavy, who read the initial posts in *The Public Ledger*, the first paper to report the story. Having learnt about John Moore's involvement, Kent went to visit him. Moore reluctantly showed him the accusatory list of questions and answers. Though Moore was rather embarrassed by confronting Kent with the allegations, his conviction in the spirit was nevertheless boosted when Kent admitted he had never married Fanny. Later, when the affair began to unravel for the clergyman, he was certain that this transgression by Kent somehow explained and justified the presence of Fanny's revenging spirit. Naturally Kent was keen to hear directly from the ghost itself, and did so on 12 January 1762. The same affirmative answers as before were given regarding his involvement in the death of his partner. Kent was even persuaded to ask the ghost if he should hang for his crime. When one knock was given in response, Kent made a protest reminiscent of the one given by Carrots earlier: 'Thou art a lying spirit, thou art not the ghost of my Fanny. She would never have said any such thing.'

While for William Kent potential life and death decisions were at stake, for the general public the Cock Lane Ghost became a source of speculative intrigue. One commentator wrote that 'the whole town of London think of nothing else'. The preoccupation was fuelled by the newspapers, many of whom seem to have had confusingly similar names: *The St James's Chronicle; Or, The British Evening-Post, The London Evening-Post, Lloyds Evening Post, And British Chronicle, The London Chronicle: Or, Universal Evening Post* and *The General Evening Post*. As they openly plagiarised copy from each other, this synchronicity of titles seems apt. From 16 January onwards they were all devoting plenty of space to the story, mostly being content with reporting the supposed facts rather than expressing much in the way of scepticism. They knew what would sell, and stating that the ghost was fraudulent would not have helped. As one publisher put it, the object was 'only to divert the people'.

Given the media coverage, it was inevitable that many wanted to witness Scratching Fanny, as she became known, for themselves. Soon 'the narrow Avenue of Cock-Lane' turned into 'a Sort of Midnight Rendezvous, occupied by a String of Coaches from one End to the other'. It was not just the masses, who possibly believed in the ghost's existence, that wanted to see Betty. It was also the nobility. The great chronicler of eighteenth-century gossip Horace Walpole wrote about his own visit. He was accompanied by some distinguished lords and ladies, including the Duke of York, the younger brother of George III. They arrived after attending an opera and the 'wretchedly small and miserable' house was so crowded they couldn't even get in at first – until the Duke of York was recognised. 'When we opened the chamber, in which were fifty people, with no light but one tallow candle at the end, we tumbled over the bed of the child to whom the ghost comes.'

They remained there until half past one in the morning but heard nothing. The party was informed, as if it were 'a puppet-show', that the ghost would not make an appearance until seven. They departed disillusioned. The knock-about element of the Cock Lane Ghost is amusingly caught in the print *English Credulity or the Invisible Ghost* [Fig. 20]. Young Betty is lying in bed next to her sister – she was actually thirteen years old at the time, while her sister was nine: she looks about three! Her hands are outside the blankets, showing that she couldn't possibly be responsible for any noises. Directly above her is the iconic image of the rapping Fanny, complete with mallet in her hand. The responses of the visitors range from awestruck ('I never shall have any rest again') to mocking ('I'll lay 6 to 4 it runs more nights than the coronation,' a reference to George III's coronation that had taken place some five months before on 22 September 1761). One gentleman is holding up a timepiece and saying 'If a

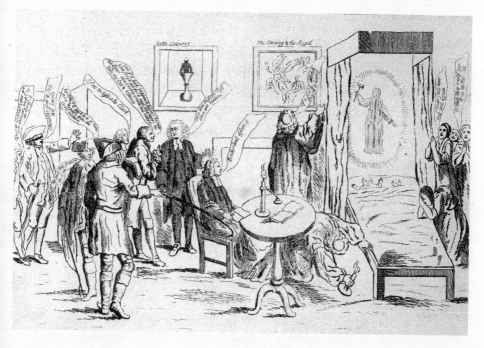

Fig. 20. *English Credulity or the Invisible Ghost*, an engraving published in February 1762.

Gold Watch knock 3 times.' The pictures on the wall of the Bottle Conjurer and Elizabeth Canning make it clear that the engraver believes it is all a hoax.

The more serious implications of the Cock Lane Ghost are also hinted at in this print. On the left-hand side is the blind magistrate, Sir John Fielding, half brother to the author Henry Fielding, stretching out his hand and saying 'I should be glad to see this Spirit.' Next to him a man is saying 'Your W[o]rs[hi]p had better get your Warrant backed up by his Lords[hi]p.' In other words, if you want to make any arrests then the Lord Mayor needs to be involved. The question to be answered was whether it was going to be William Kent ending up on trial or the Cock Lane Ghost herself.

With William Kent now on the scene, there was a clear divide between his supporters and detractors. Richard Parsons and John Moore were the principal advocates for Fanny's spirit. Alongside them was Robert Browne, the confidant of the Lynes family who had a vested interest in disparaging Kent. Another defender of the ghost was Richard James. He was a local businessman and friend of Moore. He had instigated *The Public Ledger* articles that were subsequently picked up by other newspapers. He was now working for *The Daily Gazetteer*. With the full co-operation of its proprietor, Charles Say, James was uncritically reporting on Fanny's deceased antics and her assertions against Kent.

Lined up against them were those with Fanny during her final days. Apart from William Kent, these included his friend Leavy, the servant Carrots, Dr Cooper and his colleague, the apothecary. There was also the man who would play a crucial role in disentangling the fact from the fiction, the Reverend Stephen Aldrich. He had given Fanny absolution as she lay dying, and it was in his church, St John the Baptist, that her body now lay in the crypt. More significantly he was an experienced priest with good connections and with a great suspicion of Methodism.

Aldrich's initial idea to exonerate Kent was to logically demonstrate that the ghost could not possibly be Fanny. He did this by asking her personal questions about herself. What was your father's name? Was he buried at L—? Was your sister married at M—? How many sisters have you alive? How many children had your uncle C—b when he died? Many of the answers were indeed wrong, but the scheme backfired. By engaging with the spirit in this way, Aldrich seemed to be accepting that some sort of supernatural force was at work. He changed his tactics. From now on he would try to prove that Betty was the architect of the knocking and scratchings, and therefore that the ghost didn't exist at all.

He needed to isolate Betty in a house other than one chosen by her father, and without the presence of anybody who could be suspected of colluding with her. At present, secure in his own chosen environment, Parsons could control the proceedings if difficulties arose. On one occasion a gentleman placed himself next to Betty on her bed. He was told he was not allowed to sit there. He remonstrated by arguing that he had the 'right to place myself in any part of the room' which he was suspicious of. After 'some little altercation', he was forced to leave. Another means of keeping the upper hand was through the ghost displaying her temper by scratching, threatening to cease her rapping. When one visitor stood up and stamped his foot by the bedside, presumably to check out if the noises were made by that means, continuous scratching forced the man to sit down.

Aldrich's attempts to wrestle control from the Parsons family were fortuitously assisted by someone from the opposing camp. Charles Watson was a friend of John Moore's. He was concerned that the melee surrounding all the attendees at Cock Lane to witness the ghost might get out of hand and lead to a public riot. He therefore alerted the local Alderman, Francis Gosling, who also doubled up as a justice of the peace. Gosling did not feel that he had the necessary authority to intervene, so he wisely passed the buck to the then Lord Mayor, Sir Samuel Fludyer. Watson and Moore, along with Gosling, had a meeting with Fludyer on 19 January. The Mayor acted like a true politician. He postponed making any decision for four days, hoping that the problem might go away. Instead it escalated, but the delay gave Stephen Aldrich his opportunity. He insisted on accompanying Moore to the follow-up meeting on 23 January. Fludyer further prevaricated. He ordered that an independent committee should investigate the ghost. Following this, he would then determine if an arrest warrant should be issued for William Kent, for poisoning his deceased partner. Or for Richard Parsons, for falsely accusing William Kent of murder.

Aldrich, though, had got what he wanted. Part of the mayoral terms were that Betty could not be with her family when the official examination took place. Parsons did his utmost to circumvent the ruling. When Aldrich came to collect Betty he said 'in very rude Terms, "That his Daughter should go no where"'. He then tried to have Betty accompanied by Mary Fraser, whom 'affirmed to be *unconnected*, and *not to have been with her*'. Mary Fraser was a neighbour who often acted as the orchestrator of the rapping séances and was a co-conspirator along with the Parsons family. This offer, unsurprisingly, was rejected. Eventually Parsons had to succumb to legal pressure and he agreed that his daughter could be placed under the care of Aldrich.

Aldrich elaborated on his plan. Although Richard Parsons could be in the same house as his daughter, he was to be constantly under supervision. Betty herself was to be undressed and examined before being put to bed. The bed was set in the middle of a large room without any furniture, apart from surrounding chairs to be used by the investigators. Aldrich handpicked the committee, the best-known member of which was Samuel Johnson. Johnson was at his peak of literary fame, having completed *A Dictionary of the English Language* some seven years previously. In 1762 he was still working on *The Plays of William Shakespeare*. A year later he would meet James Boswell. Other committee members included Aldrich himself, an earl, a doctor, an army officer, a matron (who was to look after Betty), a professional investigator and William Kent.

It was on Monday 1 February 1762 that the formal examination took place. It did not bode well when, on all meeting at Aldrich's house, they were told that, while the girl was present, Fanny was not. The spirit had very explicitly given two knocks when asked if she was going to turn up. Nevertheless the intrepid investigators all trooped upstairs and sat and watched Betty for an hour. No sounds were heard. They returned to the parlour to question Richard Parsons but he 'denied, in the strongest Terms, any Knowledge or Belief of Fraud'.

Betty was unaware of this interrogation of her father and had assumed the committee had left the premises. As there were some ladies still present, she decided to put on a show – and scratchings and knockings began. This so startled one of the women that she fled downstairs, alerted the committee and they returned to Betty's room to listen for themselves. Their conclusion, as written up in a later newspaper article, was that the knockings 'were produced by her clenched Fist thumping on her Breast-bone, or by striking the two

Fists against each other; and the *Scratchings*, effected by the simple Operation of a quick Motion of her Fingers, rubbed against the Bedhead, or even against the Sheet'. This reasoning was substantiated by the observation that the noises 'proceeded from that Part of the Bed where the Child lay' and that she chose the position to lie down 'which best enabled her to use her Hands under the Bed-Cloaths'. The matron in attendance, noticed that Betty's 'Knuckles were remarkably hard', indicating that they had been extensively used in the 'Operation of answering for Miss Fanny'. When 'her Arms were pulled from under the Bed-Cloaths, and kept exposed to Sight' the noises ceased.

The article went on to detail how the noises had been enhanced in the house of Richard Parsons. Accomplices, under the guise of petticoats rather than sheets, could have produced knockings and scratchings with the noises emanating 'from some snug Corner, as well as from the Bed'. The writer thought that in a roomful of eager and curious visitors it wouldn't have been hard to find 'some proper Persons ready to produce the *Sounds*, if, by the careful Inspection of any of the Company, the Girl in Bed was prevented from contributing any Thing towards the Entertainment of the Night'. It is further noteworthy that the knockings often occurred early in the morning, after an all-night vigil. This would be at a time when those watching would have been less attentive due to lack of sleep. This very perceptive analysis was in greater detail than the much more widely disseminated mayoral committee's own report, which was written by Samuel Johnson. Johnson's conclusion was merely that 'the child has some art of making or counterfeiting particular noises', without any attempt to conjecture the actual means of her doing so.

The committee's work, however, was not complete. During some of the conversations that parties had initiated with Fanny, she had said that if William Kent went down to the vault where she was lying in her coffin, she would knock on its side. This resulted in the rather farcical spectacle of the distinguished gentlemen of the committee solemnly making their way to St John's Church. First

William was sent on his own to check whether any banging could be heard. He was followed closely by the other members, confirming for themselves that there was nothing but silence when they stood next to Fanny's present resting place.

One does wonder why the ghost – in the guise of Betty, her father or another accomplice – would have issued such a challenge. With nobody, besides the sceptical investigators and the person accused of murder, next to the coffin, how could any rappings be secretly achieved? The explanation might be that somehow the spirit's original proposal got lost in translation. There is an item in a newspaper that came out a couple of days before the committee met, which stated 'this Phantom has solemnly signified, that if the Child might be carried into the Vault of St John's Church, Clerkenwell, the Knocking shall be heard on the very Coffin in which she lies buried'. This sounds much more plausible. If Betty had been down in the crypt too, she might have found a means of hammering surreptitiously on the wooden box.

If Richard Parsons thought that the committee had somehow acted unfairly in this regard, he did not make any public complaint. He did have one sliver of hope left, which was that no one had actually caught Betty physically making the noises. This was very hard to detect, of course, given that her hands and feet were concealed under her bedclothes. Aldrich was well aware that the committee hadn't really succeeded in its objective. Johnson's official report was too lacking in factual detail to conclusively demonstrate a hoax. He therefore insisted on carrying on with the observation of poor Betty. It is arguable that any decent father would have called it a day to save his daughter from further indignities. But Parsons was happy to throw the young teenager to the wolves. He hoped that somehow, without any assistance, she might be able to fool everybody into believing that she was the conduit for the spirit of Fanny. For good measure he applied some moral blackmail to sustain her in her endeavours, warning her about the fate of 'her Daddy, who must needs be ruined and undone, if their Matter should be supposed to be an Imposture'.

She did a remarkable job. She kept her investigators at bay for two weeks as they applied measures that would now be labelled as child abuse.

Betty made short shrift of the first family that Aldrich took her to. John Bray, his daughter and servant all noted unexplained noises in her presence which they thought were supernatural in origin. They even reported a new phenomenon, which was a strong whispering, although 'the Girl's Lips were motionless the whole Time'. The final straw was when the noises that came from her room were so loud that they terrified everybody in the house. John Bray insisted she should be removed. That the Brays didn't have sufficient fortitude to carry out the investigatory task is perhaps demonstrated by their belief that 'The Knockings and Scratchings were also heard there for several Days after the Child was taken away.'

Aldrich's next choice was made of sterner material. Daniel Missiter ran a business making equipment for horses, and he was determined to expose Betty. He devised elaborate means to prevent Betty scratching or knocking. These included having a maid lie across Betty's legs, holding her hands down, waking her up to insist on her hands being outside the bed covers, and tying her hands together. Still the enterprising Betty, even under these stringent conditions, was able to produce the occasional noise. Missiter's final solution was to force her to sleep in a hammock with her hands and feet fastened and spread wide apart. This had the desired effect of silence for two nights. Having applied physical restraints, he then cunningly added some psychological torture to the mix. He told her that if no more noises were heard by the following evening, he would send her and her parents to Newgate Prison.

The trap was set. She was left to her own devices, but secretly watched through a hole by a servant. Betty was observed taking part of a chimney board, on which a teakettle was normally placed, to her bed. She told Missiter that Fanny would appear at six o'clock the following morning. On the appointed hour 'she began to knock and scratch upon the Board'. She was accused directly of the deception but denied it. She was searched and 'caught in a Lie'. Her entrappers did agree that Betty had been frightened into doing this because of the threats she had received. And they further said that the noises made were 'not the least Likeness to the former' sounds. Nevertheless it was sufficient to prove that Betty was capable of indulging in fraudulent behaviour. In possession of the physical evidence Aldrich was at last satisfied. The resourceful Betty was allowed to return home.

There was one final grisly task to undertake to support William Kent's innocence. It had been suggested, presumably by Richard Parsons, that Fanny had been removed from her coffin in St John's Church – which explained the reason she was silent when the committee visited her. So William, accompanied by various church employees, went down to see if her corpse remained. 'The coffin was opened before Mr K–, and a very awful shocking sight it was.'

Richard Parsons's fate was now sealed. In February 1762 he was arrested, along with his wife Elizabeth, the servant Mary Fraser, the journalist Richard James and John Moore. It was William Kent who made the decision about whom to prosecute. It seemed that he was reluctant to pursue Moore, whom he considered naive rather than vindictive. But he was persuaded that he should do so to 'ease the mind' of others, which presumably meant those who had an antipathy towards the Methodists. Moore's last-minute confession that the 'knockings and scratching were the effects of some artful, wicked contrivance', and his belief that William was innocent, failed to save him from incarceration. Robert Browne, the friend of the Lynes, and Charles Say, the newspaper proprietor, were also arrested and later found guilty. But because they separately paid William Kent compensation, they were set free.

The trial of the five took place on 10 July 1762, so they had all been languishing in prison for several months. It lasted around twelve hours and appears to have been conducted in a seemly fashion. William Kent spoke on behalf of the prosecution for the longest period, and his testimony was supported by Fanny's doctor and apothecary, together with the loyal servant, Carrots. Rather surprisingly the gullible landlord and friend of Parsons, James Franzen, was also called for the plaintiff. However merely by reciting the antics of the supposed ghost in the sheet, thereby illustrating the amateur theatrics of Richard Parsons, he caused 'much merriment to the very numerous audience assembled' in the courtroom. The defendants relied principally on witnesses who still believed that Fanny was a genuine ghost. Many of them said they had heard the rappings but all had to admit that they didn't know 'whence the noises proceeded'.

Lord Mansfield, the presiding judge, took an hour and a half to summarise for the jury. After deliberating for fifteen minutes, they found all the defendants guilty. Sentencing, however, didn't take place until seven months later, the postponement being given to allow the parties time to find money to pay William Kent financial reparations. Richard James and John Moore eventually managed this. They were released on 10 February 1763, having contributed no less than £588 between them, approximately £60,000 in today's money. The others were unable to raise any funds so Mary Fraser was committed to Bridewell for hard labour for six months; Elizabeth Parsons was sentenced to one year in prison, and Richard two years. More worryingly for him he was also 'ordered to stand in the Pillory at the End of Cock-Lane, and at Change, once each, within the Month'. Parsons, after receiving his punishment, disingenuously claimed he had no malice against Mr Kent as he had never arrested him. He reiterated that the knocks heard by him and others sounded as if they had been 'given with a Mallet'.

An eighteenth-century pillory consisted of hinged wooden boards forming holes through which the head and hands were inserted. The boards were locked together to secure the captive. Often the unfortunate victim would be pelted with rotten fruit and vegetables, or indeed worse, by the spectators. This could lead to permanent injury or death. Such a fate seemed to be anticipated for Parsons, as one newspaper wrote that 'a great mob was assembled' and 'had prepared every offensive ingredient in order to make a sacrifice of that unhappy and ruined man'. In anticipation of the lynching, local residents 'were obliged to shut up their shops'. It was perhaps on reading this that Parsons became a 'supposed disordered in his Mind' and the day of reckoning was postponed.

Not for long though. On 16 March Parsons stood in the pillory on Snow Hill and made what was doubtless a well-rehearsed, and desperate, speech in mitigation. He said that he was not part of any conspiracy, had never taken money from those who had wanted to see the ghost, and was still willing for his daughter to be 'examined in regard to the Deception'. His continuing willingness to sacrifice Betty for his own ends worked. Two well-dressed men began by putting five shillings in his hat. Other spectators followed. The report indicated that some passing noblemen were forced by the crowd to contribute to the collection, which amounted to about ten guineas. His other two appearances in the pillory proved equally lucrative and without incident. Parsons did though serve his full term inside, eventually emerging from the King's Bench prison on 13 February 1765.

As so often happens, very little, if anything, is known about the participants in such cases once it is all over. William Kent disappeared from the scene. Reverend John Moore returned to his position as rector of St Bartholomew-the-Great but died in July 1768, aged only thirty-five. Nothing more was heard of Richard Parsons following his release. Betty lived to the age of fifty-eight, marrying twice in the process. There was a report that she would on occasions show some specimens of her art acknowledging that 'it was by the same means that she amused her credulous attendants at Cock-lane'.

One person caught up in the hoax that we do know plenty about is Samuel Johnson. His contemporaries did not let him off lightly for being, as they perceived it, credulous enough to even conceive that a spirit might exist. The poet Charles Churchill referred to him in his poem *The Ghost* as 'Pomposo...Vain idol of a scribbling crowd' and mocked him for his 'expedition 'gainst a Ghost'. Later writers would not excuse him either. The historian Lord Macaulay wrote that Johnson had been 'weak enough to pay serious attention to a story about a ghost', while Thomas Carlyle called him 'Foolish Doctor!' His biographer, James Boswell, did not pass an opinion but was intrigued by the whole affair and asked Johnson some questions about it sixteen years after. According to Boswell he expressed much satisfaction regarding how he had assisted in detecting the cheat. But when he was pressed further on how he got himself involved in the first place, Johnson was less communicative and 'he showed his displeasure'.

III

It is conceivable that it was from Boswell's *Life of Johnson* that Dickens first heard about the Cock Lane Ghost. Other possible sources for him were *The Annual Register* of 1762, which had a full report on 'some strange noises, heard the beginning of the year, at a house in Cock-Lane' and Kirby's 1805 *Wonderful and Eccentric Museum*, which reproduced many of the newspaper articles of the day in its comprehensive summary. Dickens references both these volumes in *Our Mutual Friend*.

Dickens mentions the Cock Lane Ghost no fewer than three times in his novels. In the opening chapter of *A Tale of Two Cities*; in *Nicholas Nickleby*, where Nicholas's scatter-brained mother claims that her great grand-father had gone to school with the Cock Lane Ghost; and in *Dombey and Son*, where Paul and his friends are enjoying a game of romps 'until Mrs Pipchin knocking angrily at the wall, like the Cock Lane Ghost revived', puts an end to it. The latter two books were written well before the article 'The Ghost of the Cock Lane Ghost' appeared in *Household Words*. It shows Dickens's familiarity with the hoax and why he made the connection between Fanny's rappings and those produced by Maria Hayden.

One major difference between the two was the sophistication in the means of producing the noises. We have already noted that Betty created the knockings and scratchings with her hands and feet while concealed underneath her bed-sheets. She was assisted by her parents, Mary Fraser, and perhaps other accomplices. They would improvise as necessary, doubtless banging against the wooden walls, floorings and wainscots to produce the raps. The crowded room would help in masking where the noise came from. The astonished reactions of those who believed it was a ghost communicating would generate an atmosphere of credulity to disorientate the sceptical.

Maria Hayden could not have got away with such crude techniques. She produced the raps with her toes, cracking the joints while snapping them against the bottom of the table leg. The sound reverberated upwards, giving the impression that the knocking was occurring on the table-top. If she wanted to create the illusion that the noises came from elsewhere in the room, she rapped louder and looked directly at the spot where she wished them to be heard. Such was her skill that she could produce different sound levels, depending on the respective age of the dead spirit. A rap was quieter for a woman than a man, and even more delicate for a child. T. H. Huxley, the biologist who was a strong advocate for Darwin's theory of evolution, wrote: 'Fraud is often genius out of place, and I confess that I have never been able to get over a certain sneaking admiration for Mrs Hayden.'

Maria Hayden's methods were fully explained in the *Household Words* article. Alongside her failure to produce meaningful conversations with any of the dead spirits, it was an impressive exposure of the fraudulent nature of her séances. It had an impact on her reputation, although not the knock-out blow that Dickens might have hoped for. Mr Hayden, in a letter written two and a half months after 'The Ghost of the Cock Lane Ghost' was published, said that his wife's manifestations were even more successful than back in the US and had met with remarkably few failures. There was an admittance, though, that Dickens's friends who paid her a visit 'evidently came with the intention of having every thing wrong, and they nearly succeeded to their mind'. In another letter, some seven months later, he blamed the 'stupid and silly article' which had

Fig. 21. *Credulity, Superstition and Fanaticism* by William Hogarth, an engraving published April 1762.

appeared in Dickens's *Household Words* as prejudicing the people in Ireland against the phenomena. In October 1853 the couple sailed back to New York. Later Mrs Hayden changed careers and graduated as a doctor of medicine.

If the Cock Lane Ghost is remembered at all today, it is probably from an engraving produced by William Hogarth called *Credulity, Superstition and Fanaticism*, which juxtaposes religion, in particular Methodism, with belief in the supernatural and witchcraft [Fig. 21]. The most prominent hoax depicted is that of Mary Toft, with Hogarth reprising his print of *Cunicularii or The Wise Men of Godliman in Consultation* [Fig. 6]. She lies at the forefront with rabbits scampering out from under her skirt. References to the Cock Lane Ghost are subtler. It is most noticeable on top of a pedestal next to the pulpit, which has an angelic Fanny clothed in a ghost-like sheet clutching a mallet in one hand; in the other, she holds a scratching implement. Next to her is a child lying in a bed representing Betty Parsons. The image of Fanny is repeated in the print with some of the wild-eyed congregation, driven mad by the enthusiasm of the rabid preacher, clutching replicas of her rather than the Virgin Mary. Most provocatively a young couple directly under the pulpit are about to embrace, with the man thrusting the Fanny effigy in between her breasts. One writer has speculated that the couple are a representation of William Kent and Fanny Lynes.

Hogarth reprised Fanny in a print called *The Times Plate II*. It is one of Hogarth's rare ventures into commenting on the politics of the day, and is essentially showing his support for the Treaty of Paris to end the Seven Years War. Many prominent politicians objected to the concord, feeling the English gave too much away in their negotiations. One of those was the radical politician John Wilkes, who attacked Hogarth in issue number 17 of his journal *The North Briton*. Hogarth, responding with his art rather than words, places on the right hand side of the print John Wilkes in the pillory. He has a copy of *The North Briton* hanging around his neck, the turned-up corner of the page looking like a one and a seven. A woman is emptying toiletry waste on top of his head, while a young lad is urinating on his boots. A Scotsman – Wilkes disliked the Scots – is playing the bagpipes at his feet. Next to him, also being pilloried, is Fanny. Unlike those of Wilkes, her hands are free. In one she holds her trademark mallet, in the other a lit taper that is about to set Wilkes's magazine on fire. The message is clear. Wilkes is just as fraudulent and deserving of the same punishment as Richard Parsons, the mastermind behind the hoax of the Cock Lane Ghost.

EIGHT

'Invisible Agent'

* * *

I

The Stockwell hoax appeared done and dusted in twenty hours, with the first newspaper report both narrating and explaining the mystery. And yet there are still those today who refuse to believe the solution. *The Gazetteer and New Daily Advertiser* broke the news on 11 January 1772. Five days earlier, on Monday 6 January, household goods fell from shelves and smashed of their own accord in the house of Mrs Golding. This forced her to seek refuge in her next-door neighbour's house, owned by Mr Gresham. Similar upheavals occurred there, so she moved to her niece's home. Once again items tumbled down and broke. Her final port of call, the following day, was to the residence of Mr Fowler. His property fared no better. In desperation she returned to her own abode, where her few remaining belongings suffered a similar fate. All through this journey of destruction, Mrs Golding was accompanied by her maid who was 'quite unconcerned the whole time'. As soon as she was sent away on an errand, the wrecking ceased. On her return the servant was discharged and all untoward activities ceased.

Given such a direct line between cause and effect, it is hard to understand why the story had any traction. A reason is given, however, in the very last sentence of the newspaper's narrative. Reassuringly it stated that what it had told so far were absolute facts but also that it was 'not the hundredth part of what happened'. The full revelation was to be published very soon. In other words *The Gazetteer* had a scoop. It was teasing potential buyers that there was much more to this strange tale than first appeared. Keep subscribing and all will be revealed.

An eager readership did not have long to wait. Two days later, on 13 January, a much longer version appeared in the paper. It took up one and a half columns of densely printed text with no paragraph breaks. Much of this would later be reproduced in a pamphlet called *An Authentic, Candid, and Circumstantial Narrative, of the Astonishing Transactions at Stockwell* [Fig. 22]. So even if the story itself did not merit further elaboration, there were good commercial reasons for keeping it in the public arena. The booklet comprised testimony from Mrs Golding herself; John and Mary Pain; Mary Martin, the servant of Mr Pain; and Richard and Sarah Fowler. Mary Pain was Mrs Golding's niece. The anonymous author confirmed that the information given was not altered or exaggerated in any way. But who exactly related what, is unknown. The published chronicle is a conglomerate of all of their tales, so we don't know whether any specific happening was independently verified. Nevertheless the sheer number of witnesses interviewed is impressive. As is the speed of collating their statements, with *Astonishing Transactions* appearing at booksellers a mere four days after the extended *Gazetteer* piece.

Right through to the present day, the retelling of what happened at the London suburb has relied on the *Astonishing Transactions*, with the newspaper's variant ignored. Overall there is little to distinguish between them. However when it comes to the finer details there are some interesting differences, which tell us about memory recall and how events are interpreted. Occasionally there is a significant discrepancy. For instance Mrs Golding's maid, Ann Robinson, who had only been with her mistress ten days, is described in the pamphlet as 'a young woman, about twenty years old'. In the newspaper report she is 'aged fifteen years, or thereabouts'.

It might seem pernickety to show how the earlier newspaper

A N

Authentic, Candid, and Circumſtantial

NARRATIVE,

OF THE

Aſtoniſhing Tranſactions at *Stockwell,*

In the County of SURRY, •

On MONDAY and TUESDAY, the 6th and 7th
Days of JANUARY, 1772,

CONTAINING

A Series of the moſt ſurpriſing and unac-
countable EVENTS that ever happened,
which continued from firſt to laſt,
upwards of Twenty Hours,
and at different Places.

Publiſhed with the Conſent and Approbation of the
Family and other Parties concerned, to Authenticate
which, the original Copy is ſigned by them.

L O N D O N:

Printed for J. MARKS, Bookſeller, in *St. Martin's Lane,*

MDCCLXXII.

Fig. 22. Title Page of *The Astonishing Transactions at
Stockwell*, published January 1772.

article differs from the pamphlet, given that the trajectory is much
the same. But part of the reason why *Astonishing Transactions* on first
reading appears to be so authentic is precisely because of the in-
depth detail of what happened. People who lie are usually short
on specifics. You certainly can't accuse any of these observers of
resorting to generalising waffle, particularly when it comes to the
mysterious upheaval of household objects. If some of the supposed
facts appear to change, however, then it does bring into question

whether perhaps other minutiae are not fully reliable. So although the following expansion on the travail of Mrs Golding is based on the pamphlet, I will note in brackets, or by other means, where the newspaper conflicts with the latter's narrative.

The elderly Mrs Golding, a respectable gentlewoman, was first disturbed at about ten ['eleven'] o'clock in the morning on Monday 6 January at her home in Stockwell. She heard the china and glasses in the back kitchen fall down. Her maid, Ann, informed her of what was happening and, on entering, Mrs Golding saw plates tumble from the shelf even though no one was near them. This contrasts with the newspaper report's statement that 'no person was in that room' when some of these first breakages occurred. Soon afterwards a clock, a lantern that hung on the staircase, and an earthen pan of salted beef all crashed to the floor under their own apparent volition.

Several neighbours appeared on hearing the commotion, including a carpenter called Mr Rowlidge. He offered his opinion that the house's foundation was giving way, owing to the weight of an additional room erected above. On this news, Mrs Golding, along with her maid, immediately went next door to Mr Gresham's house. Golding promptly fainted. Mrs Pain, her niece who lived in Brixton Causeway, was sent for. She advised Mr Gardner, a surgeon who was present, to bleed her aunt. A pint china bowl of Mr Gresham's was used to collect the blood. Mrs Pain asked if the blood could be thrown away but Mr Gresham said he wanted to wait until it was cold so he could examine it. 'As soon as the blood was cold in the bason, it flew out on the floor,' and then the receptacle broke into pieces. The newspaper stated that one of the bits was now in the possession of Mr Waterfield at the Royal Oak Inn in Vauxhall.

In the meantime, neighbours were removing Mrs Golding's possessions from her house to prevent any further damage. These included a tray full of china, a breadbasket, mahogany waiters, some bottles of liquors, jars of pickles and a large mirror, known as a pier glass ['worth about five pounds']. They were taken to Mr Gresham's abode but, with Mrs Golding present, they met the same fate. Glasses and china standing on the sideboard tumbled down and smashed. Bottles of wine and rum broke into pieces before they were uncorked. Mrs Golding promptly sought refuge with another neighbour, Mr Mayling. Ann stayed on at Mr Gresham's to help clear up the mess. While she was there, a jar of pickles turned upside down, and a jar of raspberry jam ['pot of jelly'], two tables for ornaments and a box for the card game quadrille all broke.

Mrs Golding remained for only a short, incident-free, time at Mr Mayling's before Mrs Pain decided to move her aunt to her own place, 'for fear of being troublesome'. Here they were joined by Mr Gresham and his daughter. They all had dinner, while Ann was sent to check up on her mistresses' house. She reported back that all was well. With calm seemingly restored, Mr and Miss Gresham left. But then about eight ['seven'] o'clock, it all kicked off again. It began with a whole row of pewter dishes except one ['seven out of eight'] falling off the shelf and rolling onto the floor. They lay there for a time but then turned upside down. Another row of plates fell off the dresser. All were returned but repeated their *kamikaze* dive. Next an egg on a shelf flew off, crossed the kitchen and struck a cat on the head. In the newspaper article the egg-flying incident took place later and there was no mention of the feline bombardment.

The Pains' servant, Mary Martin, must have reported the next part because she went to stir the kitchen fire, whereupon a pestle and mortar jumped about six feet off the floor. Following that, candlesticks and other brasses fell over. Glasses and china were placed on the floor to keep them safe. They began to 'dance' – the word 'dance' was never used in the newspaper article – 'and tumble about'. A teapot struck Ann's foot. There then follows an inventory of other household objects performing various gymnastics. A glass tumbler jumped about two feet; a china bowl leapt from the floor, between seven and eight feet, to behind a table; a candlestick flew across the kitchen about fifteen feet; a teakettle under the dresser was thrown out about two feet; a tumbler, with rum-and-water in it, cavorted about ten feet. Other items that met a similar fate were a silver tankard, a case-bottle that shattered, a mustard-pot and a single cup that flew across the kitchen, ringing like a bell. Two hams, hanging up in the chimney to dry, collapsed from their hooks ['nails and strings']. A flitch of bacon also fell.

Around ten in the evening Richard Fowler was invited over, but by one in the morning he was so terrified that he returned home. Mrs Pain went upstairs on the pretext of comforting her youngest child. In reality she could not bear to witness any more destruction of her property, which by now had amounted to 'some pounds'. About five o'clock on Tuesday morning, Mrs Golding went up to tell her niece she couldn't stay in the house any longer as 'all the tables, chairs, drawers, &c., were tumbling about'. She and Ann went over to Richard Fowler's. Ann then returned to help Mrs Pain dress the children in the barn where she, along with her own maid, had taken them for safe-keeping. In Ann's absence, all was quiet at Mr Fowler's.

Alongside Mrs Golding and her maid, Mrs Pain and her nine-year-old son assembled at Mr Fowler's. The owner lit a fire in his backroom. Soon after, a candlestick, a tin lamp and a lantern, which was lighting Mrs Golding, all fell to the ground. A basket of coals tumbled over. It was Ann who took the initiative and persuaded Richard Fowler to order Mrs Golding to leave. She said that wherever her mistress was 'the same things would follow'. Returning home, this proved to be true. A nine-gallon cask of beer in the cellar turned upside down with 'no person near it'. A box of candles fell from a shelf, a round mahogany table toppled over in the parlour and a pail of water standing on the floor boiled like a pot. The newspaper didn't mention anything about the status of the water, beyond the fact that some of it spilt. It was Mr Pain who suggested Mrs Golding send Ann to fetch his wife. In Ann's absence all was normal. On her return, sometime between six and seven o'clock on Tuesday morning, she was dismissed. A final inventory of damages was noted: the glasses, china and other broken items of Mrs Golding's fitted in three pails, while Mrs Pain's losses filled two similar containers.

Through the pamphlet, but not mentioned in the newspaper article, are periodic references to Mrs Golding's state of mind. As the destruction continued unabated, her surprise and fear increased. 'Her mind was one confused chaos.' She noticed, along with the other witnesses, that Ann was never still, always walking backward and forward. In the middle of the confusion Ann was composed and acted very coolly. Her mistress could not understand how a girl of her age wasn't as frightened as everybody else. By the end, she could only come to the conclusion that Ann was 'not altogether so unconcerned as she appeared to be'.

With such overwhelming evidence pointing to Ann's guilt, it is perplexing that the pamphlet does not categorically accuse her of being the culprit. Others clearly thought the same. One journal wrote that given 'the maid is the suspected person, it is a little extraordinary that no means were used to detect her'. A newspaper similarly queried why in the narrative, although there was a 'small Hint of the Girl' being the cause, 'it gives us not the least idea of by what Means such a Scene could be carried into Execution'. Instead *Astonishing Transactions* ends by stating that anything written that might appear unfavourable to Ann was done not with the intention of accusing her of the misdemeanours, but rather in keeping with a strict adherence to the truth. It would leave it to others to determine how this astonishing 'affair may be unravelled'. There were a number of reasons why the author might have taken such a stance. It could be that he was genuinely unsure that Ann was to blame, or at least solely to blame. It could be that his witnesses didn't think that Ann was the cause, and he didn't want to put words into their mouths. If they did accept that Ann had somehow bedazzled them, then they would have come across as naive and credulous at best. It could be that he was aware that implying it was somehow a mysterious and unsolved case would ultimately prove better for sales.

Astonishing Transactions would run to a second edition, so maybe keeping an open mind did work. Critics in the monthly journals were not impressed. 'An impertinent attempt to impose upon the credulity of the public,' wrote one. Another stated that it was merely 'a new edition of the Cock-lane Ghost ... with additions, but no amendments'. The newspapers, at least in the immediate aftermath, appeared less cynical. *The Gazetteer*, which had kick-started the story, added some more speculation. It elaborated on the anecdote about the water boiling in the pail when Mrs Golding returned to her own house. A farmer, clearly a reference to Mr Pain, had thrown the water away and then set the bucket back down. After about a minute, it 'jumped up, and turned bottom upwards'.

It is understandable, though, based solely on a reading of *Astonishing Transactions*, why many could not accept that Ann Robinson was responsible for what happened. There seem to be just too many reliable witnesses claiming that they saw numerous household items falling, tumbling, crashing, dancing, flying, jumping and breaking of their own accord. None of the testimonies directly implicated the maid in causing the mayhem, just stating that she was the only participant who appeared 'unconcerned'. One of the witnesses, Mr Pain, was prepared to back himself legally for what he contributed to the pamphlet. Responding to the 'calumnies' he and his family had received, he voluntarily took an oath before the Bench of Justices at St Margaret's-Hill as to the truth of his statement. Paradoxically, therefore, even though the husband of Mrs Golding's niece had been instrumental in getting rid of Ann Robinson – as a result of which action all activities ceased – he was still convinced that the destruction was wrought 'by an agent unknown to them, and unseen by them'.

So if Ann was not the cause, who, or what, was?

II

One alternative solution was given early on in the papers. Some Stockwell inhabitants thought it was the result of 'the effects of the Hounslow explosion'. This was a reference to the shocks emanating from two powder-mills detonating in the nearby borough of

Hounslow. The possible link was also implied in the January 1772 issue of *The Gentleman's Magazine*, where the two stories were run together. 'About the time the explosion was felt at London, some families at Stockwell were terrified with the rattling and breaking of their china.' The timings were indeed very close, both commencing on the morning of Monday 6 January. The Hounslow devastation started about half an hour in advance of the happenings in Stockwell. What is especially intriguing, though, is that the two share other characteristics: in particular in the over-the-top detailed reporting of the damage done and in the refusal of some to accept the obvious explanation of what took place.

Two out of nine mills owned by Edmund Hill, used for producing gunpowder, blew up at his factory on Hounslow Heath. As gunpowder was stored in nearby warehouses, there were a number of separate explosions – reports varied from three to seven. It began when one of the drying houses caught fire. The conflagration spread to other buildings but 'in so gradual manner' that everybody had a chance to flee the scene. As a result, and also because many of the workmen were at breakfast, nobody on the premises was killed, although three were wounded. However, several died when a wagon overturned. In addition, a child was buried in the ruins of a nearby dwelling-house that was demolished. And a boy, harrowing a field, was thrown to the ground and run over by his plough pulled by four bolting horses. Initial estimate of the cost to the proprietor was £5,000. George III ordered £200 to be paid out as compensation to any victims.

These were the basic facts but, as with the hyperbolic description of what household goods were displaced in Stockwell, the newspapers seemed similarly intent on giving absurdly exact descriptions of the impact of the shocks from the explosion. A gentleman walking over the bridge from Chelsea to Battersea was lifted up three times under his feet. Mr Thomas, an eminent surgeon and apothecary in Hounslow, had a great number of pots, bottles and glasses knocked over, so that the shop flowed with distilled water, tinctures and syrups. The horses in a carriage at Kensington reared up, resulting in the coachman's foot slipping and dropping into the storage compartment. At a gentleman's chambers in the Temple, a tall bookcase fell down. In Cecil Street, in the Strand, two flowerpots were thrown off the ledge of a window. In Salisbury Court the shop door of a cork cutter was forced open. A pregnant lady in a post chaise was so terrified that she miscarried. At Henley the explosion blew down a barn, broke several windows and threw a young woman, who was looking out of a parlour window, into the garden. Such an inventory of damaged utilities wouldn't have looked out of place in the *Astonishing Transactions* pamphlet.

One person directly affected was Horace Walpole at his residence in Strawberry Hill in Twickenham, a district next to Hounslow. According to the newspapers he lost a small quantity of painted glass. We can confirm this was true as there are three letters from Walpole describing the incident. He was alerted when the door of his room shook so violently that he thought somebody was breaking it open. Eight of his painted glass windows were broken, along with a couple of other windows and two statues. He escaped relatively unscathed, claiming that, as the tremors 'came from the northwest, the China Closet was not touched, nor a cup fell down'. A neighbour, about a quarter of a mile away, fared worse with his bow-window 'massacred'. Even royalty was not immune from the blast. The King and the Prince of Wales were riding in Richmond 'when the concussion of the earth was felt'. They alighted and went into the Queen's palace to comfort those members of the family who were 'much alarmed'.

The newspapers seemed to be competing in suggesting how far away the shocks could be felt. At first it was confined to damage done to houses in Hounslow and the neighbouring boroughs of Twickenham, Isleworth and Brentford. It then extended to other parts of London, such as Greenwich and Blackheath. At Hammersmith and Kensington it shook not only tables, chairs and dishes but the houses themselves. The steeple of a church in Battersea was shaken, while a lady in Hampstead had her china thrown down from the shelves. It was felt in the heart of the City and also at Hyde Park Corner. The tremors drifted further out to Sydenham and Deptford in Kent, and Stanmore, about twelve miles from the blast. The earth's trembles occurred at Alton, Godalming and Haslemere in Surrey, but also reached into Middlesex and the interior parts of Essex. Finally it was reported that many inhabitants of Wotton-under-Edge in Gloucestershire had run out of their houses in confusion and, furthermore, 'the Noise was heard very distinctly ten Miles below Bristol'. This was about 100 miles from the centre of explosion.

Many at first thought the shock was caused by an earthquake. This was as true for those close by as for those further afield in Dartford and Guildford. The former were quickly proved wrong as they saw smoke rising and could smell the gunpowder, 'as plainly as if a gun had been discharged near them'. However, witnesses more distant from the epicentre had no such evidence to disillusion their theory. As one paper put it, it was inconceivable that an explosion could shake the ground in all directions for a distance of some 120 miles. There was little doubt, therefore, 'that the blowing up of the mills near Hounslow was occasioned by an earthquake'. Further scepticism was expressed by another paper in stating that there must have been a natural cause as there was no instance of 'three mills blowing up so regularly in succession after each other'.

Some, even if they acknowledged that the explosion took place, could not accept that it was merely an accident. An eyewitness to the event, who was thrown to the ground while out walking with a companion and was both blinded and deafened by the smoke and noise, wrote that it had to be something much more serious: he did not offer an opinion of what that might be. One paper did offer a plausible alternative. It strongly suspected that the blowing up of the powder-mills at Hounslow 'was done by such villains as set Portsmouth dock-yard on fire'.

The Portsmouth fire had begun on 27 July 1770, well over a year before. It had burnt down the warehouses storing hemp and masts and the carpenters' shops at the harbour. In the process it destroyed 300 tons of hemp and a sufficient amount of pitch, tar, sails, rigging, timber and masts to equip thirty war vessels. Lives were lost and 'many limbs broken'. Three thousand men attempted to put out the flames, but it was still burning four days later. The estimated loss was half a million pounds, subsequently revised to nearer £130,000. Initially the fire was thought to have been caused by a pitch-kettle boiling over. This was altered to the belief that the fire was deliberate, as combustibles were found where it first broke out. Possible culprits were people looking to create employment for thousands of out-of-work ship-carpenters, sail- and rope-makers. But most imagined it was foreign intervention, with inevitably the French being the principal suspects. One correspondent claimed that 'two wan, long-nosed, slim fellows with bag-wigs and swords' were seen hovering around the dockyard the evening before. It was noted a couple of days later that 'a certain foreigner of rank' was highly disgruntled at the suspicions aimed at his nation.

The arsonist was never found, but in November 1771 Joshua Dudley confessed that he had accepted a bribe of £200 to assist some Frenchmen to enter the Portsmouth docks in order to start the fire. It turned out that he had invented the story in an attempt to extricate himself from a debtors' prison. He was prosecuted for wilful perjury. He pleaded guilty and was sentenced to transportation. Although the fire itself happened nearly a year and a half before Mrs Golding's tumbling utensils, Dudley's false confession was in the news precisely when the latter story broke. Indeed, on 14 January 1772, The Public Advertiser carried the news that a boat-builder and purveyor of the yard had been sent to London from Portsmouth to testify that Dudley was lying, while simultaneously reporting in full about the events at Stockwell. And it was this paper that tied all three incidents together when it reported that the 'curious Account from Stockwell' and the 'Fire at Portsmouth, and the late Explosion at Hounslow', were all 'occasioned by the same invisible Agent'.

The writer obviously didn't believe there was a genuine connection between the three events. What they all had in common, though, was they were clouded by false rumour and imaginative supposition. In the case of the Portsmouth dock fire it was a conviction that it must have involved some foreign malpractice: precisely the reason why Dudley's initial confession was believed. Similar underhand methods could have come into play to account for the Hounslow gunpowder mills blowing up. Alternatively the explosion was the result of an earthquake. Or the former didn't happen at all and it was therefore solely an earthquake which produced the tremors. Or the explosion did occur but, as that wouldn't explain how shockwaves were felt so far away, perhaps an earthquake and an explosion took place simultaneously.

When it came to Stockwell, following a reading of *Astonishing Transactions,* some might have initially thought the mysterious goings-on had something do with the detonation of the Hounslow mills. But surely they could not have retained that conviction for long. If they discarded the likelihood that it was carried out by Ann or another person – in other words by natural means – this left only a preternatural interpretation. The first hint of this as a possible explanation appeared in *The Gazetteer* on 14 January, where it was stated that some of the Stockwell inhabitants thought the happenings to be supernatural. Ten days later there was a note about the curious visiting the Royal Oak at Vauxhall where the enterprising landlord, Mr Waterfield, had accumulated some of 'the Spoils of Stockwell Witchcraft'.

In the eighteenth century, if you thought that what took place in Stockwell had occultish origins, there was not an appropriate term to classify the phenomenon. Now days we would use the word poltergeist. The term was popularised by Catherine Crowe in her book *The Night Side of Nature,* published in 1848. Harry Price, a prominent psychic researcher of the twentieth century, describes poltergeists as mischievous, destructive, noisy and cruel. While a 'ghost *haunts*; a Poltergeist *infests*'. In particular 'they throw things, or cause things to be thrown'. Price later wrote that if he were asked to choose an example of what best represented the popular conception of what a poltergeist is, and does, he 'would unhesitatingly single out the case' of Stockwell. Similarly Mrs Crowe, herself a believer in hauntings, reproduces the whole of *Astonishing Transactions* as her first, and strongest, example of their existence.

There were, though, a couple of earlier, seemingly unexplained, poltergeist-like incidents that provided support for those who believed unseen forces were at work at Stockwell. In March 1662 John Mompesson, who lived in North Tidworth (then called Tedworth) on the border of Wiltshire and Hampshire, ordered the arrest of a drummer called William Drury. Mompesson confiscated his drum and kept it at his house. For nearly a year after, the occupants heard unexplained thumpings, scratchings, drum sounds and other noises, with sundry items thrown around the room. Thanks to a book written by the clergyman and witchcraft apologist Joseph Glanvill, the case became known as the Drummer of Tedworth. Hogarth's print *Credulity, Fanaticism and Superstition*, which featured Mary Toft and the Cock Lane Ghost [Fig. 21], has the drummer on top of a pedestal with the word 'Tedworth' written on it. He is banging his drum immediately above the edifice depicting Fanny holding her mallet next to Betty Parsons lying in bed.

The second example was of particular significance as it took place in the family home of John Wesley, at Epworth in Lincolnshire. The future Methodist leader was away at the time at Charterhouse school. At the rectory were John's parents, Reverend Samuel Wesley and Susanna, and several of his sisters. It began on 1 December 1716 when one of the servants heard mysterious knockings at the door and, when in bed, 'the gobbling of a turkey-cock'. A fellow maid scoffed at this anecdote, but the next day was so startled by taps on a shelf in the dairy that she threw down the butter tray she had been carrying and fled. Wesley's sisters then encountered similar sounds under a table, the clattering of an iron casement and a warming pan, and the latch of a door moving up and down. Their mother was convinced it was preternatural when she listened to the violent rocking of a non-existent cradle in the nursery. When she told her husband of her fears, he admonished her for her lack of sense.

However, when he was praying for the King that evening, a

rapping echoed around the room. This was reprised every morning and evening when the prayers were repeated. Samuel also heard similar sounds in his study. One night in bed he and Susanna were woken up by loud noises. They went downstairs to find bottles scattered under the staircase and 'it seemed as if a very large coal was violently thrown upon the floor and dashed all in pieces'. They expected to see that the pewterware had been thrown around the kitchen, but all was fine. The bangings continued unabated, so much so that Samuel couldn't get to sleep until four in the morning. The culprit was believed to be Old Jeffrey, who had died in the house years before. The creaking soon became such a regular feature of the house that, when the girls heard them late at night, they would say 'Jeffrey is coming: it is time to go to sleep.' They continued for a month until they gradually became more intermittent and faded away. After the event John asked his sister Nancy, then about fifteen years old, whether she had been afraid. She said not during the day, when the knockings followed her around as she was sweeping the floor. Her only thought was that Jeffrey 'might have done it *for her*, and saved her the trouble'.

Susanna was not so chilled, and she wrote to her oldest son, also called Samuel, for his advice. He sensibly asked the type of questions you might anticipate. Was there a new maid or servant in the house who might play the tricks? Did all the family hear the noises together, or one at a time? Could not some form of animal, like a cat, rat or dog, be the cause? Have you seen *and* heard the disturbance, as 'the truth will be still more manifest and undeniable, if it is grounded on the testimony of two senses'? Her responses didn't satisfy him so he wrote to his father asking for a full account. His reply was that it was all over and 'we are now all quiet'. The family had braved it out, despite several clergymen urging Samuel to leave the house. His retort had been: 'No: let the devil flee from *me*: I will never flee from the devil.'

The haunting at Epworth undoubtedly contributed to John Wesley's own belief in witchcraft, even though his sister Emily was the only one at the time who directly attributed it to such a cause. She had noted that there had been a recent disturbance near them that was 'undoubtedly witches', so, rather like a spread of a virus, she suggested that it may have reached them. Furthermore her father had for several Sundays spoken against his congregation consulting cunning men. These were village astrologers, faith healers and fortune-tellers who dabbled in black magic. Maybe this was a revengeful attack by an evil entity against Samuel's preaching. She also reported a strange creature that was seen three times. It was described as similar to 'a badger, only without any head that was discernible' and, on another occasion, 'like a white rabbit, which seems likely to be some witch'.

John Wesley put together his own notes concerning Epworth in 1720 after speaking directly to those involved. These were later published in the 1784 edition of *The Arminian Magazine*. Wesley doesn't directly attribute his family's experiences to witchcraft but it is clear, given that his journals and letters are littered with references to the supernatural and to divine interventions and satanic manifestations, that this is what he thought. As he famously stated, 'giving up witchcraft, is, in effect, giving up the Bible'. He also showed his belief in a supernatural explanation of the Drummer of Tedworth, after his brother Samuel had been told by Mr Mompesson's son that Glanvill's chronicled account was 'punctually true'.

Wesley never referred to what happened in Mrs Golding's house. Nevertheless some claimed that the Methodists were behind those who attributed the tumbling household items to witchcraft. A correspondent in *The Gazetteer* wanted to know if Mrs Golding and the other witnesses were Methodists, if they had a favourite preacher, and if they had been chatting to anyone about preternatural appearances before the strange events. In practice, though, the supposition that the Methodists were successfully promoting witchcraft to the populace was grossly exaggerated. On sheer numbers alone they could not have been so influential: they were still a fledgling organisation. In 1770 Methodist membership stood at a mere 25,000; fifty years later

204   THE CENTURY OF DECEPTION

it would be more than ten times that number.

In theory, anyway, witchcraft was outlawed. Under the Witchcraft Act of 1736 no member of the legislature, judiciary or Anglican Church could express a belief in witches, nobody could be prosecuted for witchcraft, and it was an offence to denounce someone as a witch. There were not many instances of the legislation being enacted, but one example took place soon after the Stockwell incident. In March 1773 a woman living in the village of Seend in Wiltshire, who was dying of a fever, cried out that 'she is pinching me to death'. Her neighbours assumed the 'she' was an old woman, long considered to be a witch. They ducked her in the water to see if she would float or swim. Because she was clothed, she remained on the surface, thereby confirming her guilt. Her tormentors temporarily relented, assuming she would now cease her witchcraft. However by the next day the woman's fever had increased, so they were determined to subject her to further tests. Fortunately an intervention by a magistrate prevented it.

What this shows is that, despite the legislation, many continued to believe in the existence of witches. Indeed this continued to be the case until the mid-nineteenth century. The Anglican Church was caught in a dilemma. Prior to the 1736 Act their clergymen were often complicit in denouncing people as witches. Now that it was officially outlawed, but given the views of their congregation, it suited them to blame the Methodists for sustaining the myth. It helped that the Methodists' core support was politically excluded and socially diverse, precisely the same group who were likely to embrace witchcraft anyway.

One of those who undoubtedly fell into that category was Mrs Golding's neighbour, Richard Fowler. In *Astonishing Transactions* he is singled out as the exception to the assertion that the witnesses were in 'reputable situations and good circumstances'. We have already seen how, when invited over to visit the Pains, he was so frightened by what he saw that he returned home. Later, when Mrs Golding and Ann moved temporarily into his house, Fowler asked Mrs Golding to consider whether or not she had been guilty of some atrocious crime 'for which providence was determined to pursue her on this side of the grave'. Although the word 'witch' was not mentioned, it must have been hanging in the air.

Mrs Golding was from a different social class, described as 'a lady of an independent fortune'. As an educated and enlightened woman she would have held the view that witchcraft belonged to a bygone age. As Samuel Johnson put it, it might once have existed but, for whatever reason, it had now ceased. Her response to Fowler is therefore revealing. She informed him that 'her conscience was quite clear' and, because of his accusation, she could no longer stay in his house. Mrs Golding's viewpoint was mirrored by the majority of those who wrote about the Stockwell happenings. Nobody claimed outright that witchcraft was the cause; the closest the newspaper reports came to it was that some sort of 'invisible agent' was behind it. One journal stated there was 'no witchcraft in the matter'. *Astonishing Transactions* made no inference that anything supernatural was involved.

The newspapers also by and large refrained from any outright mockery of those who might suspect witchcraft. Unusually, too, there were no satirical prints ridiculing those involved. Instead the mantle was picked up by another form of entertaining the public: the stage. 'The superstitious belief the vulgar entertain of the witchcraft at Stockwell' was to be exposed by incorporating Mrs Golding's 'animated furniture' into a pantomime called *Harlequin Skeleton*. *Harlequin Skeleton* was not new; it had made its first appearance in December 1746 and, over the following decades, was frequently reprised. This particular production was different in that it introduced a scene that represented 'the *wonderful* and *surprizing* feats lately performed at *Stockwell*'. It premiered at the Covent Garden Theatre on 31 January 1772 as an afterpiece to *The Busy Body*, a comedy by the popular female playwright Susanna Centlivre.

The setting was Mrs Golding's kitchen. When the comical characters of the Pantaloon and Clown entered, in pursuit of the

Harlequin, the table rose and threw off its contents; the beer-barrel, along with two or three large jars and pans, became animated; the clock, table, chairs and cupboard followed suit; while the crockery on the dresser and shelves flew off and cracked into pieces. Columbine, Harlequin's mistress, joined in the action. She was hidden under a china jar and, when she was discovered, it danced out of the room. All 'was received with the greatest applause'. An addition to the entertainment was made on 4 February when Mr Dunstall, in the character of a female ballad singer, sang some new lyrics relating to the adventures at Stockwell, to the traditional English tune *Derry Down*. It 'occasioned much Laughter' and 'a universal Encore'. The words were later reproduced in the papers, the last two lines being:

A sweet girl was the cause, and girls wonders are rich-in,
For we all know sweet girls – are extremely bewitching.

'From such Poetry, Heaven deliver us!' wrote one reviewer.

The amusing re-enactment became so popular that it was sometimes referred to as the 'Stockwell Scenes' in subsequent advertisements in the papers. The Drury Lane Theatre, the rival to its Covent Garden counterpart, wanted to get in on the act and came up with its own interlude on 21 April called *All Up at Stockwell; Or, The Ghost No Conjuror*. It was even picked up by provincial theatres, with the Theatre Royal in Bath introducing 'the late wonderful transactions at Stockwell' into their own pantomime called *Harlequin at Stockwell*. One enterprising nobleman elected to dress up his family as a beer barrel, water jar, cupboard, clock and speaking statue for a masquerade in tribute to the Covent Garden's animated furniture and crockery.

All of this contributed to the general feeling of ridicule aimed at any who thought the Stockwell Ghost was the result of witchcraft. One reviewer of the *Harlequin Skeleton* certainly hoped this would be the case, rather pompously intoning anticipation that the production would 'meet with encouragement', so as to 'prevent that mysterious affair making improper impressions on the minds of the Ignorant and Superstitious'. But even if the theatrical productions were successful in their intention, it still left unanswered how one individual, with or without the aid of witchcraft, could possibly have achieved the carnage set out in *Astonishing Transactions*. As one correspondent put it, given the witnesses' statements, surely it required 'more than one person's contrivance'. You can see why even those who weren't that credulous were still left unsatisfied. How could they be so certain that Ann Robinson was solely responsible for the hoax?

III

In 1825 William Hone published his *Every-Day Book or, The Guide to the Year*. It goes through each day of the year and, as well as offering an eclectic recording of popular pastimes and ancient and modern festivals and holidays, it covers events of significance for every date. For 7 January, after relaying why the day after Twelfth Night is called 'Rock-Day', it reproduces the pamphlet *Astonishing Transactions*. At the end it notes that many people recall the Stockwell Ghost and that those around at the time attributed 'the whole to witchcraft'. Indeed Hone himself knew a woman who had been an eyewitness to 'the animation of the inanimate crockery and furniture', and she said it was impossible to have been carried out by human means.

Having set up the readers to think that supernatural forces were involved, Hone neatly pulls the rug from under their feet. The publisher had spoken to a Mr J. Brayfield, who had met Ann Robinson some years after the event. She gave him a detailed explanation of how she had achieved many of the manifestations. She fixed long horsehairs to some of the crockery and put wires under others. When she pulled them, they tumbled over. She loosened the hams and bacons and attached them by their skins. This meant that they would fall without her being near them. Many of the items she simply threw herself when nobody was watching, specifically mentioning about chucking the egg at the cat. She made the water in the bucket look as though it was boiling by surreptitiously slipping in some chemical powders as she passed.

There were other factors in her favour that enabled Ann to get away with it. She said that Mrs Golding and the other witnesses were too afraid to examine anything, so they wouldn't have spotted any of her hidden gimmicks. They couldn't even bring themselves to look at the utensils, keeping their distance. She was therefore able to orchestrate the wreckage undetected even when they were in the same room as her. When they turned around and saw the item in motion or broken, they attributed it to an unseen agency. Mrs Golding and her neighbours were old. Their reaction time was slow and their eyesight and hearing below par. In contrast Ann was 'quick in her motions'. Her most significant confession, though, was when she confided that their 'terrors at the time, and their subsequent conversations magnified many of the circumstances beyond the facts'.

This, to me, is the key to how Ann single-handedly pulled off her hoax. Harry Price writes in *Poltergeist Over England* (1945) that the exposure by Mr Brayfield is 'sheer invention, and there is no evidence to support it'. He backs up this questionable allegation by claiming that 'the greatest conjurer living could not produce the Stockwell effects by means of wires, etc', given that they were surrounded by people on 'the look-out for tricks' and in a well-lit room. Such subterfuge would be instantly detected. He justifies this authoritative statement by telling us, 'I know what can, and cannot, be done in this way.' Price here is laying down his own credentials as a magician.

Harry Price was indeed a member of The Magic Circle and, more significantly, accumulated one of the world's largest collections of books on conjuring and psychic matters, now held in Senate House at the University of London. However it is questionable how much of a performer of magic Price was, as opposed to a researcher and historian of it. The distinction is important because professional magicians know that the average spectator's recall of what actually happens during a trick is extremely poor. They 'remember' what didn't occur and 'forget' what did. Part of this is predicated on the proficiency of the magician at focusing on what he or she wants the onlooker to recollect. But it is also down to the audience member justifying in their own minds why they were fooled. In order not to appear in any way naive or simple, they will heighten the impossibility of what the performer did.

Of course modern day audiences don't believe that the magician has any unexplainable powers. They attribute their bewilderment to the individual's skill. Ann Robinson, though, had the advantage that her onlookers from the onset thought that something supernatural was involved. It is not correct to argue that Mrs Golding and her neighbours were on the 'look-out for tricks'. Indeed the very opposite was true. They assumed that all the tumbling and breakages were caused by a mystical phenomena; and the more these things happened, the more convinced they were. Once they had established this mind-set – or to use a modern term, confirmation bias – then nothing was going to alter that conclusion.

When it came to giving their testimonies, the tendency to exaggerate kicked in. Like the spectators at a magic show, they didn't want to come across as credulous. So they made out that they saw a lot more than they did, outdoing each other in the wondrous sights they supposedly witnessed when questioned. The very detail in *Astonishing Transactions* shows this. There is no way, in the midst of the confusion and terror expressed in the testimonies, that they could give exact measurements in feet of how far a glass tumbler had jumped or a candlestick had flown. That is not to say they were deliberately making it up. By the time they had told their version of events, and listened to what the others had to say, their recall of what they truly saw would have been corrupted and replaced by a false memory.

Some of the amendments can be seen by comparing the pamphlet with the earlier newspaper version. For instance: the times when events start; Ann's age increases by five years; Mrs Golding herself directly sees the plates tumble; greater damage is inflicted on her

210 THE CENTURY OF DECEPTION

property when she returns home for the final time; and the word 'dancing', with reference to the activities of some of the glasses and china, is introduced. They may be minor, and might only be down to the compiler of the pamphlet making editorial alterations, but they provide an example of how scenarios can subtly alter in the re-telling. Most of the discrepancies between the reality and what was imagined, though, would have occurred in the immediate aftermath when, to repeat Ann's perceptive phrase as relayed by Mr Brayfield, the witnesses in their conversations 'magnified many of the circumstances beyond the facts'.

According to the account in Hone's *Every-Day Book* there was a motive behind the maid's activities. Mr Brayfield rather cryptically said that 'there was a love story connected with the case', but did not elucidate any further. This was later interpreted as Ann wanting 'to have a clear house, to carry on an intrigue with her lover'. This doesn't make a lot of sense in line with what happened. If she had wanted Mrs Golding away from her own property, then she wouldn't have driven her back to it by indulging in similar pranks at the houses of her neighbours. However, it is possible that this was her original intention. Mr Brayfield goes on to say that, when she saw the impact of her first feats, she was tempted to continue 'beyond her original purpose for mere amusement'. Delighted at the astonishment she caused, she continued 'from one thing to another'.

The confession given by Ann to Mr Brayfield has an authentic ring about it. And that, coupled with the cessation of all the animated household items on her dismissal from service, is conclusive proof in my mind that she was the perpetrator of the hoax. As we have seen, there was rather more to it than Mr Brayfield's conclusion that 'the only magic in the thing was, her dexterity and the people's simplicity'. Nevertheless, condensed down to its core, it is a good summary of how the maid bamboozled so many. Sadly Mr Brayfield was unable to fulfil his original aim of committing the whole story to paper, as he was ailing and infirm; but he has still given sufficient information for us to be certain that Ann Robinson was the sole culprit.

On 17 February 1772, a newspaper correspondent calling himself Agricola asked some pertinent questions with regard to the case. These included: with whom did Ann Robinson live before she went to Mrs Golding's? How did she come to be recommended to that gentlewoman? Where was she now? Unfortunately we have very few answers. There was a report that, having been dismissed from service, she returned home to her father who was 'the clerk of Louisham parish' (a variant spelling of Lewisham). But no trace of a Mr Robinson in this position has been found to help us discover more about her family and circumstances. There is a contemporary reference in 1792 that, following the deaths of Mrs Golding and her daughter a few months earlier, there was an auction at their house where 'the dancing furniture sold at very extravagant prices'. The same source states that some had suspected Mrs Golding's daughter, as well as the maidservant, of the deception. This is the first time, though, that any relative of Mrs Golding, besides her niece, is mentioned as possibly being involved.

For those who believe in the supernatural, the Stockwell Ghost, unlike the Cock Lane Ghost, still remains relevant. The throwing around of cutlery and china brought about by some type of paranormal activity appears more credible than a dead person accusing someone of murder. Yet at the time many thought Fanny's spirit-rapping was genuine; while comparatively few, as we have seen, thought flying household objects were caused by witchcraft. The fact that the events at Stockwell are now considered more significant than those at Cock Lane is down to psychic researchers making a distinction between ghosts and poltergeists. And, for modern sentiments, a poltergeist has more credibility than a talking ghost.

The concept of what could have brought about Mrs Golding's and her neighbours' animated belongings has therefore changed over the centuries. Harry Price would have dismissed as absurd the idea that witchcraft was involved. But the notion that the untoward activities were the result of some invisible force working through Ann Robinson – even if she was 'absolutely helpless in the matter'

– is deemed valid and reasonable. Witchcraft as a plausible cause has been superseded by the paranormal. Between 1977 and 1979 the Enfield Poltergeist occurred, with claims of unexplained moving furniture, objects thrown, and loud noises in the presence of two adolescent girls. Not only was a full-length book written in support of it at the time, but more recently there have been a television series and in 2018 a BBC Radio 4 programme reuniting some of those involved. If the Stockwell hoax occurred today, it is likely that even more people than back in the eighteenth century would refuse to accept that it was carried out by a mischievous maid; instead, they would look towards some mystical source as an explanation.

NINE

'A CHINESE TEMPLE RISING
OUT OF THE CLOUDS'

* * *

I

The wider the gap between the anticipation and the outcome, the more likely it is that people will feel they have been hoaxed. Chevalier de Moret knew how to raise expectations to a fever pitch. In early August 1784 the man from Switzerland announced in a series of advertisements that he was going to fly into the air in a 'Grand and Magnificent Air Balloon, the Chinese Temple'. You would have thought this claim alone would have generated sufficient excitement, given that no manned flight had yet been achieved in Great Britain. But de Moret also wanted to stress that his floating vehicle was far from typical. It was 65 feet high, 120 feet in circumference, weighed 1,600 pounds and contained 43,982 cubic feet of air. Anybody worrying that such a vast entity might take an inordinately long time to inflate could relax. Despite its enormous weight and capacity, sceptics were reassured that it would be 'filled in an instant'.

If de Moret truly thought the speed of erecting a balloon was a major selling point in promoting his adventure, than he should have opted for hydrogen. This produces far greater lift than hot air and so a much smaller inflatable vehicle is required. It was, though, more expensive and complex to produce and, as its initial name of 'inflammable air' implied, potentially more hazardous. Given, however, that for de Moret size was apparently no object – indeed it was a promotional bonus – lighting a fire underneath the mouth of the balloon and filling it with hot air was more straightforward, cheaper and, at least in theory, a safer solution. He had, after all, done such experiments previously in Paris. Admittedly the balloons were smaller, and no human was attached to them, but the principle was the same. Crucially the Montgolfier balloon, the first-ever peopled flight, had been launched in France on 21 November 1783 by this method.

Over the previous nine months de Moret had learnt how to maximise the revenue from his ventures. So it was typical of his financial acumen that, even before he stated the admission price of witnessing the ascension, the public were informed where they could buy an engraving of his balloon. If the resulting image [Fig. 23] sold is an accurate representation of what de Moret had built, then you can certainly understand why people would be keen to see the actual construction. Instead of having the flattened sphere shape of the conventional balloon, this looks more suited to adorn a church tower, being similar in appearance to the dome of St Paul's. The additional detail on the canvas of rectangular cross-hatched windows and two large doors with steps genuinely gives the impression of a floating building. Hanging off the bottom of the cupola, held on by ten ropes, is a chariot-type vehicle with a ship's wheel attached to the side. Continuing the nautical theme, a masthead of a bearded man is on the bow while a vast sea-shell, alongside the heads of two dogs, is at the stern.

For his launch de Moret had selected the bowling green at the old Star and Garter, Chelsea, in London. Ticket prices to obtain the best view of the take-off ranged from half a crown to one guinea. This was not cheap. The most expensive seat at a prestigious London theatre cost a crown, and that was to enjoy three hours of entertainment. As Samuel Johnson cynically commented, 'to pay for seats at the balloon' is unnecessary as 'in less than a minute they who gaze at

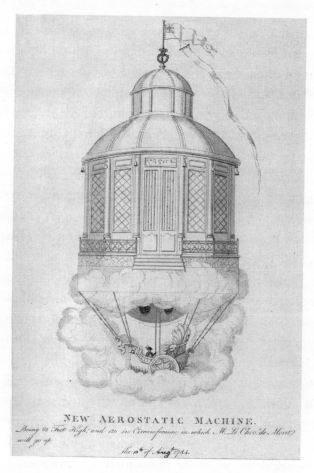

NEW AEROSTATIC MACHINE.

Being 65 Feet High, and 120 in Circumference in which M. Le Chevr. de Moret will go up.

the 10th of Aug. 1784.

Fig. 23. *New Aerostatic Machine,* an engraving sold by Chevalier de Moret before his aborted flight on 11 August 1784.

a mile's distance will see all that can be seen'. But by attending a launch, you were as much buying into the rising excitement of the anticipatory climax as you were paying for your brief sight of the flight itself. The spectators were there to watch the sagging, lifeless canvas gradually evolve into an animated floating Chinese Temple.

The scheduled date of departure for de Moret was Tuesday 10 August. But the weather proved inclement and he was forced to cancel. This didn't prevent many hopeful spectators turning up. De

Moret went to a nearby restaurant to apologise, although he was far from contrite. He stressed that if the public had taken the trouble to read his advertisements properly, they would have known he had given explicit notice that, if it was too wet or windy, the experiment would be adjourned until the first fine day afterwards. This proved to be 24 hours later on Wednesday 11 August. Spectators were summoned by the firing of seven guns at various locations around London, including Hanover Square and Tower Hill. According to eyewitnesses, this led to a huge throng traipsing down to Chelsea to find a strategic viewing spot, with one newspaper claiming there were as many as 30,000. These were watching for free. Those paying to enter into the bowling green itself numbered only around a hundred, producing for de Moret either £50 or £80, depending on which report you believed. Among the attendees were two of the pre-eminent statesmen of the era: Lord North, the prime minister when Britain lost the American colonies in 1782; and Charles James Fox, the leader of the Whigs.

These two wily politicians had entered into an alliance of expediency the previous year, even though they were on opposite ends of the political spectrum. Their much-derided coalition eventually collapsed over what seemed to be an attempt by Fox to line his own pockets through his suggested reforms of the East India Company. This was the final straw for George III, who anyway disapproved of Fox's relationship with his eldest son. He seized the chance to dismiss the administration and appointed William Pitt the Younger as the new prime minister. After a bumpy start, Pitt convincingly won an election called in March 1784. By August, both Fox and Lord North were in the political wilderness, so they had plenty of spare time to be present at the landmark balloon ascension.

The scene they saw as they took their seats at one o'clock that afternoon did not look promising. The deflated balloon was described as constructed of very coarse, porous and rotten canvas, with a slight covering of paper. In the opinion of an eyewitness it didn't have the substance to bear the weight of the air – quite a major setback given its intended usage. It was held in place by two perpendicular poles as it was filled with the smoke of burning cork and straw. The result was apparently a very beautiful spectacle as it enlarged. But there was insufficient pressure to produce any strain on the cords holding it to the ground. Twelve days later, de Moret gave his own explanation of its failure to rise. He began by claiming he could prove, with testimony from reliable witnesses, that in a rehearsal a few days before his failed launch the balloon had ascended with so much force that ten people were unable to restrain it. However, after this initial experiment, it was left lying outside on the damp ground. The canvas absorbed moisture and this, along with paint and paste repairs, increased its weight to such an extent that it was far harder to inflate it. He also said they had been unable to disengage the filled balloon from one of the major cords. This obstacle had prevented the whole contraption rising.

The newspapers reported that it took over 'three tedious hours of preparation' to attempt to fill the balloon with hot air from the fire, far removed from the publicised claim it would all happen 'in an instant'. De Moret was prominently involved in these efforts and towards the end was overcome by smoke fumes. He threw himself down on the grass groaning and panting for breath. At some point, according to another report, the rope that was holding the contraption gave way. However instead of majestically floating upwards, the balloon 'found more attractions in the earth than the air, and immediately came to the ground'.

Those who had paid for the expensive seats in the garden had compassion towards de Moret, aware of how exhausted he had become through his exertions. Not so those who had witnessed it all for nothing by climbing on the tops of surrounding hedges and trees. Enraged by being deprived of their entertainment, 'the mob' pulled down the gates of the bowling green, burst through the fences into the grass area, and tore the balloon to pieces. Some parts were carried away as trophies, but most of it was chucked on the fire, along with the fencing, benches and seats set up for those who had

Fig. 24. *The New Mode of Picking Pockets*, an engraving published August 1784.

paid. Many were injured in the riot. Several limbs were broken, and a great number of watches and other items were pickpocketed in the fracas. De Moret escaped serious injury at the hands of the revengeful crowd only when he was rescued by two or three gentlemen. One of them included Sir Harry Englefield, a meteorologist, who was presumably hoping to add some knowledge to his field from his observations of de Moret's intended flight.

Just over a month later Vincent Lunardi became the first man to fly in a balloon in England.

II

The backlash against de Moret's debacle was instant. Here was yet another person, and a foreigner to boot, motivated by money to con the credulous English public. De Moret was aware of the prevailing interest in balloons and that the French had already demonstrated the possibility of a manned flight. He had taken advantage of this, so popular opinion had it, by duping the unsuspecting public into paying exorbitant prices in the expectation he would be the first person to achieve the same in England. All this while knowing that, although his vessel had no chance of leaving the ground, he had every opportunity of leaving the country with his ill-gotten gains. The likelihood that the heralded flight was never intended in the first place rendered it comparable with the Bottle Conjurer fiasco that had taken place thirty-five years earlier.

The General Evening Post called it the second part of the Bottle Conjurer. Those caught up in it were credulous and easily 'bubbled'. Every person who had been fooled out of his money was made the subject of pointed ridicule, commented The Whitehall Evening Post. Another paper was cruder, concluding that de Moret was indulging in 'the old trade of bumming the people'. The Morning Post and Daily Advertiser almost seemed to support a lynch mentality when it stated that only de Moret's life could atone for his contemptuous and ignominious conduct in the eyes of some. A few weeks afterwards, The Public Advertiser warned about another Frenchman trying to exploit money by a similar ploy to that of de Moret.

Two satirical prints encapsulate the prevailing mood. The first is titled The New Mode of Picking Pockets [Fig. 24]. It shows a corpulent, entranced man staring up at a balloon while exclaiming how wonderfully strange it is and remarking that the French have the most ingenious hands. Directly behind him is an evil-faced, much leaner-looking man drawing his attention to the flying object by holding one arm up to point towards it, while his other hand is dipping into the gaping man's pocket. The Frenchman distracts his pickpocketing by whispering into the Englishman's ear informing him that the balloon is one of the greatest curiosities the world ever saw and that it will travel 3,000 miles before the sun sets. Although de Moret's name isn't mentioned, a sign in the background with the words 'To Chelsea', with a number of people walking in that direction, makes it clear his failed venture is the inspiration for the xenophobic caricature.

The second print is less coarse, drawn by a far more talented artist. It is *The Chevelere Morret taking a French Leave* [Fig. 25]. At the top is a grinning de Moret, displaying a bag of 'guineas' in his hand, sitting on top of a balloon – it has 'To Ostend In A Few Hours' written on its side. The balloon is propelled by an infusion of 'Gratitude'. In its ascension it splits a Chinese Temple in half. Falling from the balloon, as it rises upwards, are five emblems of other hoaxes, all of which have been covered in previous chapters: 'Bottle Conjurer', 'Rabbit Women', 'Cock Lane Ghost', 'Trial of Eliz. Canning' and 'Stokwell Wonder'. By prominently featuring these well-known hoaxes, de Moret's failed balloon ascension is labelled as one too.

In the bottom left-hand corner of the engraving two men, Lord North and Charles James Fox, are witnessing the departure. Fox is telling de Moret that he is a man after his own heart. Lord North is informing the departing balloonist that he will provide him the breeze, which he does by blowing out hot air. Four days before this print was published, *The Morning Post and Daily Advertiser* had facetiously suggested that the public ought to forgive de Moret. Allegedly, while lying on the ground, he had asked for an apology from Lord North for the failure of his mission. In doing so he represented the British nation who had prostrated themselves in the same manner for seven years at the feet of a man who had filled Great Britain with *'inflammable air'*. It is likely that the newspaper cutting inspired the amusing image.

Fig. 25. *English credulity or the Chevelere Morret taking a French Leave,* an engraving
published 17 August 1784.

But was this unequivocal verdict of writers and artists a fair assessment of de Moret's motives? Was he really planning to hoax the citizens of his host country in such a blatant manner? To find out if this was indeed his intention, we need to consider his behaviour both before, and after, that fateful day.

Up until January 1784 there is very little known about de Moret's whereabouts or his activities. It is believed that he was born in Switzerland in 1760, and there is evidence that before coming to England he assisted at some trials in Paris to launch the same type of balloons used by the Montgolfier brothers. Once he had gained this experience, possibly at the end of 1783, he crossed the Channel. England was behind France in its enthusiasm for ballooning as well as its practical application. The French were far-sighted in that they saw the potential benefits, which included 'weather prediction, telescope observation of the stars, geographical exploration, military reconnaissance and heavy cargo carrying'. There was therefore a general encouragement of ballooning that emanated down from society's elite. English scientists were rather more cynical about what balloons could accomplish. They felt there were other, more productive ways, of achieving equivalent outcomes.

But an unexpected offshoot of ballooning, irrelevant to men primarily interested in the pursuit of knowledge, was its inherent fascination to the general public. Spectators were willing to pay to watch the novel innovation of a balloon in flight. On his arrival in England, de Moret set about tapping into this potential market. He first set out his credentials as an expert on 12 January 1784 in an advertisement in *The Gazetteer and New Daily Advertiser*. He described himself as having a 'genius' for distinguished discoveries, being a lover of the arts and sciences, and zealous in promoting what may prove useful and satisfying to the King and Government. He said a collection of skilled persons, under his direction, were engaged in the building of an entirely new air balloon. It was in the form of a Chinese cabinet sustained by four eagles with their wings spread. Reluctant to let readers think this might be his sole claim to brilliance, de Moret stressed that his ingenuity would not be restricted to these experiments alone. He was involved in ruling and directing all kinds of other aerostatical machines, although to what end was never stated. Optimistically, as it was still in the process of construction, he stated his balloon would be launched on or before 20 January – whether he would be riding in it was not clarified.

De Moret's pledge was premature, as no more was heard of this venture, the project presumably abandoned. Fortunately for him there was still an opportunity to make money without venturing into the sky. At this time in London there were a plethora of exhibition spaces providing the opportunities to display the weird and wonderful. The Lyceum in the Strand had opened in 1765. It was large enough to hold an inflated balloon. De Moret, following his failure to build one, had managed to acquire one. It was a smaller model than his prototype Chinese cabinet. This was reflected in the change of description from an 'Enormous Size Air Balloon' to a mere 'Grand Air Balloon', and the reduction in its circumference from 95 feet to 40 feet. On the plus side, it was definitely ready to be exhibited, although this had little to do with the 'genius' of de Moret.

It was a Monsieur Montgolfier balloon. Brought over from Paris, it was on its way from London to Oxford University. There is no evidence it ever reached its destination, but the mention of this centre of learning helped promote the balloon's academic and scientific credentials. Fortuitously for the British public it was making a temporary stop at the Lyceum for a few days. It could be seen at the cost of one shilling. According to the advertisement on 6 February, Monsieur Montgolfier requested that the balloon be shown without any charge. The price of admission was therefore only to cover the cost of advertising and its accommodation at the exhibition centre. The description of the balloon sounded enticing. It was doubly overlaid with gold and gave the appearance of a huge world floating in the 'incomprehensible infinity of space'. If it had been made out of solid gold, it would weigh more than 4 million lb. A specially constructed viewing arena was erected in the Lyceum, a

40-foot-long gallery that was attached to the balloon.

It clearly attracted the crowds, as the residency of days stretched into weeks. Furthermore, to maximise revenue, people were later admitted not only from nine in the morning until five at night, but also on some evenings from seven until ten, when the Lyceum was illuminated with covered lamps. This candlelit vigil was touted as a far more brilliant spectacle than that seen by daylight, a declaration that must have rather annoyed those who had previously visited. By 23 February interest was slightly waning, since a print of Montgolfier filling the balloon was given free to every visitor. On 1 March the price of admission was halved to six-pence. A week later it was announced that the gallery attached to the balloon was an exact replica of that in which Dr Alexandre Charles and his assistant, Monsieur Robert, performed their aeronautical excursions in France. They, unlike the Montgolfier balloon, had used hydrogen in their ascent. On Monday 15 March, potential spectators were informed it was positively the last week. The exhibition eventually closed on 26 March. During the seven-week run, de Moret had shown his skill at writing alluring advertising copy, whether it promoted evening visits, free prints, reduced prices or threat of imminent closure, to bring customers through the door.

Having had plenty of time to study the balloon at the Lyceum, de Moret was now in a better position to genuinely produce his own. Indeed in his next advertisement of 5 April, where he claimed he had a new aerostatic machine, he openly admitted that it was built using Montgolfier's plan. You get a feeling of de Moret's frustration that, once more, he hasn't been able to show an actual example of his own genius. However it was undoubtedly an upgrade on his first construction as it was now described as a 'Chinese Temple', rather than a 'Chinese cabinet'. Furthermore he optimistically hoped 'to execute some machinery of his own invention' that would send a balloon in whichever direction it needed to go. The inability to steer balloons was one of the major handicaps to using it for practical purposes. In actuality neither de Moret, nor indeed anyone else, would come up with a solution.

As we have seen, de Moret's skills lay more in promoting than in engineering. For two days he was charging two shillings and sixpence for people to see the completion of the balloon at his new premises, the Pantheon in Oxford Street. The Pantheon was another huge exhibition space with a central dome. It was built initially for assemblies, masquerades and concerts. In addition he was already selling tickets at one guinea and half a guinea for the proposed launch. His intention was to go up in the machine and perform all the experiments previously made in France, along with several new ones. One suspects there weren't too many advance sales for a yet-to-be-announced location for an unfinished balloon. Another advertisement, the following day, gave a little more information about where the launch might take place. De Moret would choose somewhere that had high walls – to prevent the prying eyes of non-payers. The size of the launching pad would be dependent on the number of subscribers. Again it was probably too vague to persuade people to part with their money.

De Moret's display of his balloon at the Pantheon was limited because on 14 April he announced that the exhibition would close three days later, on the Saturday. He had, though, come up with a new scheme to entice last-minute visitors. They could watch the balloon inflating. As he put it, what could be more astonishing and magnificent than the sight of a temple, richly decorated, rising instantaneously from the midst of its own ruins and floating in the body of a thick cloud. Reassuringly he informed the visitors that all his experiments had infinitely exceeded expectations. Again, eager to show his own abilities as a scientist, he wrote that the balloon would be filled with a gas of his own invention, which was far better and quicker in its effect than any previously known. This was a strange boast given that his balloon was a Montgolfier model, which normally used hot air. However his earlier reference to Dr Charles and Monsieur Robert, the first to fly in the more sophisticated and reliable hydrogen balloon, suggests he was experimenting with this substance. It is quite possible that his claims of a speedy inflation in his practice runs were because he was using hydrogen. But when it came to the actual launch he reverted to hot air.

With the Lyceum and the Pantheon no longer available, de Moret chose a new tack. Explaining that for greater convenience his balloon, now completed, had been moved to Pimlico, he advertised for people to pay to see it inflate outdoors. The cost was the same as at the Pantheon, two shillings and sixpence, whether you were watching in the garden or from an apartment. Given that this performance was weather dependent, this must have been a hard sale. De Moret, as always, gave his all in the copy of 11 May. He re-emphasised that the machine was a Chinese temple superbly decorated with columns, and that it required the weight of twenty men to keep it from ascending once it was filled. Despite this there was no further reference to de Moret himself going up in the balloon. Reading between the lines, one can deduce that the Swiss adventurer had realised his prototype was not airworthy. No more was heard from de Moret until the beginning of August.

Unfortunately for him a rival made an appearance in his absence, a man who was rather better prepared. On 9 July 1784 an advertisement stated that a balloon was in the process of being built at the Lyceum by an anonymous gentleman. It would be filled with inflammable air and flown from the Chelsea Hospital Gardens. Tickets could be purchased to see the construction. Just over two weeks later it was announced that the same balloon, under the direction of the now-named Mr Lunardi, was complete. Before the launch, you could pay one shilling to see the machine in its floating state in the Lyceum. The Italian, too, was taking advantage of charging people to see his balloon in order to defray the expense of its design and building. Lunardi was using the same place to build his balloon, asking for the same price to view it, and promising exactly the same aim of launching it, as de Moret had done. You could imagine this might be a little galling to the man from Switzerland. It provoked him into returning to the fray.

On 4 August, in adjacent advertisements in *The Morning Herald, and Daily Advertiser*, the two balloonists went head-to-head. Lunardi informed the readers that his Grand Air Balloon, 33 feet in diameter and 102 feet in circumference, was truly an object of curiosity and one of the most admirable exhibitions ever presented to the public. It repeated the information that it could be viewed at the Lyceum for a few days before its ascension. Tickets could also be purchased at the Lyceum for admission to the Chelsea Hospital Gardens on the day of take-off. De Moret countered that his Grand and Magnificent Air Balloon, being a Chinese temple in shape, was more curious than anything seen before. Unlike Lunardi, de Moret had nowhere to display his balloon. But he played his trump card. He had an actual date, 10 August, when he would fly it. The venue was also Chelsea and the ticket prices were commensurate with those charged by Lunardi.

There can be no doubt this was the same balloon that de Moret had first advertised back in April. The stated dimensions were slightly altered – 65 feet high compared with 56, and 120 feet in circumference rather than 115 – but not sufficiently divergent to suggest different models. Both were named as the Grand Air Balloon, the Chinese Temple. Given de Moret's propensity to extract as much mileage out of his balloons as he could, the public would have been informed if he had indeed built a replacement. All of this did not portend well. The balloon had not proved airworthy back in April and May, despite de Moret's confident assertions that sundry launches would take place. It is conceivable that he had been working hard on overcoming whatever the engineering deficiencies were. If this was so, he had uncharacteristically kept quiet about it. Rather endearingly, de Moret displayed his lack of confidence in a successful flight. In his advertisements from 4 August onwards, having listed no fewer than five different places where tickets could be bought, he wrote, as an N.B., that the money would remain in the hands of the ticket-sellers until after his engagement had been fulfilled.

One does wonder if de Moret was half hoping Lunardi might

bring forward his own launch to pre-empt him. Seemingly some of Lunardi's supporters were urging him to do just that. The Italian was having none of it. On 9 August, the day before de Moret's scheduled flight, he posted a notice that the earliest he would be ready to ascend was the 14 or 16 of August. Only when all his apparatus was ready would he be launching. The public would be duly notified when that was. In the meantime, his balloon was still on display at the Lyceum with a price of admission of one shilling. He had called de Moret's bluff. Unless de Moret wanted to lose face, he was now forced to fulfil his promise, the disastrous results of which have already been covered.

At this stage it must have been hard for the public to assess which of the two balloonists had the most likelihood of success. When it came to advertisements taken out between 4 August and his aborted flight a week later, de Moret's ouput exceeded Lunardi's three to one. From sheer weight of publicity you can imagine that de Moret had the upper hand. One man that was persuaded of this was Thomas Moore. He was the publisher of *Breslaw's Last Legacy*, an early book on magic tricks, puzzles, paradoxes and simple scientific experiments. The first edition, produced in November 1783, contained a description of the 'Air Balloon', with an explanation of how to make one. This followed the launch of a recent unmanned balloon flight by Michael Biaggini. With the interest in ballooning escalating, the second edition, published in March 1784, expanded the number of pages devoted to the topic from three to twelve. It also included a frontispiece of a group of people staring up at a balloon, looking duly amazed. In early August an advertisement for this same edition appeared stating that in its pages was a clear and entertaining description of that wonderful invention, as it is to be 'launched and navigated at *Chelsea Garden* by Chevalier De Moret'.

A month later, in a similar promotional blurb, de Moret's name was replaced by Lunardi's.

III

Right up to the flight itself, there is no indication de Moret was trying to hoax anyone. Instead he comes across as a man overconfident about his own abilities, his aspirations getting ahead of what he was capable of achieving. He had come to accept that his Chinese Temple would not sustain a manned flight, and in May had quietly abandoned the enterprise. But then along comes Lunardi, capturing the public's imagination with his good looks, confident bravado and flair for publicity, following the same path de Moret had pursued but apparently abandoned. De Moret's only recourse, whether goaded by jealousy or just a desire to be the first, was to gamble that his balloon, against all expectations, would somehow take to the air.

This is a different interpretation of de Moret's actions to that taken by the newspapers and satirical prints in the immediate aftermath of his debacle. As we have seen, their angle was that his primary motivation in staging an event that had no chance of succeeding was to swindle the spectators. But de Moret had stated upfront in his publicity that he would only receive any money collected in advance from the paying punters after the completion of his engagement. It is possible that he might have been lying about that. But if that were the case, he would have fled the country with the proceeds at the first opportunity. What he wouldn't have done is to remain in England and try to explain his side of the story. He did this with the publication of an article on 23 August in *The Morning Herald, and Daily Advertiser*.

The main thrust of this eighteenth-century equivalent of a press statement was indeed to stress that he had not ripped anybody off. He began by thanking those who had assisted him 'when he made that experiment at Chelsea, which in the event proved so unfortunate', as he termed it. He went on to say that he had received none of the admission ticket money paid on the day. Some of it was returned to the spectators. The greater part was given to the proprietor of the Chelsea bowling green to compensate for the damage caused by the mob. As for those who had paid in advance to one of the four stipulated booksellers, their money was still waiting to be returned.

De Moret, though, got carried away with the 'rectitude and purity of his intentions' by promising to publish further authenticated details of his transactions in different newspapers over the next few days. He would prove that all tradesmen were promptly paid for any material used in the construction of his balloon, and that he did not receive any money himself upfront, even when he was offered it. This was especially true in the case of the tickets sold at Mr Hayes's Bookseller in Oxford Street. Mr Hayes's clerk had pressed money on him but he refused to take it. Predictably these newspaper reports never emerged.

Nevertheless de Moret's protestations over his honesty do ring true. If his sole aim was to steal money by somehow hoaxing the public, then there must have been easier ways of doing that than by orchestrating an ascension which he knew had no chance of success. To an extent he had found a far better method previously, by charging money for spectators to see a balloon that supposedly was, but almost certainly wasn't, capable of a manned flight. Furthermore, if his avowed intention were to disappear with the ticket money, then it is unlikely he would have stated in advance his intention to repay monies received if the venture failed.

Perhaps as a direct result of his statement, on the following day the first sympathetic report of de Moret emerged. *The Gazetteer and New Daily Advertiser* wrote that they were uncomfortable with humiliating the man who had narrowly escaped with his life, given that his intentions were just and that he had lost considerably because of the scheme. However the accompanying anecdote – that he had borrowed a small sum of money from a gentleman a few days before the failure, and had repaid him the day after – has the feel of a story planted by de Moret. Another indication of at least some understanding was a letter a month later in *The Public Advertiser* by a man calling himself Justus. He said he had been one of those convinced that de Moret had gained much from his enterprise. But he was now thoroughly satisfied that his losses were close to £200.

Justus's conclusion that de Moret was not a 'swindler', but a 'successless though honest experimenter' would seem to be a fair summation of his character. Unfortunately for him, it is what people thought in the immediate aftermath of his flight failure, fuelled by the newspaper coverage and the satirical prints, that cemented his reputation. The propaganda that de Moret was a hoaxer had already been established and the odd letter or article in his support was not going to change that perception. And this is so, even today. For although most modern books on the history of ballooning tend to dismiss de Moret as a footnote to Lunardi's historic flight – delayed until 15 September because the Governor of the Chelsea Military Hospital, following the rioting that attended de Moret's launch, withdrew his permission to let the Italian use the venue – some still emphasise his supposed fraudulent culpability. It was obvious to the most gullible that the so-called Chevalier was a 'charlatan', wrote one twentieth-century author. A second stated that de Moret's disastrous attempt had no other result than 'fostering incredulity'.

De Moret is an example of conjecturing that someone is a hoaxer even though the evidence doesn't substantiate it; a swiftness to condemn the credulous which is undeserved; and a general concern about universal gullibility that isn't as extensive as was originally thought. In the case of Chevalier de Moret all three of these false assumptions prevailed. De Moret wasn't deliberately trying to deceive anyone with his failed balloon flight. Rather he had let his self-inflated opinion of his own 'genius', and his jealousy of a rival balloonist, corrupt his judgement on the capability of his flying machine. Spectators weren't revealing their naivety by turning up to watch the manned attempt. Their knowledge that the feat had already been achieved in France, and the confidence emanating from de Moret's advertisements, were good reasons for anticipating a successful venture. And finally, there was no indication that this showed how easily the populace could be deceived. It was more of an excuse for the propagandists to have another go at the evil foreigners taking advantage of the good-natured English.

It would be fitting to leave the final word with de Moret. But after his *mea culpa* on 23 August, there were no more public pronouncements, and indeed we have no indication of what happened to him, either in England or abroad. It is thought he died in 1810. De Moret disappeared into obscurity, leaving behind the only existing image of him: a smirking man perching on top of a balloon headed for the Continent while grasping a sackful of money – the very epitome of a hoaxer.

TEN

'WHEN THIS SOLEMN MOCKERY IS O'ER'

* * *

I

Here is a poser for your pub quiz. From which play of Shakespeare do these memorable lines come?

Give me another sword! I have so clogg'd,
And badged this with blood and slipp'ry gore.
That it doth mock my gripe. A sword, I say!

Not instantly recognisable, but memorable enough to make somebody well versed in the output of the Bard attempt an informed guess. *Henry V*? *Richard III*? *Coriolanus* maybe? Unsurprisingly, given the subject of this book, the question is a trick one. The words come from *Vortigern*, not a work that you will find in any of Shakespeare's folios. But for one night, towards the end of the eighteenth century, a London theatre was packed out with spectators anticipating that they were about to see a new masterpiece from England's most famous playwright. The drama they were to witness was actually written by the nineteen-year-old William-Henry Ireland.

William-Henry was born on 2 August 1775 [Fig. 26]. His father was Samuel Ireland. The only living son – there were also two daughters

Fig. 26. Portrait of William-Henry Ireland, an
engraving by Mackenzie.

and another boy, Samuel Junior, who had died in infancy – never
knew who his mother was. It was probably Mrs Freeman, who was
ostensibly the housekeeper for the family. She never displayed any
maternal instincts; indeed she occasionally taunted William-Henry
that Samuel wasn't even his father. The family were comfortably off.
This was partly because of money that belonged to Mrs Freeman
who, in her previous life, had been Anna Maria de Burgh Coppinger,
the mistress of John Montagu, the Fourth Earl of Sandwich. William-
Henry attended a number of schools in England before being sent
away to complete his education in France. This proved to be the
happiest period of his life. As William-Henry approached the age of
seventeen, his father arranged for him to be an articled clerk with
Mr Bingley of New Inn, who specialised in real estate transactions.

Samuel Ireland was making a good living through writing travel books illustrated by himself. On the back of the money earned from these, Samuel and his family moved to a more fashionable part of London, Norfolk Street. He could also afford to indulge in his primary interest, that of collecting books and antiquities. His taste was wide-ranging but he was especially attracted to items that had an association with famous people from the past. Within this obsessive interest one person particularly stood out: William Shakespeare.

In the summer of 1793 Samuel Ireland made a pilgrimage to Stratford to see if he could unearth any original papers that might have been missed by others. His son accompanied him, to assist in carrying his engraving equipment, as he was also working on a book which emerged two years later as *Picturesque Views on the Upper, or Warwickshire Avon*. The guide for the Irelands on their excursion was a consummate con man called John Jordan. Jordan was a self-appointed expert on Shakespeare, not averse to forging a few Shakespearian items himself. These included a poem and a Profession of Faith, supposedly written by the playwright's father, John Shakespeare. Jordan had hoodwinked people with greater Shakespearian credentials than Samuel, so the enthusiastic collector was easy meat. Among Samuel's purchases were a bugle purse Shakespeare had supposedly given Anne Hathaway, and the chair he had allegedly sat on with Anne on his knee. The latter would take pride of place in Samuel Ireland's London residency. He was also fooled into believing that he had missed by only a few weeks priceless Shakespearian manuscripts that had been burnt by a local resident in order to create some space to house some young partridges.

Reinvigorated in his enthusiasm for Shakespeare following his visit to Stratford, Samuel Ireland waxed lyrical about him. Every day he extolled his genius and on many evenings he read one of his plays aloud to his family. William-Henry was becoming similarly preoccupied with the playwright, absorbing 'a similar fondness and veneration for every thing that bore a resemblance to the mighty father of the English stage', even to the extent of copying out all of Shakespeare's plays. It is assumed that around about this period William-Henry had the idea of using his own knowledge of Shakespeare to produce what his father craved: an original piece of documentation attributable to the Bard himself. Sensibly, though, he first chose to practise his forgery skills with a comparatively innocuous piece of ephemera.

He bought a book of prayers that was dedicated to Queen Elizabeth I and inserted a presentational letter from the author to Her Majesty in the binding of the cover. He wrote the inscription on old paper but took the precaution of getting it checked out by a local bookbinder. One of the assistants suggested a different formula for making the ink to render it more realistic. Once it was written down, he was advised to hold it over a fire for a few seconds in order to darken the colour. The young man was quite open with the shop owner as to his intention – it was merely a prank to play on his father. He presented 'the book to Mr. Ireland, who had no doubt as to its authenticity'.

He followed that up by buying a comparatively modern terracotta head of Oliver Cromwell. He fixed a label to the back suggesting that it was a gift from Cromwell to John Bradshaw, one of the judges at the trial of Charles I. He also signed the sculpture with Bradshaw's name, reproducing fairly accurately his actual signature. Samuel Ireland was again taken in, even to the extent of attributing the work to Abraham Simon, a prominent engraver and modeller of the time. If he hadn't realised it before, William-Henry now learnt that, once somebody believes a fake is genuine, they are likely to find connections that the forger hadn't even intended.

Confident now of his abilities, William-Henry ventured into Shakespearian territory. He created a lease agreement from Shakespeare and John Heminges, an actor and editor of the first folio, to the unknown Michael Fraser and his wife Elizabeth. It was written, with the same ink that he had perfected earlier, on a piece of parchment that came from the end of an old rent-roll at his chambers. Using a similar deed from the period of James I, he imitated the style of handwriting as best he could. Shakespeare's signature was copied from a facsimile in the 1773 *The Plays of William Shakespeare* edited by George Steevens. He forged Fraser's signature with his left hand 'in order the better to conceal it as being from the same pen'. More tricky was producing a verifiable seal for both parties. These needed to be attached to a piece of parchment hanging directly below the two signatures. After some trial and error he extracted an old seal, sticking it on with modern wax. To disguise the different colouring he rubbed soot and coal ashes over the finished product.

With his document complete, he needed to prepare his father for its discovery. In his diary Samuel Ireland reveals the story he was told by his son. William-Henry was invited to dinner at the house of the banker Mr Mitchell on 22 November 1794, where he met a Mr H, a wealthy gentleman. William-Henry chatted to the elder man about his interest in old autographs and handwriting and was told that if he came and visited he would find plenty of examples of deeds and papers that Mr H had lying around. William-Henry went around on 2 December, which was fortunate timing as Mr H was thinking of selling them. Rummaging through the documents, William-Henry came across the 1610 lease granted by Shakespeare and Heminges.

On 16 December he presented Samuel Ireland with the deed. The first of William-Henry's Shakespearian papers, as they came to be known, was inspired. The very banality of the agreement seemed to give it authenticity. Why would anyone bother to forge such a dull piece of legal paraphernalia that told nothing new about the playwright? When the Shakespearian scholar Edmond Malone later made a forensic dissection of Ireland's papers, he found faults with the lease, but they were relatively technical and only an expert on Elizabethan legalese would have discerned them. For Samuel by far the most significant aspect was the signature. He knew that there were only five known signatures by Shakespeare in existence, two of them discovered by one of the Irelands' neighbours twenty-six years earlier. He had previously said that he would willingly give half his library to obtain one. 'It is impossible for me to express the pleasure you have given me,' he informed his son on receipt of the lease, which William-Henry magnanimously permitted him to keep.

Samuel was not so naive as to completely ignore all due diligence. He consulted Sir Frederick Eden, an authority on heralds. Eden not only pronounced the seal to be genuine but added that the emblem on Shakespeare's stamp represented a piece of apparatus called a quintain, a specially constructed post used by young men to instruct them in the art of tilting on horseback with a lance. Given that part of the Bard's name comprised the word 'spear', it was obvious to this expert why he should have chosen such a picture. With an objective eye it is hard to discern anything more than a five-star cross emblazoned on the seal. William-Henry's laconic observation was that he hadn't really looked at the impression and, furthermore, had never heard of a quintain until the image was scrutinised by Sir Eden.

Now that William-Henry had convinced his father that he had a reputable source for the discovery of Shakespearian documents, he could become more creative. He reproduced some of the great man's actual words. Sensibly he kept it comparatively bland. This was not going to be imitation of Shakespeare as an artist, but rather as a businessman. It was a promissory note given to his friend John Heminges agreeing to pay five guineas in recompense for work he had done at the Globe Theatre. It was short, fewer than seventy words in total, again signed, and dated 9 September 1589. That the Globe Theatre wasn't built for another ten years didn't seem to faze Samuel. He also produced an accompanying acknowledgement from Heminges that he had received the money owing from Shakespeare. Here was a man who was honest in his financial dealings. By moulding Shakespeare in the image that appealed to Samuel's idealistic characterisation of him, William-Henry had another means of convincing his father that the Shakespearian papers were authentic.

Whether or not William-Henry could successfully extend his forgeries beyond administrative paperwork was answered by his next 'find', easily his most ambitious to date. This was a Profession of Faith written in Shakespeare's own hand and running to several hundred words. Its objective was to show that Shakespeare had no sympathy with Catholicism, as some feared, but was a true Protestant. In executing it, William-Henry tried to use as many letters as he could that corresponded to those in Shakespeare's existing signature, which presumably restricted his creative skills a little. He also dropped all punctuation, doubled up on his consonants and placed numerous 'e's at the end of the words.

His father was undaunted by Shakespeare's idiosyncratic spelling, embracing the sentiment of the piece which included a comparison of the Lord forgiving our sins with the sweet Chicken (spelt 'Chickenne') spreading her wings to protect her little brood. Later there would be a dispute as to whether in Elizabethan times a chicken meant a hen, as chickens would be too young to have their own offspring. To add credence to the piece, William-Henry learnt it by heart and informed his father that he repeated it twice a day at his prayers. Two respected gentlemen, the Reverend Samuel Parr and (editor of the works of Alexander Pope) Dr Joseph Warton, were invited to look at this and other manuscripts. They interrogated William-Henry about his discoveries and then heard Samuel Ireland read the Profession of Faith aloud. The teenager feared that this might be the moment when he was exposed. But their verdict was that they had heard many fine passages in their church service but this 'distanced' them all.

This verification from such experts gave William-Henry the incentive to let his imagination run free. Among the items that he faked over the next months were financial agreements between Shakespeare and various colleagues; numerous slips of paper noting monies that Shakespeare had received and paid; correspondence between Shakespeare, John Heminges and the actor Richard Cowley; negotiations with his agent, William Holmes, over a play; several letters from Queen Elizabeth to the Globe Theatre company commanding them to put on a performance for her; a letter of thanks from the Earl of Southampton to Shakespeare; a letter from Shakespeare to

Anne Hathaway; verses and a lock of hair to his beloved; signatures and margin notes in books supposedly owned by Shakespeare; a new version of *King Lear*, an extract from *Hamlet*; a letter from Queen Elizabeth to Shakespeare; and a receipt acknowledging money from the Earl of Leicester.

The sheer quantity of material was in itself an alibi for William-Henry, which he further enhanced by acting the part of a rather imbecilic youth. He wanted to world to think of him as 'a giddy thoughtless young man, incapable of producing the papers'. His father, and indeed many others too, could not conceive that one man, yet alone the intellectually challenged William-Henry, was capable of such an output. And the papers kept on coming. As early as 26 December 1794 Samuel wrote in his diary that William-Henry had told him Mr H had further materials at his country residence that were of even more consequence than those that had already been discovered. Overwhelmed by what he was getting, Samuel didn't have the time to properly evaluate what he was receiving. More fundamentally he knew that if he disputed even one piece of work, then it would inevitably call into question all that went before. His whole facade as an authority on Shakespeare would collapse.

William-Henry had therefore effectively entrapped his father into believing in the veracity of whatever came his way. The receipt from Leicester was dated 1590, two years after the Earl had died. The discrepancy was dealt with by the simple expedient of tearing off the offending part of the paper. William-Henry claimed that a childish drawing of Shakespeare which he brought home was a self-portrait. Samuel who, if nothing else, did know about engravings and art, dismissed it as of no consequence. The next day the son produced a letter from Shakespeare to a fellow actor that enclosed a whimsical conceit (spelt 'whymsycalle conceyte'), a reference to the image. This was all the proof Samuel needed to add another important possession to his burgeoning collection.

William-Henry just had to present his papers and Samuel would conjure up connections that didn't exist. He purchased from a shop in Butcher Row an old drawing of a Dutchman on one side and a young man dressed in the attire of James I on the other. He made a few alterations to make the older man look as though he might be playing the part of Shylock, and the other to appear to be a portrait of Shakespeare. Samuel persuaded himself that the latter represented the Bard in the character of Bassanio in *The Merchant of Venice*. A friend who was expert on antiquarian writing examined it, and was convinced he could trace the signature of John Hoskins, an artist of this period. 'I could never perceive any thing like a resemblance to the name in question,' was William-Henry's conclusion. In warming up the ink on some of these papers to make them look old, occasionally the edges of the manuscripts became scorched. This seemingly obvious indication of his duplicity was turned to William-Henry's advantage. Samuel knew a fire had taken place at the house of a certain Mr Warburton some thirty-six years before. It had destroyed all his property, including many manuscripts that were thought to have belonged to Shakespeare. It was surmised that some of William-Henry's discoveries had been rescued from the conflagration, thereby further validating his findings.

More radical steps needed to be taken when outsiders raised queries. The same neighbour and lawyer, Albany Wallis, who had earlier discovered the two genuine Shakespeare signatures, now also turned up in his papers an authentic signature for John Heminges. It differed substantially from the ones forged by William-Henry. The young man was asked for an explanation. He said he had to speak to Mr H. Memorising the genuine signature, he hastily drew up another receipt with Heminges's name attached. This was shown to Wallis, who agreed it was sufficiently similar to his own to demonstrate its validity. William-Henry said he had obtained it from his benefactor, who had informed him there were two John Hemingeses at the time of Shakespeare. One of them was tall and attached to the Globe Theatre. The other was short and worked for the rival Curtain Theatre. The original papers had been signed by short Heminges. William-Henry had managed to concoct the story and produce the face-saving note within an hour and a quarter of hearing the news about his dubious signature.

It is possible that Samuel Ireland might have been more suspicious about the discoveries if his own conviction as to their genuineness hadn't been reinforced by the endorsement of visitors to his house. Surrounding himself with fellow believers cut out any possible dissenting voices. This was enshrined in writing, for any prominent person was requested to sign a petition agreeing they had inspected the Shakespearian papers and were sure of their authenticity. The best-known name among the signatories was Samuel Johnson's biographer, James Boswell. It was alleged that when he saw the documentation, he fell down on his knees to thank God and exclaimed that he could now die in peace. In his defence, he wasn't that well at the time: he died three months later.

Samuel Ireland was keen to publish the documents he had accumulated so far. On 4 March 1795 he issued a tantalising prospectus stating the forthcoming book would consist of a variety of 'authentic and important documents respecting the private and public life of this wondrous man'. The price to a subscriber was a mouthwatering four guineas. However, there was the proviso that anyone who viewed the papers and doubted they were genuine would 'instantly have his subscription returned'.

William-Henry was against any publication. When it came to the external evidence, the paper, seals and ink used in the forgeries, William-Henry was on strong grounds. There were no forensic methods to date any of them. And whenever possible he had used artefacts of the period, even to the extent of stealing some of the worsted thread off an old tapestry on a visit to the House of Lords. This was subsequently used to string documents together. As Joseph Ritson, a scholar of Shakespeare, privately wrote, 'the most remarkable circumstance' of the whole affair is 'that the parchment and seals of the deeds are indisputably ancient and authentic'.

What concerned William-Henry was that, if his papers were published, Shakespearian experts who so far had been denied access to them or had chosen not to inspect them, could thoroughly check out the words themselves. Ritson's conclusion on inspecting them, again never publicly expressed, was that the perpetrator of the hoax must have deliberately inserted 'anachronisms and inconsistencies' with the express purpose of revealing them at a later date to prove the 'ignorance and gullibility of the Shakspearian connoisseurs'. It was a damning verdict on William-Henry's output. Even at his most optimistic, he must have known that his works could not survive prolonged scrutiny. In desperation William-Henry raised the possibility with his father that they were forgeries. Samuel insisted that this was impossible. Only the genius of Shakespeare could have penned them. In the end William-Henry was worn down by his father's insistence. He could only go so far in denying publication without admitting the real reason for his reluctance. Eventually he obtained 'permission' from Mr H to publish, providing the latter's name wasn't associated with the project. He hoped that this might give his father second thoughts. However, Samuel instantly accepted the terms.

Samuel Ireland's *Miscellaneous Papers* appeared on 24 December 1795. Nearly two thirds of the book was taken up with William-Henry's version of *King Lear*. He had copied it, in Shakespeare's hand, from a rare folio possessed by his father 'making interpolations where I conceived they would answer my purpose'. These related to censoring anything considered 'ribaldry'. He claimed that his original proved beyond doubt that Shakespeare was a better writer than had previously been imagined. It was surmised that the subsequent alterations had been made by actors, and were afterwards inserted in the playhouse copies of his productions. There was also a short extract from *Hamlet*, which he called *Hamblette*. He had originally intended to transcribe the entire play but, becoming 'weary of this plodding business', only produced a few leaves.

Less than three weeks after the *Miscellaneous Papers* appeared, the first negative response was published. It was written by James Boaden, who was the editor of the newspaper *The Oracle*. For a time, he had been an avid supporter of Samuel. He was turned in his opinion by the Shakespearian expert George Steevens. The pamphlet was called *A Letter to George Steevens*. Much of the *Letter* was taken up in critically comparing William-Henry's *King Lear* with an earlier version, but it did make some telling points about a number of the other manuscripts. It was not a knock-out blow, though, particularly as Samuel Ireland immediately orchestrated replies from a couple of his friends. *A Comparative Review of the Opinions of Mr James Boaden* was written anonymously by 'A Friend To Consistency', Samuel thereby pointedly contrasting himself with the duplicity of *The Oracle*'s editor. Francis Webb, secretary of the College of Heralds, also withheld his name in penning *Shakspeare's Manuscripts, in the Possession of Mr Ireland*, using the pseudonym Philalethes. His identity was revealed by Boaden himself in *The Oracle*: 'The official *defender* of the *Pseudo* Shakspeare is a Mr *Webb*. – It is feared he is inextricably *entangled*.'

Webb did his best in supporting the published Shakespearian papers but was unconvincing. If they were forgeries, he argued, then they must have been done in Shakespeare's time – and why would anyone bother to do that and not make use of them? No forger would fabricate legal instruments as they knew they would eventually come unstuck due to their complex nature. William-Henry, in order to try to prove he was the rightful heir to his own papers, had earlier concocted a story about his ancestor rescuing Shakespeare from drowning when he had fallen off a boat on the Thames. In gratitude Shakespeare had drawn up a deed of gift that was now in William-Henry's favour. Webb's response was that nobody would risk making up such an unlikely tale. 'Imposture, in general, keeps within bounds of probability,' he wrote. He also contended that the quality of writing was consistent with other known works by Shakespeare. One reviewer let Webb off lightly by saying he was honest and well meaning, although ultimately credulous.

There was one major omission in the *Miscellaneous Papers*. And for most people, until that could be scrutinised, the jury was still out on whether the Shakespearian papers were genuine or not. The reason it was not included was because it was 'intended for theatrical representation'. Ultimately it was the staging of the historical play *Vortigern* that would determine if William-Henry's hoax was sustainable.

II

Samuel Ireland was first told by his son of the existence of a new play by Shakespeare on 26 December 1794. It was tied up in a bundle with a copy of *King Lear*. Up to this point interest in Ireland's papers was mostly confined to scholars. Dry, legal documents were not going to excite the general populace. News of a previously unknown work by Shakespeare, called *Vortigern*, was something else though. When information about this discovery leaked out, the media were quick to publicise it. If the report that a tragedy called *Vortigern* by the immortal Bard had been unearthed was true, triumphed *The London Packet* on 9 February 1795, 'the literary world will have enough to talk of for seven years to come'. Three days later Samuel Ireland was revealed as the owner, alongside the confident statement that there was no doubt about the authenticity of the manuscript. 'The idea of seeing an original Play of our great Poet brought upon the Stage in these times, fills the mind with a mixed emotion of wonder and delight', wrote *The St James's Chronicle*. It also noted that many experts had come to examine the papers and expressed 'their surprise and rapture at the discovery of such a literary treasure'. At this stage *Vortigern* was still being written. William-Henry composed it in his own handwriting, claiming he was copying it out as Mr H wouldn't release the original. It took him two months to complete.

As soon as it was finished, around March 1795, Samuel Ireland had aspirations to produce it on stage. It was overly long and Samuel asked his friends to suggest alterations and amendments to render it more suitable for a live performance. Negotiations began with the Covent Garden and the Drury Lane theatres, both keen to produce the play. Samuel Ireland opted for the latter because the owner, the playwright Richard Sheridan, was an old friend of the family. Sheridan was sceptical about *Vortigern*. On a read-through he commented that the Bard always wrote poetry and that, if he had written it, he must have been very young. Nevertheless, Sheridan was nothing if not pragmatic. He knew a box-office hit when he saw one. He drew up an agreement with Samuel Ireland in which they would split the profits for the first sixty nights. In an age when new plays were lucky to see three performances, Sheridan was anticipating a windfall. His manager, John Kemble, who did not have a direct financial interest in the theatre, did not share his boss's enthusiasm. Following 'a few minutes conversation' with the Shakespearian expert Edmond Malone, he was convinced *Vortigern* was spurious. He chose not to promote the forthcoming production, informing a newspaper that it was up to the audience to determine its provenance. To make matters worse, he was going to be playing the eponymous lead role.

Samuel Ireland's original intention was that the play would appear before his *Miscellaneous Papers* were published. There were sundry reasons for the delay including time spent negotiating terms, Sheridan's procrastination and disputes over the scenery to be used. The longer it was postponed, the more time it gave critics to express doubts and create an air of incredulity about the authenticity of the Shakespearian papers generally and *Vortigern* in particular. The most fun was had with William-Henry's spelling. One newspaper imagined Shakespeare writing to a cheesemonger: 'Thee cheesesse youe sentte mee werree tooe sweatttie, ande tooe rankee inn flavourre'. Another had Queen Elizabeth suggesting to Shakespeare that 'wee shalle *drinke Tea* withe thee bye Thames Tomorrowe, thou Monarche offe the *Globe*.' It was dated 1580 when the Globe was 'not then built'. 'Shakespear, it has been said, never blotted a word,' noted a third. 'Where is the wonder, when he wrote with such apparent eeeee!'

The first public announcement that *Vortigern* was to appear at the Drury Lane theatre was made in January 1796. It stated that 'The Manuscript of the Play of Vortigern being now placed by Mr Ireland in the hands of the Manager, will be speedily brought forward, with appropriate Scenery and Decorations.' This rather bland pronouncement was repeated underneath the announcement of that night's play right up to its eventual staging. The startling omission was the lack of reference to Shakespeare as the author. Newspapers queried why neither Kemble nor Sheridan were prepared to advertise the play as Shakespeare's. In doing so they showed to the public 'an offensive indifference'. More worryingly for Samuel, John Kemble had no intention of withdrawing from the production, unlike his equally famous actress sister, Sarah Siddons, who pulled out from the part of Rowena claiming ill-health.

Edmond Malone took full advantage of the gap between the *Miscellaneous Papers* and the staging of *Vortigern*. He had made it clear a mere five days after Samuel Ireland's publication that he was going to respond in print. *An Inquiry into the Authenticity of certain Miscellaneous Papers* eventually came out on 30 March 1796. Running to over 400 pages, the book was too long and complex for mass appeal. But the newspaper reviews had only to quote its conclusion, together with some selective examples, to sabotage William-Henry's forgeries. Readers were informed that the authors of the Shakespearian papers knew nothing about the spelling, the words, the dates, the theatrical contracts, the legal instruments and the handwriting of the period. This was supported by the failure to provide any provenance when it came to authenticating the works; the conflicting penmanship for those Elizabethans where there were samples already in existence; the absurd manner in which almost every word was over-laden with both consonants and vowels; the anachronistic use of Arabic numbers; the incorrect use of the titles of noblemen; the ridiculously high remuneration for young actors; and the mistaken insertions of double Christian names.

Malone's book was published three days before *Vortigern* was staged on 2 April. Kemble had wanted it performed the day before. He was thwarted in his April Fool reference but did manage to insert *My Grandmother*, a farce about a gullible art collector, as an afterpiece.

Samuel Ireland attempted some damage limitation. He produced a playbill, handed out to the audience as they entered the theatre, stating that it was impossible to produce an answer to the 'most illiberal and unfounded assertions in Mr Malone's Enquiry'. He therefore requested that *Vortigern* may be 'heard with that *Candour* that has ever distinguished a *British Audience*'.

The plot of *Vortigern* has much in common with *Macbeth* in particular, but also echoes of *Richard III*, *King Lear* and *Henry IV*. Vortigern was possibly a British fifth-century warlord. In William-Henry's version, based on *Holinshed's Chronicles* – the same source that Shakespeare used for many of his plays – Vortigern betrays the trust of King Constantius and kills him to seize the crown. He falls in love with Rowena and makes her his Queen. Eventually Constantius's son, Aurelius, defeats him in battle. The victor spares Vortigern's life as he has fallen for his daughter, Flavia, who he marries. There were a total of five acts. Interspersed with the derivative writing, poor characterisation and unlikely plot twists, there is the occasional spark of genuine inspiration from William-Henry. For that reason, despite events stacking up against them, the Irelands nearly got away with it.

The omens to start with were good. People were waiting at the doors of the Drury Lane theatre as early as three o'clock to get in. It was said that the auditorium, which could accommodate up to 3,500, could have been filled twice over. Samuel Ireland took pride of place in a box at the centre of the house. William-Henry was less sanguine and spent most of the play 'in the green-room'. There was an initial stumble in the prologue, with the actor Mr Whitfield, according to one paper, so overcome by the applause 'as apparently to deprive him of all recollection'. He had to be assisted by the prompter to complete his rendition. However, this didn't reflect badly on the author, as neither the prologue, nor indeed the epilogue, were written by William-Henry. As was normal, they were separately commissioned. Samuel had encountered considerable difficulty finding a poet prepared to come up with some words that didn't question the authorship of *Vortigern*. His original choice was

Henry James Pye, the Poet Laureate. On reading it Pye had declared it a 'very excellent play' and said that he would be delighted to write a prologue that 'shall be worthy the name of Shakespeare'. Soon after this Pye met up with John Kemble, in consequence of which, he informed Ireland, 'I must lower my tone a little.' His draft was lowered too much as far as Samuel was concerned and was rejected. The eventual author was the amateur poet Sir James Burgess.

The first three acts went well and Mrs Jordan, playing the part of Flavia, kept reassuring the nervous William-Henry that it was going to be a success. That the audience began to get restless in Act Four, was as much due to the cast as it was to the more enfeebled script. Kemble had deliberately chosen a player with a high-pitched voice to pronounce the words 'bellow on', which produced convulsions of laughter. Another actor, killed in action, managed to fall on the exact spot where the drop curtain came down, resulting in his legs being exposed while his head was hidden from view. Groaning and straining he eventually extrapolated himself to the further delight and merriment of the audience. The *coup de grâce* was provided by Kemble himself. Reciting Vortigern's best speech, as he contemplates the defeat of his army, he paused just before the line: 'And when this solemn mockery is o'er.' He then delivered it in the 'most sepulchral tone of voice possible', which resulted in ten minutes of laughter. After that had subsided, he said the line again 'with even more solemn grimace than he had in the first instance'. It was the killer blow from which the play never recovered. At the finish, when it was announced that the play would be repeated on the following Monday, the roars of disapproval brought about a reversal of that decision. Instead it would be replaced by Sheridan's own *The School for Scandal*.

The contribution of the actors to the demise of the play was pointed out by reviewers the following Monday. Some of them were 'hardly qualified to be candle-snuffers', while Kemble himself was deemed guilty of the 'most execrable acting'. Judged on his performance, and the play itself, 'both would be prevented from ever appearing again upon the stage'. However even first-rate thespians probably wouldn't have saved *Vortigern* from the universal drubbing it received. It was 'Shakespeare in Masquerade' – in a format an English audience had never seen him in before and which 'they will never wish to see him again'. In listing other Shakespearian plays by which *Vortigern* had clearly been inspired, a paper wrote that his characters were not drawn 'in the exercise of his usual Faculties'. Shakespeare 'is remarkable, in seldom borrowing from himself.' A reporter claimed impartiality before he walked in. Leaving aside who was the author, he would have been happy to proclaim another Shakespeare, 'but alas we found not even the shadow of *one*'. Only one newspaper demonstrated a degree of sympathy: 'We are persuaded, that if many of Shakespeare's plays were to be now *exhibited* for the first time, they would not meet with a better reception than that which *Vortigern* has experienced.'

With *Vortigern* condemned by the public and critics alike, and the remaining Shakespearian papers lacerated by Malone, it was effectively the end of the hoax. For William-Henry it was a relief it was all over. As his father, along with his supporters, conducted a post-mortem at the end of the long and disastrous evening back at Norfolk Street, he 'retired to bed, more easy in my mind than I had been for a great length of time, as the load was removed which had oppressed me'. Samuel Ireland did not see it in that light. He still passionately believed in the authenticity of his manuscripts and was determined to prove his detractors wrong. He refused to take the sage advice of one newspaper to 'acknowledge that he has been deceived'. If he didn't, he was warned, 'he must take the consequences'.

Samuel's primary aim was to track down the elusive Mr H and, to that end, William-Henry was interrogated by a committee of his father's friends. Samuel was confident of the gentleman's existence as he was aware of another man who was present with his son when the papers were first discovered. This was William-Henry's friend Montague Talbot, a fellow conveyancer. Early on in the hoax Talbot had caught William-Henry forging his papers in the attorney's office.

He had promised not to tell anyone. Later, in order to strengthen the validity of the manuscripts, he was persuaded into admitting that he too had met Mr H. Demanding more information about Mr H, Samuel begun writing to Talbot, who was now an actor in Dublin. Talbot, though, remained loyal and schtum.

William-Henry was running out of wiggle room. Rather than speaking to his father directly he confessed to the lawyer Albany Wallis. He was advised to stay quiet for the present about the illusory Mr H. Wallis would keep his father at bay by 'stating that it was his opinion, as a professional man, that the supposed gentleman was not exactly safe in committing his name to the public.' This tactic didn't work for long. They tried another means to appease Samuel. William-Henry published an affidavit swearing that he had given the papers to his father as the genuine 'manuscripts of Shakspeare' and that the recipient was totally 'unacquainted with the source'. It was still not sufficient and, with parental pressure mounting on William-Henry, he decided to tell all in a letter to Samuel.

The result was perhaps predictable. Samuel Ireland went straight to Wallis and informed him there was not a word of truth in what he had read; that he knew the papers were genuine; and that his son could not possibly have produced them. William-Henry considered his only option, against the advice of Wallis, was to go public. Surely his father would believe him once the story was in general circulation? In December 1796 he published *An Authentic Account of the Shaksperian Manuscripts*. The forty-three-page booklet failed spectacularly in its aim. Not only was his father still unconvinced of his duplicity, the critics now didn't believe he wrote the papers either. According to *The Herald*, based on 'the literary merits of the pamphlet now before us', William-Henry could not possibly be the author of *Vortigern*. This was a view endorsed by *The True Briton*, which thought his *Authentic Account* displayed 'not a single spark of genius, talent' nor even 'the smallest portion of that *feeling*' of any of the original papers. 'Young Vortigern certainly might have written the Shakspeare MSS, as they are now called – But who composed the play that he copied,' queried *The Gazetteer*. His attempted *mea culpa* was summed up by *The Morning Chronicle*: 'if it be true' it 'goes to prove that the writer is a great liar'.

Samuel Ireland devoted the next year to producing two pamphlets to salvage his reputation. The first, *Mr Ireland's Vindication of his Conduct*, set out to show how he had always behaved in the most appropriate and laudable manner throughout the affair, relying on what he was told by his son and reaffirming how other experts had agreed the papers to be authentic. In the second he took on the harder task of rebutting Malone's claims. In some he is reasonably successful. He shows an example in which the Earl of Leicester did spell his name differently from Leycester, and argues that handwriting can change over time. Some of Malone's criticisms he dismisses. What stress could possibly be laid on the frivolous and accidental ommission of the letter 'r' in Stratford? Similarly he wouldn't detain his readers with the distinction between a hen and a chicken. But it didn't stop him taking issue with Malone as to which came first, a bud blooming or blossoming. The sad fact was that no one was that interested. People knew the papers were fake. Ireland would have taken little comfort in the verdict of one newspaper that in point of style it was 'by far the best written book we have seen since the commencement of the dispute'.

Samuel Ireland died in July 1800, still believing in the authenticity of the Shakespeare papers and still unable to accept that his son might have written them. It is hoped that he forgave him at the end, as he left him his watch and £20 in his will. William-Henry survived for another thirty-five years, making a scratchy living as a prolific author on a wide variety of subjects, many of them written under a pseudonym. His major confession was written in 1805, expanding on what he had stated in his *Authentic Account*. It was summed up by one journal as 'the whole taken together will excite pity from some, indignation from others, and great astonishment from all'. Three years before he died in 1835, William-Henry published a version of *Vortigern*, with a preface reminding contemporary readers of his duplicitous past. He supplemented his income towards the end of his life by selling interested parties the 'original' forgeries he had produced while in fact duplicating his own fraudulent papers. Today there are close to twenty copies of William-Henry's Shakespeare's love letter to Anne Hathaway in various institutions.

III

There are two unresolved questions about the Shakespearian papers. The first is whether Samuel Ireland was truly ignorant throughout of his son's involvement in the forgeries, even to the extent of denying his culpability after William-Henry had made a full confession. One modern-day writer has postulated that Samuel deliberately refused to accept that his son was the hoaxer in order to protect him. He was aware that if it were universally agreed that he was duplicitous, then his character would be so maligned that never again would he be trusted in society. The evidence for this is that Samuel wrote to William-Henry telling him that under no circumstances should he confess, otherwise 'no person will admit you into their house'. There is the added argument that Samuel wasn't entirely scrupulous himself, happy to sell off artefacts of dubious provenance. And there is no doubt that he had a substantial financial interest in ensuring the papers were deemed authentic, an excellent reason for denying his son's involvement in their manufacture.

Public pronouncements at the time skewed towards implicating Samuel as part of the conspiracy. *The Gazetteer* called him a 'Shakespeare humbug' who was 'determined not to be outdone' by his son in putting more money into the family purse. *The Morning Chronicle* labelled him a 'literary impostor'. Newspapers also criticised him for failing to repay the subscription money he had taken for the purchase of his *Miscellaneous Papers*. A satirical print of the period, *The Oaken Chest or the Gold Mines of Ireland* [Fig. 27], depicts the whole Ireland family in league. Samuel is kneeling beside a chest with the letters WS engraved on the side. It is full of forged documentation

Fig. 27. *The Oaken Chest or the Gold Mines of Ireland*, an engraving by John Nixon, 1796.

including 'My Alterd Playe of Titus Andronicus All Written by Myself' and 'Ould Deeds ready Drawn to Fill up as Occasion may require'. He is holding out a huge chunk of hair, with a label 'A Lock of my Dear Williams Hair', to a delighted woman, presumably Mrs Freeman. On the right are Samuel's two daughters hard at work churning out the manuscripts. In contrast, William-Henry is depicted as a simple youth, grinning inanely while reading *Giles Gingerbread*, a children's book. The inference is explicit that William-Henry is incapable of writing the Shakespearian papers himself.

In November 1797, the satirical engraver James Gillray produced a caricature of Samuel Ireland, titled *Notorious Characters. No. 1* [Fig. 28]. It is a head and shoulders portrait in which he is holding a book called *Ireland's Shakespeare*. Underneath is some verse about four forgers: William Lauder, who claimed Milton plagiarised other writers for *Paradise Lost*; James Macpherson, who wrote under the name of an almost-certainly fictitious third-century bard called Ossian; and Thomas Chatterton, who took on the persona of an imaginary fifteenth-century poet, Thomas Rowley. The fourth is Samuel Ireland. Samuel wanted to sue the publishers of the etching and he sought legal advice to find out if he had a case. Included in the information sent to the barrister was that William-Henry had made a solemn avowal that he was the author of all the documents. 'This declaration, therefore, totally exculpates the father Mr S. Ireland, from all share or participation in the forgeries, if forgeries they can be called.'

Samuel received differing opinions as to whether he had any chance of a successful prosecution. One lawyer agreed it was a 'gross libel'. Another, in contrast, thought the proceedings were 'perfectly absurd and unadvisable'. Samuel eventually opted not to pursue the matter, perhaps partly because even the more bullish barrister realised that William-Henry would have to give evidence on Samuel's behalf, and that the court might well consider him an unreliable witness. What is significant here, though, is that Samuel was seriously considering going to law over the matter. You would have thought that if he were somehow complicit in the deception, he would not have risked perjuring himself.

Contemporaries who knew Samuel Ireland were divided in their opinion as to his guilt. George Steevens felt there was a complex conspiracy hatched up between father and son. In Steevens's version, William-Henry admits the entire forgery, exculpating Samuel from any involvement. Samuel claims William-Henry doesn't have sufficient ability to carry out the task. The result is a 'pretended quarrel' whereby nobody suspects they are acting in concert. John Taylor, who attended the first and last night performance of *Vortigern*, initially thought Samuel was 'concerned in devising' the 'fabrication'. But on reflection he concluded that the father really went along with 'the story of his son'. Joseph Farrington, another attendee at the play,

Fig. 28. *Notorious Characters. No. 1*, an engraving by James
Gillray, published in November 1797.

wrote that the elder Ireland 'thoroughly believed his son's honesty'.

My own instinct is that Samuel was innocent of any complicity.
William-Henry cleverly drew him into accepting the relatively
nondescript early manuscripts, so that by the time he was receiving
the sensational papers written by Shakespeare himself, he was unable

to back out from thinking them authentic. By only speaking to those who agreed with him, Samuel surrounded himself with people happy to confirm his own opinion. Furthermore he trusted his own instincts as to what constituted great writing. For him, the Profession of Faith and the newly discovered *Vortigern* fell under this banner. He was also convinced that William-Henry was quite incapable of imitating Shakespeare. There is plenty of evidence that he considered his son less than bright. By the time Malone's devastating book came out, Samuel was so locked into his own belief system that he was ready to accept any theory, however contrived, to explain away all the flaws the critic had exposed. He just had too much invested – emotionally, personally, financially and in his own self-esteem – to admit an error of judgement.

The second question, harder to evaluate, concerns William-Henry's motive. Was it for money? To win the love and respect of his father? To humiliate Samuel? To show up Shakespearian experts as frauds? To test the general gullibility of the public? To prove he was the smart one after all? Or for the sheer thrill of it? One person who met him said that he had a gleam in his eye that 'forbad you to trust him' – but that was written after the hoax so may well have been a retrospective character assessment. Maybe he did just get a kick out of lying. There was a period, after the debacle of the staging of *Vortigern*, when he was apparently making up facts for no reason, surely knowing that he would be caught out. He claimed, for instance, that he was engaged to a wealthy woman, and also that he had written a play about William the Conqueror which the Covent Garden Theatre had wanted to stage. Both, when investigated further by his father, were found to be fictitious. It has been postulated that he maybe went through a mental breakdown that might explain such actions. One contemporary indeed wrote that his 'brain was affected'.

Is it possible to tease out William-Henry's motives from his own writings? He is keen to stress that he never did anything for financial gain. When the agreement was drawn up with Sheridan to stage

Vortigern, his father, who had conducted all the negotiations, was paid £300. He gave only £60 of that to his son. No one, William-Henry therefore maintains, should accuse him of avarice. The idea of obtaining money didn't enter his mind, he says, during the whole period he was occupied in his forgeries. However one feels there is an element of protesting too much. The imaginary Mr H is at pains on at least a couple of occasions to stress to Samuel how much the Shakespearian papers are worth. William-Henry regrets that Samuel didn't agree to publishing *Vortigern* before it was staged, after a bookseller informed him he would have paid 1,000 guineas for the copyright. Furthermore part of the reasoning his father used to persuade his son that the manuscripts should be published was because they would 'prove a source of benefit' to the family.

In his *Authentic Account*, published not long after the hoax, William-Henry writes that he began the project to 'occasion a little mirth' and to show how credulous some might be in their search for antiquities. He expands on this a little in the preface to his first novel, written in 1799, arguing that he didn't deceive the world, but rather the world deceived itself. He claims he knew that 'men of superior genius' would fall for the papers. 'I knew how far the credulity of mankind might be imposed upon.' He is being disingenuous though, as the forgeries, at least initially, were directed only at his father. It was a joke played on, and a gullibility test of, just one man. He is probably being more honest when he writes later that, because his father and others believed the initial papers to be valid, he was urged on by his 'own vanity' to attempt something further.

In his fuller confessions, written in 1805, there is no mention of testing anybody's credulity – indeed, very little about his motives generally. Rather than conducting any self-analysis, he just wants to be excused and forgiven. He lists at the end of the book a defence for his actions, including that he did not intend to injure anyone and repeating that he never benefited himself from the papers and that the experts who fell for the fakes had only themselves to blame. He also makes much of his young age, 'being scarcely seventeen years and a half old'. He continues:'My boyhood should have in some measure screened me from the malice of my persecutors.' This supports an earlier comment that he was 'considerably under the age of eighteen when I wrote the play of Vortigern'.

Using his age as an excuse reoccurs in the 1832 preface to *Vortigern* where he says his actions were the 'thoughtless impulse of a head-strong youth, under seventeen years of age'. So he has managed to shave another year off his life! Unfortunately this contradicts with his admission in *Authentic Account* that he was nineteen years old at the time, which was indeed his true age. Seen in this light his plea that Edmond Malone surely wouldn't have bothered to write his *Inquiry* had he known the Shakespeare papers to be written by 'a boy of seventeen years of age', and asking for forgiveness on the basis of his 'boyish folly', falls on deaf ears.

Towards the end of his life William-Henry does seem to acknowledge that the relationship with his father played a larger role. His only aim, he writes, was 'to afford pleasure to a parent'. He had wanted the 'permanent gratification' of seeing his father pleased. He excuses his behaviour stating that 'my father's enthusiasm', and the fact that his desire to possess even a signature of the Bard would render him 'the happiest of human beings', sealed his fate. It is entirely possible that he did begin with the best of intentions to find for his father what he wanted above all else. The praise that he received from fulfilling this need then became addictive. In order to earn the same amount of parental affection, the Shakespearian documents he produced had to become exponentially more desirable and rarefied. Even after *Vortigern* was staged, William-Henry told his father about treasures that he had discovered which he couldn't possibly have successfully forged. These included a full-length portrait of Shakespeare, verses to Queen Elizabeth, Sir Francis Drake and Walter Raleigh, and a record of the playwright's life. It was only by promising Samuel such riches that he could retain his love.

But to pass off his deeds as just a means of trying to obtain some sort of compassion from his father is surely to over-simplify. What also comes out is an arrogance and self-aggrandisement through what he did. Many years after the hoax James Boaden, the editor of *The Oracle* who had first supported Samuel Ireland and then turned against him, confronted William-Henry. The erstwhile forger listened to a diatribe whereby he was informed of 'the enormous crime you committed against the divinity of Shakspeare'; it was 'nothing short of sacrilege'. The unrepentant hoaxer merely wanted to laugh out loud at this 'sample of mingled pedantry and folly'. And for him to finish his confessions by categorically stating he 'injured no one', knowing that his father's reputation had been ruined by his behaviour, again shows a man who is self-obsessed and who finds it hard to empathise with anyone taken in by his actions.

The only conclusion is that William-Henry is just too complex a man to be shoehorned into any easily identifiable motivational box. It is part of the reason why he, like the other hoaxers in this book, still provide plenty of material for discerning the complexity of human nature when it comes to the art of deception.

EPILOGUE

* * *

What can be learnt from the ten hoaxes I have looked at in *The Century of Deception*? It is hard on initial scrutiny to find any obvious connections between them. I accept that this is partly due to the variety of my selection. For instance, I could have included more literary hoaxes – the attempt to pass off your writings as authored by someone deceased – of which there were several in this period. As it is, I opted for only one, the subject of the final chapter. Arguably I have chosen two associated with the supernatural. But apart from this shared feature, the Cock Lane and Stockwell Ghost have little in common. However, I don't believe my choices markedly skewer the comments below. I have concentrated on what are considered to be the major hoaxes of the eighteenth century. The only one that falls outside that remit is Chevalier de Moret's balloon flight which, as I have shown, wasn't really a hoax at all. I have included it because it was perceived as such at the time.

The first observation is that the hoaxes are spread fairly evenly over the century. George Psalmanazar's book on Formosa is published four years after 1700. William-Henry Ireland's *Vortigern* is dramatised four years before 1800. Five hoaxes are pre-1750 and five post-1750. Hoaxes were occurring regularly and there is therefore no basis for assuming that people became more sophisticated in detecting them. Some of this comes down to the diversity of the hoaxes. There was not necessarily much that you could learn from a previous one to expose a current one. Mary Toft and the Cock Lane Ghost were similar, in that they involved physical exertions by the hoaxer, required accomplices and lasted several months before they were finally resolved. But both needed a different skill set to investigate them. In contrast you have the Bottle Conjurer, instigated and executed in under a week, and the Polly Baker Speech, where several decades passed before anyone even knew it was a hoax. The forensic analysis of language and anachronisms that exposed William-Henry Ireland's Shakespearian writings would have been little use in uncovering *An Historical and Geographical Description of Formosa* as fraudulent.

When it comes to those taken in by the hoaxes, there is no single class that is particularly vulnerable. While it was the poor and uneducated who mostly believed in the Cock Lane Ghost, only the comparatively wealthy could have afforded to buy the tickets to see the Bottle Conjurer. Mrs Golding, the woman duped in Stockwell, was described as 'a lady of an independent fortune'. The Elizabeth Canning case was universally discussed by all sections of society. Mary Toft managed to convince highly respected physicians as well as the general populace. Both the 'mob' and the gentry were present at Chevalier de Moret's aborted balloon ascent. The instigators of the hoaxes, too, came from differing sections of the social order. Hoaxers in privileged positions were Jonathan Swift, Benjamin Franklin, Chevalier de Moret, the Duke of Montagu and William-Henry Ireland. Set against those, you have Betty Parsons, Ann Robinson, Elizabeth Canning and Mary Toft.

What stands out here, of course, is that all the female hoaxers came from an impoverished background, while the male hoaxers, with the exception of the Frenchman George Psalmanazar, were advantaged and rich. However, whatever they might lack in schooling and money, the women certainly make up for it in cunning, hard work and perseverance. Apart from de Moret, the men, in order to instigate their hoaxes, just had to write. Swift penned an astrological almanac, Psalmanazar a fake autobiography, Franklin a newspaper article and the Duke of Montagu an advertisement. Admittedly William-Henry Ireland's output was huge by comparison, but at least it was all done from the comfort of his lawyer's office.

Contrast that with the physical endurance of the women. Mary

Toft imitating labour pains and inserting rabbits into her vagina; Betty Parsons counterfeiting the noises of ghostly scratching and knockings;Ann Robinson rushing around throwing about household items; and Elizabeth Canning, even if her story wasn't true, enduring some sort of ordeal for several weeks.And that wasn't the half of it.All of them, apart from Mrs Golding's maid, were ruthlessly interrogated by groups of high-status men, their bodies were probed and examined and they were threatened in order to obtain confessions. The only one that didn't crack from all this psychological torture was Elizabeth Canning, who then had to undergo the ordeal of two court trials. The fallout for them must have been grim. Mary Toft was forever more referred to as the 'Rabbit Woman'. Betty Parsons lived with the realisation that her father was imprisoned for two years, indirectly because of her duplicitous behaviour. Canning probably had it best in being exiled to another country, away from all the incessant public scrutiny and spiteful comments. The trauma they must have suffered post-hoax can only be speculative. The women were of interest solely because of their hoaxing and, once that was laid bare, as individuals they were forgotten about.

Very different for the men. The achievements of Benjamin Franklin and Jonathan Swift outweigh any preoccupation with their hoaxes. And, far from being vilified, both men were admired for their clever deceptions. Admittedly George Psalmanazar is now best known as the Formosan imposter. But he never received any comeuppance for his deceit. He became a competent hack writer and a good friend of Samuel Johnson. William-Henry Ireland is the man who suffered the most because of the exposure. However, he maintained a good life-style and continued to make money from his Shakespearian forgeries right up to his death. The Duke of Montagu kept his involvement in the Bottle Conjurer under wraps, so much so that it was only twenty-three years after he had died that the truth came out. The only man as anonymous as the women after his hoax was Chevalier de Moret, but then he did leave England soon afterwards, thereby avoiding any retribution.

If we measure the hoaxes by the amount of publicity they generated, and how long they were remembered for, the most significant are Mary Toft, the Bottle Conjurer, the Cock Lane Ghost and Elizabeth Canning: they are the big four. All sections of society knew about them, and doubtless had a view, in the cases of the three women, as to their authenticity. It is no surprise, therefore, that they are often linked together, whether in text or satirical prints. Examples of the latter have been given throughout the book. The first instance is when Elizabeth Canning is associated with the Bottle Conjurer in the engraving *Jumpedo and Canning in Newgate* [Fig. 17]. It depicts the two of them consorting together in prison. *The Conjurers 1753* [Fig. 19] is rather more subtle. There is a bottle placed, without elaborating on what it represents, in the middle of those either supporting the maidservant or Mary Squires. Nine years later *English Credulity or the Invisible Ghost* [Fig. 20] shows a scene in Betty Parsons's bedroom. Hanging on the wall are two pictures. One is the Bottle Conjurer, the other is Elizabeth Canning with an angel, the inference being that it needed divine intervention for her to have survived for so long without food or water. In the same year there is Hogarth's masterly *Credulity, Superstition and Fanaticism* [Fig. 21]. Mary Toft is in the foreground with rabbits emerging from under her clothing. A Methodist preacher is ranting in the pulpit, while sprinkled around the rest of the etching are numerous references to the Cock Lane Ghost. In 1784, in *English Credulity or the Chevelere Morret taking a French leave* [Fig. 25], all four hoaxes, together with the Stockwell Ghost, are featured.

A pamphlet written in 1753 contrasts 'the grossest credulity' of the Elizabeth Canning case with that of 'the rabbit-woman' and 'the adventure of the quart-bottle'. In 1762 a spoof creed is published, supposedly recited by the Cock Lane Ghost's advocate, John Moore, in which he states his belief in '*Mary Tofts*, who conceived' and gave birth to rabbits; and in '*Elizabeth Canning*, who lived a whole Month' on six crusts of bread and half a jug of water. There is also a send-up of the séance with Fanny, in which one of the questions asked is whether she would enter a 'Pint Bottle'. Once those connections are established in people's minds, subsequent hoaxes pick up on them. The alleged kidnapping in 1764 of the androgynous French spy Chevalier d'Éon happens when 'the Scratching of the Cock-Lane Ghost is scarce out of our Ears'. The Rabbit Woman, the Bottle Conjurer and Elizabeth Canning are all used to support the contention that 'Wonders' of this sort, 'will never cease'.

When a theatre critic reviews two shows the same night, there are suggestions that he is either the 'famous Bottle Conjurer' or 'the scratching Ghost of Cock-Lane'. But it is decided that he is Mary Squires, as he has 'the supernatural Power of being in two Places at once'. The Bottle Conjurer is juxtaposed with a 'famous Water Walker from Lyons' intimating that he is going to walk from Calais to Dover. Similarly in William-Henry Ireland claiming he has discovered Shakespeare's *Vortigern*, the 'bottle-conjurer himself would not have calculated so grossly'. Future hoaxes are anticipated on the back of the four. Having reiterated the hilarity caused by 'Bet Canning', 'a Cock-lane ghost', 'bottle conjuror' and 'the rabbit woman', a journal forecasts that 'the period is probably at hand, when we may expect such impositions' once more. A year later it is pondering what next may astonish or surprise, given that 'ghosts are out of date, no Bet Cannings can arise; all the Bottle Conjuror's are flown, and not a rabbit woman to be met with'.

Yet the repetition of these four reveal that in practice there really weren't as many hoaxes of consequence as writers were implying. The truth was that recurrent examples of so-called 'English Credulity' were few and far between. And when they did come along there were usually rational and understandable explanations for believing the story. All the hoaxes covered in this book worked for a variety of reasons. Take your pick from ignorance, prevailing beliefs, a societal survival strategy that assumes people don't lie, confirmation of our own prejudices, gut instinct, the unreliability of witnesses, lack of existing forensic tools, a network of fellow supporters, failure to consider contrary evidence, over-reliance on an authoritative source, instinctive antagonism to those who take an opposite view, reluctance to admit you might be wrong, and a desire that, however absurd and ridiculous it might be, wouldn't it be fun if it was true.

Often there were a number of factors involved. So, in the case of the Bottle Conjurer, the Duke of Montagu primarily persuaded people to attend the theatre on the evening of 16 January 1749 because he posted a cleverly worded advertisement that sounded authentic. In addition, though, there was the apparent support from a prestigious venue; a price that appeared commensurate with the anticipated quality of the performance; the endorsement by others in the same social group; the realisation that a decision had to be made quickly otherwise you would miss out; an inherent desire to witness something miraculous; and a commendable natural instinct to believe that nobody was lying.

And, of course, all of these examples of behaviour are applicable today. Right through to the twenty-first century, the hoaxes might change, but the reasons why we fall for them don't. Many believed in the *Hitler Diaries* because they were endorsed by the respected historian Hugh Trevor-Roper. George Psalmanazar's career as an imposter was predicated on the authoritative figure of the trusted Bishop of London. Clifford Irving nearly got away with forging the autobiography of the eccentric billionaire Howard Hughes because people were desperate for his story – and it seemed compelling that he should write one. William-Henry Ireland succeeded in fooling his father because Samuel was obsessed in finding lost Shakespearian documents – and it was a reasonable assumption that such papers existed.

Anthropologists accepted Charles Dawson's find of Piltdown Man, the apparent link between man and ape, for over forty years because the tests weren't available to date the bones. This scientific ignorance was akin to physicians believing in the theory of maternal imagination to explain Mary Toft's birth of rabbits. Orson Welles caused a panic in the 1930s with his radio adaptation of H.G. Wells's *The War of the Worlds* because the audience had no time to properly scrutinise it: if there was an invasion they had to instantly flee to save themselves. In the same way those attending the Bottle Conjurer hoax were given insufficient notice to find out if the Bottle Conjurer performer really existed: if they wanted to see him, they only had one opportunity. Faith in a non-corporeal entity explains why Sir Arthur Conan Doyle wrote *The Coming of the Fairies*, based on photographs taken by two teenage girls from the village of Cottingley. Similar naivety accounts for why many thought that the Cock Lane Ghost was genuine. We saw in Chapter 8 how the 1970s Enfield poltergeist mirrored the activities of the events at Stockwell. Reliable witness statements suggest to many that the Loch Ness Monster really exists. The rebuttal of Elizabeth Canning's kidnapping story was based on sworn affidavits that Mary Squires had been seen many miles away from Enfield Wash.

So eighteenth-century commentators were wrong in their supposition that they were living in a unique era of gullibility. It turns out that people of this period were no more credulous than later generations. The offshoot of this is that many of today's concepts that we associate with hoaxes, thought to be modern in derivation, were prevalent back then: they were just not given a name. An obvious example is 'fake news'. Mary Toft giving birth to rabbits, a ghost talking through rapping and Elizabeth Canning surviving on a quarter loaf of bread and a pitcher of water for nearly a month – these were all frequently stated as facts. The speed at which intelligence was transmitted might be slower than today, but there was still a swift dissemination of information equivalent to 'going viral'. For instance the widespread circulation of the Polly Baker speech, which happened through newspapers and journals both in England and abroad; or the incident at Stockwell, which was rapidly dispersed through the swift publication of a pamphlet.

The eighteenth-century version of 'social media' were the coffee houses, where the influential met and gossiped about the topic of the day – which occasionally was a hoax. For a week in January 1749, 'Politics made a Halt, and Scandal held her Tongue, all to

make Way for the Conversation of the Bottle [Conjurer],' wrote
one pamphleteer. Another claimed that Mary Toft was 'now the
Topic of every Conversation'. Different coffee houses catered for
differing social groups and political viewpoints. This meant the
chattering classes could mingle with like-minded people, equivalent
to logging into an internet forum that shares similar views to you.
There was even an understanding of 'confirmation bias', with one
correspondent noting that certain 'minds are fertile in inventing' in
order to 'confirm their credulity'.

'Conspiracy theories' are all over these hoaxes. Chevalier de Moret
was out to rip people off with his aborted flight; the entire family
of Ireland were involved in the forging of the Shakespeare papers;
the tremors from the gunpowder explosion at Hounslow, which
coincided with the events at Stockwell, could be felt 120 miles away;
or rival theatre owners must have been responsible for staging the
Bottle Conjurer fiasco at the New Theatre in the Haymarket. The
whole concept of English Credulity, which as we have seen was
continuously referenced from 1749 onwards, was itself a chimera.
There is no evidence that the British were any more gullible than
other nationalities. A very modern conspiracy theory was flagged
by one correspondent in *The Public Advertiser* in 1777. He said that
'the Bottle Conjurer, Rabbit Woman, Cock-Lane Ghost' were
deliberately organised to distract the populace from 'some villainous
Scheme'. In his view the culprit was 'the Government'!

I would like to be able to say that through reading this book
people might be able to detect hoaxes rather better in the future,
working on the theory that we learn from studying history. I don't
buy that. Admittedly if someone comes along claiming to have
given birth to rabbits, you might be a tad suspicious – although,
with genetic engineering, who knows? This might be achieved for
real one day. It is my belief that even if some of these eighteenth-
century hoaxes were repeated virtually verbatim, they would still
work. Watch out for someone predicting the death of a psychic
medium, a poltergeist running amok in a suburban house, a person

surviving for a month on just a tube of Pringles or, to bring it full circle, the author advertising that he is going to climb inside a bottle of Prosecco on the stage of the Theatre Royal Haymarket. If *The Century of Deception* tells us anything, it is that human nature has not altered one iota in 300 years.

ACKNOWLEDGEMENTS

* * *

My first generalised thank you is to The Magic Circle. It is so much more than a club for magicians to exchange secrets. Its library and its members have given me lifelong knowledge and friendships and provided me with the seeds out of which this book has grown.

I am specifically grateful to Thibaut Rioult, a French historian, who checked to see if there was any further information about Chevalier de Moret before he came to, and after he left, England. Valerie Rumbold kindly indulged me with some exchanges over Jonathan Swift's role as a hoaxer. Sharon DeBartolo Carmack, the biographer of Maria Hayden, tracked down hard-to-find references: we have agreed to disagree on the psychic abilities of Mrs Hayden. Karen Harvey, in addition to helping me through her excellent recent book, assisted me with some thoughts on Mary Toft. I thank Sally Eaton, the Archivist for London Borough of Lewisham, for her attempts to discover more information on Ann Robinson. William Gibson (along with Daniel Reed) helped me enormously in understanding the role of William Nicholls as a Curate and Vicar. Cindy McCreery clarified some points about the Tête-à-Têtes column in *The Town and Country Magazine* and the originator of an engraving. Helen Bates gave me encouragement with my researches into the Bottle Conjurer. Elizabeth Einberg courteously gave me some pointers with regard to interpreting an obscure print. Andrew Rouse, in inviting me over to speak at his Pécs conference in Hungary, allowed me to formulate the connection between Charles Dickens and the Cock Lane Ghost.

My primary institutional source has been the British Library, where I have always found the staff exceptionally helpful. Also thanks to Virginia Mills, the Archivist (Early Records) of The Royal Society; Lindsay McCormack, Archivist, Lincoln College; Ross MacFarlane at the Wellcome Collection; and Peter Lane at The Magic Circle Library. I would have to single out Crispin Powell, the Archivist for Boughton House, the ancestral home of the 2nd Duke of Montagu. He unearthed papers relating to the Duke that I would never have found myself.

I have only ever encountered show business agents before, so it was quite a shock to discover a literary agent who actually took an interest in my work and helped shape a proposal that was worth submitting to publishers. Thank you to Peter Tallack, from The Science Factory, for restoring my faith in the profession of agents.

Even with Peter's assistance, none of this would have come to anything if Lynn Gaspard from The Westbourne Press hadn't trusted me to produce a finished manuscript. Her enthusiasm for the subject matter has more than matched my own. Thank you, too, to Brian David for his diligent editing which means, I think, I can blame any mistakes on him! And to Elizabeth Briggs, Ruth Killick and Amy Stewart for their work in helping me promote the book.

A special thank you to Ruth Stratton who read much of the book as I worked through it. Her positivity and encouragement has kept me going. And to Brian Sibley who read through the final manuscript and assured me it was worth the writing.

The following have been supportive of the project in various ways: Jonathan Allen, Neal Austin, David Britland, Charlie Burgess, Paul Cato, Janet Clare, Geoffrey Durham, Careena Fenton, John Field, David Harry, Will Houstoun, Stephen Jarvis, Cathy Keable-Elliott, Paul Kieve, Peter Lamont, Julie Marshall, Pietro Micheli, Andy Nyman, Marco Pusterla, James Smith, Chrisann Verges and Richard Wiseman. None of this would have got off the ground if it hadn't been for the pioneering books and articles by Edwin Dawes and the late Ricky Jay. The former has also provided direct support and given freely of his extensive knowledge in too many ways to list them all.

Thank you to The Arts Society, U3As, National Trust, Rotary, Probus and other groups that have allowed me to refine my knowledge about eighteenth-century hoaxes and satirical prints through numerous talks.

Finally, and most importantly, thank you to Elizabeth, who has allowed me to research and write without complaining (too much) that my time could be better spent earning more money in a better-paid activity. And, of course, to George and Carly for being there.

BIBLIOGRAPHY

* * *

Whenever possible, contemporary sources have been consulted, which include eighteenth-century newspapers, journals, pamphlets, court transcripts and satirical prints. The following resources have been extensively used, all of them accessible online:

17th-18th-Century Burney Collection newspapers
Eighteenth-Century Collections Online
HathiTrust Digital Library (https://www.hathitrust.org)
Internet Archive (https://archive.org)
British Museum Collection Online (https://www.
    britishmuseum.org/collection)
JSTOR (https://www.jstor.org)
Library of Congress: Cartoon Prints, British (https://www.
    loc.gov/collections/british-cartoon-prints)
Old Bailey Online (https://www.oldbaileyonline.org)
Oxford Dictionary of National Biography

The bibliographical list has been restricted to books and articles post 1900. Comprehensive notes and references for each chapter can be viewed here: www.centuryofdeception.com.

General

Ackroyd, Peter, *The History of England, Volume IV: Revolution*, London, Macmillan, 2016
Atherton, Herbert M., *Political Prints in the Age of Hogarth*, Oxford, Clarendon Press, 1974

Avery, Emmett L., ed. with a critical introduction by, *The London Stage, 1660-1800, Part 2: 1700-1729*, Illinois, Southern Illinois University Press, 1960

Baines, Paul, *The House of Forgery in Eighteenth-Century Britain*, Hampshire, Ashgate, 1999

Beattie, J. M., *Policing and Punishment in London, 1660-1750*, Oxford, Oxford University Press, 2001

Brewer, John, *The Pleasures of Imagination: English Culture in the Eighteenth Century*, Chicago, The University of Chicago Press, 1997

Clarke, Bob, *From Grub Street to Fleet Street: An illustrated history of English Newspapers to 1899*, Brighton, Revel Barker Publishing, 2010

Dawes, Edwin A., *The Great Illusionists*, New Jersey, Chartwell Books, Inc., 1979

Dickie, Simon, *Cruelty and Laughter: Forgotten Comic Literature and the Unsentimental Eighteenth Century*, London, The University of Chicago Press, 2011

During, Simon, *Modern Enchantments: The Cultural Power of Secular Magic*, London, Harvard University Press, 2002

Gatrell, Vic, *City of Laughter: Sex and Satire in Eighteenth-Century London*, London, Atlantic Books, 2007

Grafton, Anthony, *Forgers and Critics: Creativity and Duplicity in Western Scholarship*, New Jersey, Princeton University Press, 1990

Harris, Michael, *London Newspapers in the Age of Walpole*, London, Associated University Presses, 1987

Harris, Michael, 'The structure, ownership and control of the press, 1620-1780', in *Newspaper History from the seventeenth century to the present day*, ed. George Boyce et al, London, Constable, 1978

Hibbert, Christopher, *George III: A Personal History*, London, Viking, 1998

Hill, Draper, *Mr Gillray The Caricaturist*, London, The Phaidon Press, 1965

Jay, Ricky, *Jay's Journal of Anomalies*, New York, Farrar Staus and

Giroux, 2001

Lynch, Jack, *Deception and Detection in Eighteenth-Century Britain,* Hampshire, Ashgate, 2008

Mangan, Michael, *Performing Dark Arts: A Cultural History of Conjuring,* Bristol, Intellect Books, 2007

Morison, Stanley, *The English Newspaper, Between 1622 and the Present Day,* Cambridge, Cambridge University Press, 1932

Rosenblum, Joseph, *Practice to Deceive,* Delaware, Oak Knoll Press, 2000

Scouten, Arthur H., ed. with a critical introduction by, *The London Stage, 1660-1800, Part 3: 1729-1747,* Illinois, Southern Illinois University Press, 1961

Shoemaker, Robert B., *The London Mob: Violence and Disorder in Eighteenth-Century England,* London, Hambledon and London, 2004

Stone, Jr, George Winchester, ed. with a critical introduction by, *The London Stage, 1660-1800, A Calendar of Plays etc., Part 4: 1747–1776,* Illinois, Southern Illinois University Press, 1962

Uglow, Jenny, *Hogarth, A Life and a World,* London, Faber and Faber, 1997

Chapters

Prologue

Griffiths, Cerian Charlotte, *Prosecuting Fraud in the Metropolis, 1760–1820,* Liverpool, University of Liverpool, PhD Thesis, September 2017

Raven, James, 'The Abolition of the English State Lotteries', *The Historical Journal,* Volume 34, Number 2, June 1991

Chapter 1

Day, Robert Adams, 'Psalmanazar's 'Formosa' and the British reader (including Samuel Johnson)', in *Exoticism in the Enlightenment*, ed. G. S. Rousseau and Roy Porter, Manchester, Manchester University Press, 1990

Keevak, Michael, *The Pretended Asian: George Psalmanazar's Eighteenth-Century Formosan Hoax*, Detroit, Wayne State University Press, 2004

Chapter 2

Capp, Bernard, *Astrology and the Popular Press, English Almanacs 1500–1800*, London, Faber and Faber, 1979

Curry, Patrick, *Prophecy and Power: Astrology in Early England*, Cambridge, Polity Press, 1989

Glendinning, Victoria, *Jonathan Swift*, London, Pimlico, 1999

Mayhew, George P., 'Swift's Bickerstaff's Hoax as an April Fools' Joke', *Modern Philology*, May 1964

Rumbold, Valerie, ed., *The Cambridge Edition of the Works of Jonathan Swift: Parodies, Hoaxes, Mock Treatises*, Cambridge, Cambridge University Press, 2013

Rumbold, Valerie, Chapter 4, 'Burying the fanatic Partridge: Swift's Holy Week hoax', in *Politics and Literature in the Age of Swift: English and Irish Perspectives*, ed. Claude Rawson, Cambridge, Cambridge University Press, 2010

Thomas, WK, 'The Bickerstaff Caper', *Dalhousie Review*, Volume 49, Number 3, 1969.

Walsh, Marcus, 'Swift and Religion', David Oakleaf , 'Politics and History', in *The Cambridge Companion to Jonathan Swift*, ed. Christopher Fox, Cambridge, Cambridge University Press, 2003

Chapter 3

Altick, Richard D., *The Shows of London*, Massachusetts, Harvard University Press, 1978

Boucé, Paul-Gabriel, 'Imagination, pregnant women, and monsters, in eighteenth-century England and France', in *Sexual underworlds of the Enlightenment*, ed. G. S. Rousseau and Roy Porter, Manchester, Manchester University Press, 1987

Buckley, Jenifer, *Gender, Pregnancy and Power in Eighteenth-Century Literature: The Maternal Imagination*, London, Palgrave Macmillan, 2017

Cody, Lisa Forman, *Birthing the Nation: Sex, Science, and the Conception of Eighteenth-Century Britons*, Oxford, Oxford University Press, 2005

Cody, Lisa, 'The Doctor's in Labour: or a New Whim Wham from Guildford', *Gender & History*, Volume 4, Number 2, Summer 1992

Da Costa, Palmira Fontes, 'The Medical Understanding of Monstrous Births at the Royal Society of London During the 1st Half of the Eighteenth Century', *History and Philosophy of the Life Sciences*, Volume 26, 2004

Harvey, Karen, *The Imposteress Rabbit Breeder: Mary Toft and Eighteenth-Century England*, Oxford, Oxford University Press, 2020

Haslam, Fiona, *From Hogarth to Rowlandson: Medicine in Art in Eighteenth-Century Britain*, Liverpool, Liverpool University Press, 1996

Leslie, Glennda, 'Cheat and Impostor: Debate Following the Case of the Rabbit Breeder', *The Eighteenth Century*, Volume 27, Number 3, 1986

Newman, Gerald et al., *Britain in the Hanoverian Age, 1714–1837: An Encyclopaedia*, New York, Garland, 1997

Park, Katharine and Daston, Lorraine J, 'Unnatural Conceptions: The Study of Monsters in Sixteenth-and Seventeenth-Century France and England', *Past & Present,* Number 92, August 1981

Todd, Dennis, *Imagining Monsters*, Chicago, University of Chicago Press, 1995

Todd, Dennis, 'Three Characters in Hogarth's *Cunicularii* – and Some Implications', *Eighteenth-Century Studies*, Volume 16, Number 1, Autumn, 1982

Todd, Dennis, 'The Hairy Maid at the Harpsichord: Some Speculations on the Meaning of Gulliver's Travels', *Texas Studies in Literature and Language,* Volume 34, Number 2, 1992

Wilson, Dudley, *Signs and Portents: Monstrous Births from the Middle Ages to the Enlightenment,* London, Routledge, 1993

Wilson, Philip K., "'Out of Sight, out of mind?": The Daniel Turner-James Blondel dispute over the power of the maternal imagination', *Annals of Science,* Volume 49, 1992

Chapter 4

Amacher, Richard E., 'Humor in Franklin's Hoaxes and Satires', *Studies in American Humor,* Volume 2, Number 1, Special Issue in honor of Walter Blair, April 1975

Burleigh, Erica, *Intimacy and Family in Early American Writing,* New York, Palgrave Macmillan, 2014

Hall, Max, *Benjamin Franklin & Polly Baker, The History of a Literary Deception,* Virginia, The University of North Carolina Press, 1960

Klepp, Susan, *Revolutionary Conceptions: Women, Fertility, and Family Limitation in America, 1760–1820,* Virginia, The University of North Carolina Press, 2009

Lemay, J. A. Leo, *The Life of Benjamin Franklin,* Three Volumes, Philadelphia, University of Pennsylvania Press, 2006-9

Lemay, J. A. Leo, 'The Text, Rhetorical Strategies, and Themes of "The Speech of Miss Polly Baker"', in *The Oldest Revolutionary, Essays on Benjamin Franklin,* ed. J. A. Leo Lemay, Philadelphia, University of Pennsylvania Press, 1976

Maestro, Marcello, 'Benjamin Franklin and the Penal Laws', *Journal of the History of Ideas,* Volume 36, Number 3, July to September, 1975

Weinberger, Jerry, *Benjamin Franklin Unmasked: On the Unity of His Moral, Religious, and Political Thought,* Kansas, University Press of Kansas, 2005

Chapter 5

Bates, Helen, *Boughton and Beyond: An investigation of the local, national and global estate interests and activities of John, 2nd Duke of Montagu, 1709–1749*, Leicester, University of Leicester, PhD Thesis, 2018

Battestin, M. C. and R. R., 'Fielding, Bedford, and the Westminster Election of 1749', *Eighteenth-Century Studies*, Volume 11, Number 2, Winter, 1977-1978

Einberg, Elizabeth, 'Music for Mars, or the Case of the Duke's Lost Sword', *Huntington Library Quarterly*, Volume 56, Number 2, 1993

Elias Jr, A. C., ed., *Memoirs of Laetitia Pilkington*, Georgia, The University of Georgia Press, 1997

Falk, Bernard, *The Way of the Montagues: A Gallery of Family Portraits*, London, Hutchinson & Co., 1947

Gibson, William, "Mischievous snares': bonds of resignation', *Journal of the Society of Archivists*, Volume 10, Number 1, January 1989

Guest, Alan D., Charles Adams and John Gilbert-Cooper, *Theatre Notebook, A Quarterly Journal of the History and Technique of the British Theatre*, Volume 11, Oct 1956 - July 1957

Highfill, Philip H. et al., *A Biographical Dictionary of Actors, Actresses etc. In London 1660–1800*, Illinois, Southern Illinois Press, 1987

Kelly, Ian, *Mr Foote's Other Leg*, London, Picador, 2012

Longden, Rev. Henry Isham, *Northampton and Rutland Clergy from 1500*, Northampton, Archer & Goodman, 1938-1941

March, Earl of, *A Duke and his Friends, The Life and Letters of the Second Duke of Richmond*, 2 Volumes, London, Hutchinson & Co., 1911

McCreery, Cindy, 'Keeping up with the Bon Ton: the Tête-à-Tête series in the Town and Country Magazine', *Gender in Eighteenth-Century England*, ed. Hannah Barker and Elaine Chalus, London, Routledge, 2014

Mitchell, Eleanor Drake, 'The Tête-À-Têtes in the "Town And Country Magazine" (1769–1793)', *Interpretations*, Scriptorium Press, Volume 9, Number 1, 1977

Paulson, Ronald, *Hogarth, Volume 3, Art and Politics, 1750–1764*,

Cambridge, The Lutterworth Press, 1993

Roos, Merethe, 'Struensee in Britain: The Interprestion of the Struensee Affair in British Periodicals, 1772', *Library of the Written Word,* Volume 42, 2015

Toseland, Alan, *Estate Letters from the Time of John, 2nd Duke of Montagu 1709-39,* ed. Peter McKay and David Hall, Northampton, Northamptonshire Record Society, 2013

Whitworth, Rex, *William Augustus Duke of Cumberland: A Life,* London, Leo Cooper, 1992

Chapter 6

Beattie, J. M., *Crime and the Courts in England 1660–1800,* Oxford, Clarendon Press, 1986

Bertelsen, Lance, *Henry Fielding at Work: Magistrate, Businessman, Writer,* New York, Palgrave, 2000

Cruickshank, Dan, *The Secret History of Georgian England,* London, Windmill Books, 2010

De la Torre, Lillian, *'Elizabeth is Missing' Or, Truth Triumphant: An Eighteenth-Century Mystery,* London, Michael Joseph, 1947

Gladfelder, Hal, *Criminality and Narrative in Eighteenth-Century England,* Baltimore, The John Hopkins University Press, 2001

May, Allyson N., *The Bar and the Old Bailey, 1750–1850,* London, The University of North Carolina Press, 2003

McLynn, Frank, *Crime and Punishment in Eighteenth-Century England,* London, Routledge, 1989

Moore, Judith, 'Whose Story Is This, and Who May Tell It?: Medical Evidence Versus "Common Capacity" in the Framing of the Elizabeth Canning Case', in *Writing British Infanticide, Child-Murder, Gender, and Print, 1722–1859,* ed. Jennifer Thorn, London, Associated University Presses, 2003

Moore, Judith, *The Appearance of Truth,* London, Associated University Presses, 1994

Rousseau, George, *The Notorious Sir John Hill, The Man Destroyed by Ambition in the Era of Celebrity*, Bethlehem, Lehigh University Press, 2012

Rumbelow, Donald, *The Triple Tree, Newgate, Tyburn and Old Bailey*, London, Harrap, 1982

Thomas, Donald, *Henry Fielding*, London, Weidenfeld and Nicolson, 1990

Treherne, John, *The Canning Enigma*, London, Jonathan Cape, 1989

Wellington, Barrett R., *The Mystery of Elizabeth Canning*, New York, J. Ray Peck, 1940

Chapter 7

Carmack, Sharon DeBartolo, *In Search of Maria B. Hayden: The American Medium Who Brought Spiritualism to the U.K.*, Utah, Scattered Leaves Press, 2020

Chambers, Paul, *The Cock Lane Ghost: Murder, Sex and Haunting in Dr Johnson's London*, Gloucestershire, Paul Sutton Publishing, 2006

Christopher, Milbourne, *Mediums, Mystics and the Occult*, New York, Thomas Y Crowell, 1975

Clery, E. J., *The Rise of Supernatural Fiction, 1762–1800*, Cambridge, Cambridge University Press, 1995

Grant, Douglas, *The Cock Lane Ghost*, London, Macmillan, 1965

Heppenstall, Rayner, *Tales from the Newgate Calendar*, London, Constable, 1981

Houdini, Harry, *A Magician Among the Spirits*, New York, Harper, 1924

Keable, Ian, 'Dickens, Spiritualism and the Cock Lane Ghost', in *Charles Dickens 200: Text and Beyond*, ed. Gabriella Hartvig and Andrew C Rouse, Spechel e-ditions, Volume 2, 2014

Slater, Michael, ed., *Dickens' Journalism, Volume 3: 'Gone Astray' and other Papers from Household Words*, London, JM Dent, 1998

Wiley, Barry H., *The Thought Reader Craze: Victorian Science at the Enchanted Boundary*, North Carolina, McFarland & Company, 2012

Chapter 8

Bostick, Ian, *Witchcraft and Its Transformations, c. 1650–c. 1750*, Oxford, Clarendon Press, 1997

Davies, Owen, *Witchcraft, Magic and Culture, 1736–1951*, Manchester, Manchester University Press, 1999

Davies, Owen, 'Methodism, the Clergy, and the Popular Belief in Witchcraft and Magic', *History*, Volume 82, Number 266, April 1997

Elmer, Peter, *Witchcraft, Witch-Hunting, and Politics in Early Modern England*, Oxford, Oxford University Press, 2016

Hall, Trevor H. and Dingwall, Eric J., *Four Modern Ghosts*, London, Gerald Duckworth, 1958

Hunter, Michael, 'New light on the 'Drummer of Tedworth': conflicting narratives of witchcraft in Restoration England', *Historical Research 78 (201)*, 2005

Price, Harry, *Poltergeist Over England*, London, Country Life, 1945

Rutkowski, Pawel, 'Witches, Demoniacs and Ghosts: John Wesley's Methodism in Defence of Real Christianity', *From Queen Anne to Queen Victoria. Readings in 18th and 19th century British Literature and Culture*, ed. Emma Harris and Grażyna Bystydzieńska, Volume 1, 2009

Rutkowski, Pawel, 'Broken China and Flying Teapots: The Stockwell Ghost and the Spectacle of Fear', *From Queen Anne to Queen Victoria. Readings in 18th and 19th century British Literature and Culture*, ed. Emma Harris and Grażyna Bystydzieńska, Volume 5, 2016

Chapter 9

Hodgson, J. E., *The History of Aeronautics in Great Britain*, London, Oxford University Press, 1924

Holmes, Richard, *Falling Upwards*, London, William Collins, 2014

Holmes, Richard, *The Age of Wonder*, London, HarperPress, 2009

Marsh, Lt-Col. W. Lockwood, *Aeronautical Prints & Drawings*, London, Halton and Truscott Smith, 1924

Robins, Brian, *The John Marsh Journals: The Life and Times of a Gentleman Composer (1752–1828)*, New York, Pendragon Press, 1998

Rolt, LTC, *The Aeronauts, A History of Ballooning 1783–1903*, London, Longmans, 1966

Smith, James A, *Breslaw's Last Legacy, The Thomas Moore Editions*, pub. the author, 2013

Wichner, Jessika, 'Hot Air and Chilly Welcomes: Accidental Arrivals with Balloons and Airships in the Eighteenth Century and Beyond', in *Citizens of the World: Adapting in the Eighteenth Century*, ed. Kevin L. Cope and Samara Anne Cahill, Maryland, Bucknell University Press, 2015

Chapter 10

Bate, Jonathan, 'Faking it: Shakespeare and the 1790s', in *Literature and Censorship*, ed. Nigel Smith, Cambridge, D. S. Brewer, 1993

Grebanier, Bernard, *The Great Shakespeare Forgery: A new look at the career of William Henry Ireland*, London, William Heinemann, 1966

Groom, Nick, *The Forger's Shadow: How Forgery Changed the Course of Literature*, London, Picador, 2002

Kahan, Jeffrey, *Reforging Shakespeare, The Story of a Theatrical Scandal*, London, Associated University Press, 1998

Lynch, Jack, 'William Henry Ireland's Authentic Forgeries', *The Princeton University Library Chronicle*, Volume 66, Number 1, Autumn 2004

Lynch, Jack, *Becoming Shakespeare: How A Dead Poet Became The World's Foremost Literary Genius*, London, Constable, 2008

Mair, John, *The Fourth Forger: William Ireland and the Shakespeare Papers*, London, Cobden-Sanderson, 1938

Pierce, Patricia, *The Great Shakespeare Fraud: The Strange, True Story of William-Henry Ireland*, Gloucestershire, Sutton Publishing, 2004

Schoenbaum, S., *Shakespeare's Lives New Edition*, Oxford, Clarendon

Press, 1991

Sergeant, Philip W., *Liars and Fakers,* London, Hutchinson & Co., 1925

Stewart, Doug, *The Boy Who Would be Shakespeare: A Tale of Forgery and Folly*, Massachusetts, Da Capo Press, 2010

Epilogue

Lamont, Peter, and Steinmeyer, Jim, *The Secret History of Magic: The True Story of the Deceptive Art*, New York, TarcherPerigee, 2018

ILLUSTRATION CREDITS

* * *

9. British Library, Seventeenth and Eighteenth Century Burney Newspapers Collection, General Advertiser, 15 April 1747.

10. Courtesy of The Lewis Walpole Library, Yale University.

11. Reproduced from *Social Caricature in the Eighteenth Century*, George Paston, London, Methuen, 1905, owned by the author.

12. Reproduced from *Social Caricature in the Eighteenth Century*, George Paston, London, Methuen, 1905, owned by the author.

13. The Miriam and Ira D. Wallach Division of Art, Prints and Photographs: Print Collection, The New York Public Library. 'The Savoyard Girl.' The New York Public Library Digital Collections. 1799. http://digitalcollections.nypl.org/items/34daac60-e8f3-0130-13da-58d385a7bbd0

14. The Buccleuch Collections.

15. Sanders of Oxford, Antique Prints & Maps.

16. © The Trustees of the British Museum.

17. The Jay/Verges Family Trust.

18. Courtesy of Wellcome Collection, Creative Commons Attribution (CC BY 4.0), Mary Squires, a gypsy renowned for her ugliness. Engraving.

19. The author.

20. Courtesy of Wellcome Collection, Creative Commons Attribution (CC BY 4.0), Complete contemporary history of Cock Lane Ghost.

21. Courtesy of Wellcome Collection, Creative Commons Attribution (CC BY 4.0), An outlandish church congregation.

22. Courtesy of Eighteenth Century Collections Online (ECCO).

23. Scrapbook of early aeronautica by Upcott, William, 1779-1845, Courtesy of Smithsonian Libraries.

24. Courtesy of Library of Congress, Prints & Photographs Division, Call Number: PC 1 - 6652-X (A size).

25. Courtesy of Library of Congress, Prints & Photographs Division, LC-DIG-ds-13368.

26. A. D. 1818. W. H. Ireland, author of the Shakspear [sic] papers [graphic] / engd. by Mackenzie from an original picture in the possession of Mr. Ireland. Call No: ART File 165.5 no.1. Used by permission of the Folger Shakespeare Library under a Creative Commons Attribution-ShareAlike 4.0 International License.

27. John Nixon, The oaken chest, or The gold mines of Ireland, a farce [graphic]: the earth hath bubbles as the water has & these are them, Shakspere. Call No: ART File S527.6 no.2 copy 1. Used by permission of the Folger Shakespeare Library under a Creative Commons Attribution-ShareAlike 4.0 International License.

28. Courtesy of The Lewis Walpole Library, Yale University.

INDEX

Page numbers in *italics* are references to images.